# Dear VI…Love V

# Dear VI…Love V

*Letters to Assist in Living Life to the Full*

LEWIS SEELEY BRADSHAW V

ISBN: 1535291370
ISBN 13: 9781535291378

*Son, this book may be written for you, but it is dedicated to your mother. She is our queen.*

# PROLOGUE

16 March 2016

Dear VI,

I am out in the boundary waters of northern Minnesota, twenty or so miles from the Canadian border. The snow is falling steadily. I am absolutely alone. I don't feel alone, but I do believe this is the farthest I have ever been from other people. Six other veterans are scattered out there. All of us are a part of a dog-sledding and cross-country skiing expedition. The first three days were spent together, breaking trails and pushing sleds ever deeper into this maze of frozen bays and portages. The conditions have made the going slow, averaging about one mile per hour. One man compared our efforts to "pushing a truck with four flat tires through knee-high mud." My body is adjusting to this new kind of ache; it is a specific exhaustion that occurs when the body is simultaneously sweating and trying to keep warm. I sweat, then freeze, thaw, then sweat. Between the sleds, my inability to ski, chopping wood, setting up camp, tending to the dogs, and organizing my kit, I have had zero time or energy for reflection.

But now, in the solo phase of the expedition, I have the opportunity to sort out all that has happened these last few days. To begin with, I have no idea where I am. We marched in a single-file line through the driving snow, stopping occasionally so our instructor could point out a blip on the shoreline and say, "That's you." My spot is a small leeward stretch of pine and birch living in harmony on a gentle hill. I found a small level area, constructed my shelter (a tarp tied down with twine and rocks), gathered wood and other critical necessities for a fire, and then sat down on a snow-covered bolder to do what I am doing this very moment. The same thing I have done in some capacity every day for the last three years—write to you.

It took eighteen hours of travel to get to base camp in Ely (El-ee). The morning began at 0415 when I laid my hand on your chest to feel your heart beat and pray for your safety. It ended in a 14-passenger van with 14 crabby veterans and their gear stuffed inside. We were tired and irritable, which is close to how most men feel after a long day. One man would curse, another would remind the group how cramped they were, and then there would be about 90 seconds of silence before the cycle repeated itself. Eventually, we stumbled into a room full of cold weather gear and four ecstatic instructors. We learned the group was to be split in half with two instructors taking one group and the other two absorbing the rest. I was shocked and almost offended at how jubilant these instructors were. My life in the Navy more closely resembles the van ride, so the vibrancies of these instructors made me suspicious. No bags under their eyes, no pale, pasty skin. Strong but not buff, thin but not skinny, their hair unkempt but not unclean, their hands calloused, their teeth white. Upon meeting Lisa and Dan, I assumed the expedition would look similar to a summer camp—s'mores over a fire while I braided a friendship bracelet. Wrong!

The last four days have been some of the most physically demanding days I can remember, and my respect for the instructors has grown a mile long. Their knowledge is only trumped by their unwavering optimism, and their leadership has earned my trust. I am fascinated by these humans because they seem to thrive like humans were made to. Their bodies react positively to things like sawing wood in 10 inches of slush and pushing six-hundred-pound sleds up rocky faces. They enjoy a handful of trail mix like I enjoy a rack of ribs. They are humans doing what God created humans to do—get up early, graze, work hard in the elements, socialize, learn, relax in the feeling of physical exhaustion, go to bed early to the sounds of creation.

At first I thought these people cracked the code I have been searching for. The answer to the question I ask time and again in the pages of your book. How does a man live so that he best thrives? I thought these people found how to get the most out of body, mind, and spirit until I discovered they do not believe in any sort of higher power. How can this be? These people with a deep connection to nature are content, believing that life is nothing more than the random assortment of atoms. And what is more astounding is the fact that they spend their lives serving others. When they are not taking veterans into the unknown, they are embarking on longer trips with youth at risk! They are selfless servant-leaders in the highest capacity. Their lives mimic the precise example Christ set for us, while also believing there never was such a man. I cannot wrap my mind around living such a life without any purpose.

At the end of the day out here, I feel accomplished. Maybe this beautiful feeling of fatigue is why they don't ask the deeper questions. Out here, I am the right kind of drained. I am exhausted as a man should be. It is a deeply satisfying exhaustion that occurs when your bones scream "Uncle!" with tones of appreciation. I have been sleeping only a few hours each night on a tarp in the snow, but I awake feeling infinitely more refreshed and motivated. After a day at my desk, I feel the opposite. I feel like I took a ten-hour pass-or-fail exam. My body is begging for action, but my brain is paralyzed. I yawn a lot, and tears drain down my cheeks. I am hungry but don't feel like eating. I am excited to play with you, but I simply want to sit in my chair. I share a cozy bed with the love of my life, but my sleep is restless. I wake groggy and sore.

I have a responsibility to provide, protect, love, and impart every good thing I know into you. Some of those things are practical: a safe place to sleep, consistent, square meals, proper clothes, and medical insurance ("three hots and a cot," as they say). Other areas are less obvious but far more important: things like purpose, sound theology, how to know when you're passionate about something, persecution, and, what I am still looking into, how to avoid a career that leaves you feeling like most men do at the end of the day. I cannot, in good conscience, tell you any of those things from an armchair with the television blaring. How can I impress upon you the importance of God and the wonder of Creation if I am spending my days snacking at the computer?

A generation of men is dying a noble death, trying to provide in a way that our world would consider "successful." Comforts are exchanged for their time, energy en route to passion is redirected toward an all-encompassing fixation point called *career*. There is a way to couple practical life necessities with the necessity of living out life as humans were designed to. A man can pay his taxes and feel at home in the elements while always doing the most important thing in all of life: furthering the kingdom of God. The world is so crooked that the riddle is difficult, but it's there. I'm sure of it.

You will see from the following letters that I have dedicated myself to trying to rectify this situation. There is a solution which couples the physical ecstasy our bodies are designed to enjoy with a lifestyle that provides the basics. It all starts with the Creator of earth, body, and spirit. At the risk of boasting, I will say we have made some solid strides as a family unit, but I can see now, as I sit in the deep wilderness, we have a ways to go.

To be continued...I am going to try and get this fire started...

■ ■ ■

03 April 2016
(Conclusion of 16 March letter)
1720

We pulled the camper to King's Bay, Georgia, this weekend. Two years and a month of living like this, and we love it more than ever. My return from the boundary waters was a bear. The expedition in the wild provided a type of detox, and work took pleasure in exacting revenge. We have been stationed in Jacksonville, Florida, for nearly three years, and through that time, the stress and workload of my job has steadily increased. It's the same stuff—just more of it. Responsibility is up, morale is down, and my Minnesota education has made my senses keen to how destructively tough this type of work is on the spirit of a man.

When I started all of this writing, you were packed snuggly in your mom's tummy. Nowadays you have passed two and a half and are heading toward three at full steam ahead. When you wake up in the morning, I am reminded of a toy with newly inserted "AA" batteries. The problem is you have been waking up at 0500, which means the entire family is up at 0500. Naps are out of the question as you are too excited about life to waste a moment resting, which means your parents don't rest either.

Today when you woke up, your amazing mom kept you quiet, made coffee, then roused me to report I was to "wake up slow. Coffee is on; the boy and I are gonna take the wagon and explore." What an exceptional woman we have! I laid in that peaceful place between dreamland and reality for a while, then got up, poured a cup, read the Word for a solid chunk of time, then took this journal outside to troubleshoot a situation.

Your book is nearing completion, and I have been in touch with an editor who I feel very good about. The issue is that she is not part of the original instruction given to me from the Lord regarding your book. Up until I contacted her, almost no one knew of the existence of this project. What a challenge it has been to dedicate so much time to something while keeping the struggle and joy to myself. The question I find myself gnawing on is: am I experiencing the movement of the Holy Spirit? Or is this my will being inflicted upon a situation? I prayed, made a list of pros and cons, then looked out at the lake where, on the far side, I spotted your beautiful mom pulling the wagon against the wind with you in the back, bucket on head and stick in each hand. I have since learned this is your "helmet," and it is to be looked upon with respect. Something about that scene told me "You can't keep this to yourself." For some reason seeing you and your helmet led me to my final decision. That's how our Lord works. I do all the sensible problem-solving legwork, and He reveals the solution in the last way I would ever expect.

A couple of doors have opened. One with the aforementioned editor and another with an old friend in L.A. Writing this book is far and away the toughest assignment the Lord has ever given to me. I have faithfully pored over each word for years in the wee hours of the morning, late into the night, and every available second in between. I don't know what I am going to do after I sign the bottom of this page. Probably some sort of unattractive crying celebration dance. The experience has completely transformed me. But now, with the finish line so near, I must admit I still have no idea what the future holds for this book. Maybe I was told to write it so that I would change. Maybe you will hold the only copy. Maybe it will lay the foundation for a ministry. Only time will tell, but honestly, I have no expectations. I can say there are very few times I have obeyed God's instructions in full, but I can boldly say that I have given my all to this project. I will move forward with the editor and see where this thing goes. I hope that is okay with you. If you need more detail on what has happened between my penning these words and your reading them, just ask. My room is on the other side of the trailer.

You just rode by me on a bike. The only cement in sight is our RV pad. It's 50 feet long which is not far. You ride off into the gravel on one end, get off, turn the bike around, and then ride by me into the grass on the other side. Back and forth you go, each time as exciting as the first. You are barefoot, bare-chested, and helmetless (I just realized that is probably dangerous). Each time you pass by me, you say, "Bye, Daddy, I'm taking motorcycle to restaurant!"

By choosing to write instead of chase you around, I will be contradicting every word in the pages that follow! So I end here. I will run after you claiming to be a monster from the seashore. I will capture you. I will throw you in the air. I will kiss you. I will love you all the days of your life.

Your daddy,

V

P.S. The Bible verse at the beginning of each letter pertains to the letter but is mainly put there so you can practice finding scripture. When you read this book have your Bible beside it.

10 June 2013
#01
0510
Luke 8:25


Dear VI,


I try to start my morning in silence with my Bible. This morning the Lord commanded me to begin writing letters to you for a season. Understand that hearing God so clearly is not something I am used to. I feel cowardly admitting this, but my knee-jerk reaction was fear, doubt, and a series of questions. The first question being a foolish, "What am I supposed to write about?" I now realize that if the Lord wants me (a man without much to say and hardly any writing knowledge) to start writing, He will, no doubt, provide the content. Let the season begin.

Last night your mom and I were watching a movie, and you were positioned in such a way that I could scratch your entire back. Just because this is not unusual for a third trimester pregnancy does not make it any less amazing. In the same way, I am amazed when watching a setting sun—regardless of the fact that it is not unusual for a sun to set.

The Lord's direction has made today special for a second reason. On this day I start service at the Naval Air Station here in Jacksonville, Florida. What a life-changing transition it has been! The last 16 months have been spent ping-ponging from school to school all over the country, most of the time without your mom, my very best friend, who I am now calling "Big Momma," thanks to you.

We are almost moved into the house where you will be spending your first five years. Inspired by feeling your back, I painted a thick horizontal blue stripe around your future room. Outside of this blue stripe, your room is empty. You have nothing—not so much as a blanket. But your parents aren't worried; there is still plenty of time for collecting all those so called "baby necessities." How much could there be?

I did not choose this shade of blue because you are a male, but because it matches the color of the Pacific Ocean, my favorite place on earth. (To be honest, knowing that the Navy held the highest odds of my returning to the Pacific coast is what swayed me toward this particular branch of the service.) I get all teary when I dream of the day you and I will be playing on the beach together—the way your grandpa, Lewis Bradshaw IV, did with me. The coast is the landscape that best enables my spirit to rejoice and regroup. It is my "big, blue reset button." For now I am sure we will find contentment exploring the Atlantic, but whatever shoreline you grow up by, I pray you fall in love with it as I have. But if not, well, you will be spending lots of time there anyway.

How fitting it is that I read Luke 8 today. In verse 25 after Jesus rebukes a storm at sea, the shocked disciples ask, "Who is this? He commands even the winds and the water, and they obey him." As you grow to better understand the intricacies of the sea, how it operates, and experience its unrelenting power, I am sure you will see it demands sincere respect. What kind of weight must God's words have that, upon hearing His voice, an otherwise unmatchable power instantly obeys? Try and wrap your brain around that sort of influence!

Let me end this first letter by letting you in on some good news. This same God who controls the seas is also knitting you together at this very moment. He is the Savior of souls and the ruler of this house—yes, this house, the one with the ocean-blue stripe around your room.

Wish me a good first day at work,

V

■ ■ ■

11 June 2013
#02
0512
1 John 3:16, 4:11-12

Dear VI,

Read Proverbs again and again. This suggestion is high on the very
short list of wisdom I can offer you. There are 31 chapters in Proverbs.
Read one chapter every day of the month from the time you are able
until you cannot. This book is stuffed full of practical nuggets of wisdom guaranteed to nurture a man's spirit. A couple of them came in
very handy during my first day of work yesterday, but that is a story for
another time.

Right out of the gate, Proverbs 1 highlights the sort of crowd a man
should avoid: "My child, if sinners entice you, turn your back to them!"
The chapter goes on to list many of the specific qualities found in this
brand of sinner, one being the desire to "ambush the innocent." These
verses are referring to bullies—humans who build themselves up by tear-
ing others down. Christian men should not tolerate these people. In fact,
Christians are charged to do the opposite by taking care of the "least of
these" (Matthew 25:40) or those humans who might be considered "easy
prey"—the boy who eats lunch alone, the girl whose tough home life forces her to go to school in the same dirty clothes day after day, or even those
with special needs. A godly man must stand beside the vulnerable! To
make yourself appear superior by announcing the weakness in another is
the opposite of what Christ did for us. We are weak; He is strong. We are
lambs; He is the Lion.

You will quickly realize God has allowed you to be part of a really
fortunate family. You are surrounded by a network of selfless aunts, un-
cles, grandparents, and cousins. Your parents are madly in love with you
and each other. Your home is secure. You will not grow up wondering

where you will find your next meal. You will sleep safely in a comfortable bed.

Our greatest blessing and the true source of your home's strength is a Savior whose love is ever widening. Because we have true strength, we are obligated (out of a thankful heart) to try and repeat His example by watching out for the vulnerable. Even if we lived in a cardboard box and wore clothes made of old oil rags, our mission would be the same. Nothing will upset me more than seeing or hearing about your picking on a fellow human.

God's love for us is equal to that of His love for every human on earth. We are commanded to spend our life attempting to love like He does but, because we are not perfect, neither will our example be. This might sound discouraging when, in fact, you should be excited because it means we will never arrive. Each day carries new opportunities to grow and become that much more like our Creator. Life with Jesus is an adventure until the day we meet Him!

Never allow yourself to be deceived into thinking you deserve more. The breath in your lungs and the clothes on your back are a gift from our generous Savior. Let us show our gratitude by loving those with the love He daily shows our family.

I just kissed you through your ma's stomach! I am so proud,

V

■ ■ ■

12 June 2013
#03
0523
Psalm 55:22

Dear VI,

Someday you will love to read, so much in fact that you might even attempt to decipher my tiny script. My handwritten words are miniature. Your grandpa says my writing looks as if someone one inch tall was writing in the dark with his non-dominant hand. I began writing this way in 1998, the fall of my seventh grade year, as a way of punishing my mom for her decision to homeschool me. Talk about your all-time backfires! Not only do I credit my homeschooling years as a critical shifting point in my life, I am forever cursed to write in this tiny "font." Thank God the military demands digital! My command would throw a fit if I ever submitted a handwritten request.

   Once you are reading, your parents will buy you your own Bible—one you can write in, highlight, and make your own. You are always welcome to use mine, but I believe every man should have his own. Today I opened my Bible to Psalm 145, which gives a jaw-dropping account of how wonderful God is. When you get your own Bible, I recommend you read, meditate, and record how this Psalm impacts you. It is worth noticing, that after 13 verses of praising God for His "wonderful goodness and greatness beyond discovery," the psalmist then makes a point to mention that "the LORD helps the fallen and lifts up those bent beneath their loads."

   This promise is one reason why His majesty is a glorious splendor. The Creator of all things wants to help us. He craves our petitions. He asks for them. I have two practical thoughts for you concerning this promise: the first being, some days you will feel free of burden as if life is full of enchantment and a load capable of weighing you down simply does not exist. On those days (of which I hope you have many), keep a sharp eye out for those around you who are not feeling as you are. If you see a fellow human in a fallen condition, do not pass him by. Do not let your personal season of blessing trump your duty to lend a hand. When you are given strength, be sure to pass it on.

This directive leads me to my second thought. We have a Father who is ready to carry our burden for us. When you feel strong, tell others where your strength comes from, and when you feel burdened, do not hesitate to ask the Source for help. He is beside us ready to lift us up from beneath our heavy load. We only need to ask. Draw near to Him, and He will draw near to you (James 4:8).

As for me, your mom just made me scrambled eggs, and I need to draw near to them before heading off to work!

I hope this letter is helpful,

V

■ ■ ■

13 June 2013
#04
0515
James 1:22

*While all of these letters vary slightly from the original draft, this letter gave me a particularly difficult time. When thinking about choices, there is the ever-present temptation to go deeper down the rabbit hole until, too late, you find yourself hopelessly lost. It took stumbling upon a letter C.S. Lewis wrote to a young admirer to set me straight. His advice finally made it all click.*

Dear VI,

There is a never-ending onslaught of tasks in life I would rather not do. Sorry to break it to you, your life will be no exception. Therefore, it is best not to waste time considering how little you want to do the task. Instead, ask yourself if the task is something you ought to be doing. If a man asks himself that question, he then gives himself a chance to weigh the pros and cons. It is not until he decides that he should do the task that he can concentrate on the most important aspect of performance: attitude. Attitude determines how much benefit a person can get out of a given experience.

It is simple to have a decent attitude when doing something you must do, like putting on clothes, eating, practicing some sort of hygiene. Most people accept these tasks as necessities and, therefore, do not have a grudge held against them. It is simpler still to have a good attitude when doing something you want to be doing. Those things that we ought to do are the ones that get tricky and, unfortunately, they make up the bulk of our daily life.

I have already hinted that deciding to do something must include weighing the pros and cons. Should I go to my math class? Pro: Not going to class gives me a chance to go to the beach with my friends. Con: If I do not go, my test could suffer. If my test score is low, my grade will slip. If my grade slips, my dad will make me sit beside him for hours studying, and I will not get to go to the beach. Conclusion: I should go to class.

Everything I have written thus far is to better drive home my point which is this: the decision-making process I have described can very easily be influenced by the world around us, which will cause a man to do what he does not want to do. The world can trick a man into wearing clothes that make his skin itch or to stay up late studying a subject he hates only to pursue a career in which he has no interest. The world can cause a man to live his entire life doing neither what he wants nor what he likes.

As Christians, we are not only given the ultimate example of a man, Christ, going through with what He ought, but His Holy Spirit intervenes. That same Holy Spirit guides and helps us best judge what ought to be done. Christians are in the world but, thanks to our Savior, we are not obligated to be of it. Through His Word and a personal relationship with our Savior, we Christians are the only people who have a real shot of actually doing what we should. This excites me for three reasons.

1) Our human logic goes out the window. (This one is my favorite but does require some faith.) If a Christian feels the Lord has told

him that using his last five dollars to buy a stranger something to eat (even when his own gut is empty) is something he ought to do, that Christian can do it with confidence, knowing that whatever happens next will undoubtedly be better. Logic tells the man to use his last five dollars to buy himself some bread and peanut butter, but worldly logic is only helpful when the Holy Spirit is not in the equation. Ask any Christian. This is true.

2) There is no pressure. The Lord knows a man's heart, and therefore knows if his efforts are genuine. He is always very aware that only He is perfect; His nail-pierced hands act as a constant reminder. Therefore, He is prepared for us to slip. He only demands that we try our best to do as we ought. Remember, He really knows whether or not you give it your all.

3) When we do our best to live like our Savior (that is to say as we ought to live), life is at its fullest and most interesting. A man following Christ will often think, "I wonder what will happen next," while also knowing that he never needs to worry that his real must-haves and much more will be taken care of. To the world his situation might look unstable while, in reality, he is firmly planted on the most solid ground.

This morning as I scribble down all of these thoughts, your mom is being a great example by sleepily shuffling around the kitchen, fixing her husband a meal. I would wager my pathetic paycheck that she did not get out of bed excited about the prospect of scrambling eggs. I begged her to try and sleep more, but she insists God is nudging her to get up and help me. She insists making me breakfast is something she ought to do. Who am I to argue with that?

She just said, "I am really proud of how hard our son is kicking this morning." Me too,

V

∎ ∎ ∎

14 June 2013
#05
0510
James 1:2-4, Proverbs 14:23

Dear VI,

Friday, which has finally arrived, is the last day of my first week as an optician at the Naval Air Base in Jacksonville, Florida. To be honest, it has been a week of constant failure. (This is where reminding myself of the few Proverbs I know came in very handy.) The amount I must learn is completely overwhelming. Computer programs and machines never mentioned during my nine months in optician school seem to be popping up everywhere. I keep experiencing waves of panic that make me feel like I need to rip open my uniform just to breathe. My one comfort lies in the fact that everyone else in my department once experienced this same situation. The people I work with are encouraging, but their encouragement does not make things less intimidating.

I have found myself deeply wedged into an "If-at-first-you-don't-succeed,-try,-try-again" situation. (That "proverb" is not in the Bible.) Remember, on this day, June 14, 2013, your dad was being challenged; his palms were sweaty and his face was red as he asked his peers to repeat yet another question everyone else already knew. I feel like I have been knocked down and crawled back to my feet a thousand times.

In many places, the Bible refers to this variation of challenge as a "trial." You might be thinking "This flies in the face of my previous letter." After all, how can a man find himself in a trial if he is trying his best to do as he should? Trials are a gift from God to make a man stronger and increase his value with those he comes into contact. Trials strengthen the legitimacy of his witness. They are weights on his words.

Sometimes the reason for a trial will be obvious and, at other times, you will have no clue as to why you are in the midst of such hardship. It is less important to understand why we are going through a particular trial and more important to cling to the peace that comes from knowing that Christ has our very best interests in mind. That is the point of a trial. It is an exercise in trusting God's promises and, if we succeed, we will come out of whatever challenge we face better than ever. Our example then converts into hope and inspiration to others, which, in the end, adds up to strides taken toward life's ultimate goal: furthering His kingdom.

His idea of love is different, and far greater than ours. All week, I have been one bad thought away from writing myself off as the "World's Biggest Failure." But when that thought sinks its teeth in, I counter it with God's promise that His wonderful plan somehow involves my surviving this week. I do not understand it, but I am all in. I pray the Lord is proud of His 28-year-old friend's effort despite a gut full of nerves and the intense desire to run the other way.

Gotta bring home that bacon!

V

■ ■ ■

17 June 2013
#06
0505
Romans 15:8, Lamentations 3:22-23

Dear VI,

Well, I survived the week which means that yesterday I got to celebrate my first Father's Day! It was a quiet celebration. Nothing exceptional happened except for your old man walking around swollen with the pride that comes from having his very own son. I have yet to do any actual parenting, but you are alive in there (I have heard your heart beat), and I consider that enough for me to claim the title of "Dad."

Today, this honored daddy read Romans 15:8. In this verse, Paul mentions God's promises, which are, as they say in the gambling community, "a sure thing." In fact, they are man's only sure thing. Everything else is majorly flawed, including your parents (I know how shocking this admission must seem). Do not bother yelling, "But you said…," because I will refer you to this very letter.

Of course, your parents will always do their best to keep their word. Our desire to keep our word comes from our striving to be like Christ. But we are humans, and we will let you down; this is one of God's promises, but do not be discouraged, my boy. Just as your parents falter, so will you. Everyone will flop. No one is perfect; we are all on an equal playing field. This is part of human nature. This is why *everyone* needs a Savior. He is the example to follow *and* the One with the power to forgive when we fail—all wrapped up into one.

When I was young and fell victim to a friend's going back on his word (not meeting me where he said he would, not giving back something he borrowed, etc.), I would go to my mom and vent. Most of the time she gave the same response: "Now you know what not to do." Do not tell her I said this, but she is exactly right. When the day comes where you feel the particular pain that accompanies a human's pulling the rug from beneath you, remember the feeling and choose not to repeat it. Man is not the example you want to follow anyway.

Do not dwell in the knowledge that you and everyone you love will have times when their actions contradict their speech. It is just as foolish to spite your eyes for being whatever color they turn out to be. Instead, rejoice in the fact that our Savior's love never fails, and neither do His promises.

I love you; you can take my word on that!

V

■ ■ ■

18 June 2013
#07
0510
Psalm 12:5

Dear VI,

I just finished Psalm 142. David does a great job of provoking the reader into feeling the desperation he had while writing it. He writes as if the entire world is out to get him. Every man I know has, at some point, felt that same kind of complete desertion. I believe even David, the most powerful man on the earth, whose relationship with God was special and intimate knows perfectly well God has not deserted him. Yet he cannot shake the feeling of soul-wrenching loneliness. "I look for someone to help me, but no one gives me a passing thought! No one will help me."

David proves here that a man (Christian or not) goes through times where he feels as if he has been locked outside in the cold. It breaks my heart to think of you in such a state, which is why I want you to know your mother and I are here—during the tough times and joyful ones. Our desire as parents is to have open lines of communication with you. We want our relationship to be such that you feel comfortable coming to us, regardless of the situation. This isolated feeling David describes is one of the Enemy's favorite tricks. It is a trick that I have fallen for time and again. Never allow yourself to entertain the thought that you are alone.

I can guarantee that you will come into contact with curiosities. There will be temptations difficult to overcome and observations that will make your head spin. *This is normal.* In addition to your parents desiring your trust in coming to us, we are praying diligently that you make friends with those you can discuss the heavy issues. A primary group of friends is an important part of life but a subject for another day. Today, know that your family is here. If you want to discuss something, let's discuss it. If you need to vent, come vent. If you have a problem, let's find a solution.

I love you, my precious oven bun,

V

P.S. It would be foolish to end without pointing out that David, as he does so often, concludes his poem by acknowledging that, while his depression is all encompassing, he has not forgotten that God is greater than his feelings. And through God, his rescue will come.

■ ■ ■

19 June 2013
#08
John 19
0525

Dear VI,

Your letters are fast becoming a part of my little morning routine. Every morning before work I crawl out of bed and, while still in a dreamy haze, I manage to shave, strap on my uniform, brew some coffee, and open up the Bible. I read and sip until I feel I have benefited. Then I spend some time in prayer before getting to work on your letter.

Around that time, your mom stumbles in from the bedroom, looking like a sleepwalking watermelon on stilts! You are so active in the womb that she is hardly finding any rest. Her lack of sound sleep has turned her into a kind of reverse zombie who, instead of surviving through the nourishment of the living, survives by nourishing others. "RAAAA... Can I make you a smoothie? RAAAAA...I am folding clothes. RAAAA!" Despite her current state, she is still up shuffling around the kitchen fixing my lunch. I would be thrilled to know she was fast asleep right now. I want my best friend to receive the rest she so desperately needs. But alas, that is not the way things are shaping up. I see no better option than to accept the unchangeable and then adjust accordingly.

I read John chapter 19 today. In this chapter, Jesus is crucified and rises from the grave three days later. I grew up hearing this story every Sunday, in every way imaginable. We use to joke by saying any question asked at church could be correctly answered, "Jesus died on the cross."

Call me late to the party, but it was not until age 15, while attending a summer camp, that this concept of Christ's death and resurrection actually hit home. I realized that Jesus is the real thing. This revelation sent me to the floor for the next few hours where I lay on my face, thanking God for paying such a price for me and everyone I cared about, including you, my dear child. From that moment on, every time I read this particular part of any of the gospels, I get so charged up I want to raise my hands above my head and roar at the top of my lungs. (On past occasions I have, but because this morning I thought your mom was sleeping, I managed to refrain.)

I look forward to a day when we can discuss these matters. That being said, I do not want your knowledge of Christ to be solely based on Sunday school felt boards and your old man's microscopic ramblings. I encourage you to dig into Scripture and soak up all it has to offer. Develop an idea, then go deeper and see if it checks out or if you might prefer another. I want you to discover how blessed we are, the way I did at summer camp. Spoon-feeding salvation can end up crippling spiritual growth. Dig in, examine, pursue, figure it out!

I am fired up and ready for another week,

V

■ ■ ■

20 June 2013
#09
James 1:6
0521

Dear VI,

Yesterday I alluded to John 19, titled "Jesus Rises from the Dead." Without this, there would be no Christianity. If Christ did not come back after the crucifixion, He would have been a habitual liar psychopathic sicko. Here are the facts: Jesus was God incarnate, the Creator of the earth in a human body alive on His own planet, He gave himself as a living sacrifice on our behalf, defeated the grave, then *returned to earth* complete with scars in order to give His friends their final instructions before heading home. He sits there now, at the right hand of God until His glorious return, which could be any second! I would give my life for these truths but, even as I write them to you now, I cannot help but notice it sounds farfetched.

And so we come to the subject of faith. Faith in its most basic form (which is the only type I feel remotely qualified to explain) is confidence or trust in something or someone. I do not want to say more than that because I believe it is critical for you to investigate this subject in order to nourish your own faith. A man's faith in his Savior cannot be based on his parents' say-so. I will assist with whatever you need, but I believe putting in the work is crucial for a man's spiritual maturity. It is an adventure worth taking.

Think of this: how does a man *really* know that the food he eats is being digested and distributed accordingly? How does a husband *really* know that his wife is a faithful lover? Or even simpler, how do you *really* know that Van Gogh painted "Starry Night"? Did you see him do it? And if you did, are you sure he was the painter? Did he produce a birth certificate? And if so, are you sure the certificate was not a forgery? Eventually you will find the answer must be "because I believe. I have faith."

Romans 14:11 reads, "One day every knee will bow and every tongue will confess to God," which tells me that a day is coming when a man will not need faith to know the reality of his Creator. How glorious a day that will be for those whose faith held strong and how terrible for those whose faith lay elsewhere! Personally, I consider the ocean, the trees, the human body, the endless spectrum of animals, my connection to you, the whispering of the Holy Spirit, marriage, and a long list of other things to be very solid evidence in favor of a loving Creator, but faith is still needed.

I believe God specifically designed things so that, while He is everywhere all the time, we are always looking for Him. We are never content in who He is; we are always discovering Him. He wants us to pursue Him, so He made Himself available for discovery in infinite ways. He is under every rock, yet makes a man feel as if the pursuit must leave no stone unturned.

Because of this, I will end my ramblings by again encouraging you to engage. Your parents are a resource at your disposal, but we cannot flip stones for you.

Your faithful friend,

V

■ ■ ■

24 June 2013
#10
John 21:1-14
0511

Dear VI,

Monday has arrived again! It is always tough to get focused on Monday. I am ready, though. My head is shaved, and my boots are shined. God's got big plans for the Bradshaws this week, and I want to be a part of them.

As part of my Monday prep session, I read the story of Jesus surprising His disciples with an ocean-front BBQ. What can be more pleasant than imagining Jesus sitting on the beach, poking the fire with a stick and smelling His seafood breakfast while He waits for His buddies to show up. He endured the crucifixion, conquered the grave, and now sits in the sand, hitting bull's-eye after bull's-eye with the pebbles around Him. Whatever He is doing, I am sure He is enjoying creation in exactly the way His Father intended. This is the definition of *contentment*.

I do not often fish with a pole, but I do hunt a lot of fish while free diving with a spear. I am very excited to introduce you to this hobby of mine. We will go diving and poke a couple fish out of the deep, clean them up, and follow our Lord's example by making a fish taco breakfast feast for our queen, Mrs. Bradshaw.

I daydreamed about Jesus on the beach and our future water adventures while we spent some time on the sand yesterday. After church we headed straight for the water, again in preparation for Monday. I surfed while your mom relaxed on the beach in a custom sand recliner of my own creation. Eventually, the three of us got in the warm Florida ocean and captured our first family beach picture. Your mom said she could tell you loved the water, which made me cry. You are making me a big softy, son!

It was no easy task getting your mom in and out of the water. Even the walk from the car to the sand was a chore—but one worth the effort. A little determination was rewarded with the memory of a custom sand chair and a family picture. I would have never picked off that one wave or cried at the realization that my son was actually in the ocean enjoying himself had we stayed home. Most of the time, going the extra mile pays off.

This morning I felt led to take a break from tough topics and simply document a family adventure. This has been a different writing experience and certainly much easier! My words will always be written based on the Spirit's suggestion, but I think I like recording Bradshaw history. As you finish reading this, know that your dad got up to meet Monday with a big stupid grin on his face.

Thank you,

V

■ ■ ■

25 June 2013
#11
Genesis 2:7
0528

Dear VI,

After a couple weeks, my job description is taking shape. I reluctantly admit that after a lifetime of trying to avoid it, I have found myself the submissive owner of a desk job. How ironic! It was the Navy that finally got me—a Navy whose slogan boasts: "Join the Navy and see the world!"

Because I am not a big tech guy, I just now am beginning to truly understand the power of the computer. It will be the king of the world you grow up in. It already is. People do not know how to act when they cannot access their desktop or phone. I watch the entire medical clinic transform into a limping mess every time a network connection is lost. I know people who experience chest pain every time they discover their phone has no service. Technology has opened up new methods of correspondence, which have crippled people's ability to work together. The main ones being email, text, and instant messaging.

These "new and improved" modes of communication make it almost completely unnecessary to actually speak to other human beings. Information is passed quickly—but at the expense of relationship. Looking another person in the eye and expressing one's self is being replaced by extended hours straining against the glow of a screen. Backs are stiffening.

Bottoms are slowly spreading. The word *sedentary* has made its way into our vernacular. And while I do begrudgingly accept that description, and this is the way things are, I am not happy about it.

My job calls for me to split my time roughly 60/40 between the computer and patient care, which means I do not battle with technology as much as some—but certainly more than I like. My job is forcing me to come to grips with a new sensation. At the end of the day, I feel as if my body is at war against itself. My brain is exhausted from dealing with Social Security numbers, troubleshooting paper jams, booking appointments, and ordering glasses. But mostly, it is sick and tired of yelling "Sit still and keep working!" to my ever-wiggly body. My soul endures a constant nagging, which makes my spirit angry and understandably so. I have forced it to do something that is in many ways self-destructive, and my body has no problem reminding me that, if I keep this up, it will submit and lose the ability to function as it was designed.

We humans are animals. Have I taken you to the zoo yet? If so, I am sure you remember that animals do not thrive in a cage. We flourish in the elements. Vitamin D, which comes from the sun, is responsible for giving us a positive attitude. Who is not uplifted by the sun on their back? We have hands that we might build and climb and create. God gave us hair that we may keep warm (to the Bradshaw men He gave extra hair—just not on their heads). How clever is our Designer that something as beautiful as a woman's hair also serves such a practical purpose! How incredible it is to think that my skin absorbs encouraging vitamins via a star 92 million miles away.

I distinctly remember my childhood friends falling away one by one. A job or a woman or a substance replaced the things they knew would benefit them—like playing outside, being a part of a church community, or staying away from women in leather skirts. The curiosity to chase what adults did lured them away, and because of this, I found myself spending much more time by myself. I had many arguments with my mom over what she considered a "long adolescence," but I preferred to call that time "wisdom concerning my mental health." Our senses must be exposed to God's creation. This is how we are designed.

It dawned on me this morning that, barring a serious war, I will be working at the same desk for the next five years. The realization put me into a state of mild panic! Must a man choose between responsibility and overall health? How did it come to this? Your family puts real value on time spent in the wild. Our desire is to rear you in such a way that your body can absorb as much creation as humanly possible.

But how can this happen if your dad is at a desk 50 hours a week? How can I lead you if I am not in shape myself? What type of a husband would put such a burden on his wife? I believe achieving a balance is possible, but it will require a unique lifestyle. I guess I had better get on my knees and start figuring out this thing.

Get on out of there and play with your pa,

V

■ ■ ■

26 June 2013
#12
Genesis 1:31
0523

Dear VI,

To my untrained eye, it looks like you are surely ready to get out of that womb! If the energy you're displaying right now is any indication of things to come, your mother and I have our work cut out for us. With two months still to go, your mom is already 50 pounds heavier than she was pre-pregnancy (which is a lot when considering she started out weighing a petite 115.) Her mental toughness during this season of physical discomfort is inspiring.

Even though she is seriously uncomfortable, she considers the experience of carrying you a great pleasure. Instead of spending her time griping about her sore joints or daydreaming about the trim, fit body she once lived in, she is praising God for the opportunity to grow a baby boy. Because of this, her perspective is in its proper place. Your mom's willingness to let Christ into the experience is responsible for making her experience a great pleasure.

I want you to know that the Bible never says we are not to enjoy pleasure. People seem to think Christianity's main focus is to ruin everyone's fun. No, God filled the earth with things He considered good; He wants us to enjoy them. Rather than condemning pleasure, the Bible reminds us that the world apart from God has no *real* pleasure in it. Christ is the ingredient that makes an experience truly pleasurable. Pleasure without Christ is a question with no answer. It is a piano with no keys or a sports car with no engine.

Reading, surfing, music, camping, good food, traveling, sports, skipping rocks, working, sleeping, movies, relationships—I hope you experience all of these pleasures and much more. But if any of those things are done without getting the Holy Spirit involved, it is like getting a small sample of the feast, but never getting to sink your teeth in. The experience ends up being a tease.

The best way to get Him involved is simply by nurturing your relationship with Him. When you have the Holy Spirit living actively inside, it is easy to involve Him—just as it is natural to share your belongings with your best friend. If you play football and tackle someone, help him up. If you are the one receiving the hit, grit your teeth, look your opponent in the eye, and say, "Well done." This is how a man makes the most of a pleasure.

Writing letters to you is challenging, but it pleases me very much,

V

∎ ∎ ∎

27 June 2013
#13
John 3:23
0518

Dear VI,

Many facets of Christianity are capable of making a man scratch his head. Well, today I hope to offer you some peace. In John 3:23 our purpose is summarized in one command: "Love God and love others."

I believe the Bible has the ability to answer any question the world can throw at Christianity. But this does not exempt a man from finding himself bogged down in some areas and overwhelmed in others. That is the beauty of John 3:23. It is an anchor, a net we can depend on when balance seems uncertain. "Love God and love others." When you find yourself wedged into a corner, you cannot go wrong looking to this verse for guidance.

It is also wise to keep this command close when a discussion begins feeling like an argument. For example, suppose someone says, "I believe that the only way to take communion is by eating yeast free bread." How would you respond? I have taken communion with a baguette representing the body. Does that nullify my communion? This may seem like a moot point, but I have seen best friends become enemies and churches split over issues more hair-splitting. I have seen a church body begin a kind of Civil War over topics like women wearing earrings! I will always encourage you to dig in deep. Search the scriptures for solutions; there is no question too small to consider, but never do so at the expense of John 3:23.

I know this is easier said than done. The concept is simple, but the application is tougher than you may think. The Bible tells us we are specifically put in uncertain situations (such as disagreements) so we can grow. Never rule out the very realistic possibility that you may never reach an agreement, and that is acceptable. It is more important to love that person in Christ than it is for your point to be driven home. Lewis, love our Savior and love those around you. Everything else is simply details—important details, but details nonetheless.

Just so you know, your mom is so massive, a stranger recently asked if she was expecting twins!

V

■ ■ ■

28 June 2013
#14
0518
1 Corinthians 13

Dear VI,

Love: a word with a million meanings. How can I go on about the importance of loving God and loving others without clarifying what *love* means? Love is a word that can flip-flop between a noun and a verb or be both simultaneously. It is an idea that differs with every culture and every household. To get where we are headed, we need to be on the same page, which means a definition must be established. I choose the one found in 1 John 3:16; "We know what real love is because Christ gave up his life for us. And so we also ought to give up our lives for our Christian brothers and sisters." The Bible defines *love* as "sacrificing one's life for another." This definition includes, but does not specifically mean, "the forfeiture of a man's breath and heartbeat." A man can lay down his life by giving his time, energy, resources, strength, wisdom, or friendship.

As surely as we breathe, we love. General insight to what a man loves can be observed by what he spends his money on, but that is not always the case. Sacrifice is the *true* test that proves what a man truly loves—whether that love is godly, evil, or simply foolish. Yes, the man loves the woman as long as all he has to do is hold her hand, but what about when she expects him to buy her nice meals or spend the day cleaning her grandma's room at the nursing home? What happens when loving this woman means rearranging his finances and his Saturday?

What about when your love for Christ is tested? What will happen when you walk by a boy being teased, and the Holy Spirit tells you to intervene on the kid's behalf? Getting involved might mean getting into a fight or those spectators choosing to laugh at you. Will you show your love for Christ by sacrificing your pride or will you walk by thinking, "That isn't my problem"?

Everyone will sacrifice himself for something. Whatever a man loves most will be preserved the longest. If a man ignores the Holy Spirit's orders to stand up for a brother, he is saying, "I love my pride and reputation more than obeying the Holy Spirit." That sort of love is genuine, but it is also selfish. Loving yourself to the point of denying those in need is the opposite of 1 John 3:16. Unless a man purposely does the opposite of what he wants (which is insane), he cannot act without exposing what he loves most.

I feel bad writing letter after letter about less-than-uplifting subjects! But as I have said from the start, this entire process is one big exercise in obedience. I don't relish writing to you about such matters. I find it stressful and exhausting, but because I love you, I am doing my best to clearly express whatever the Holy Spirit puts on my heart. Today, I am loving you by giving you some information I pray helps you in the future.

I do love you,

V

P.S. Our home is all set up, but we continue to pray about a situation that will blend my work schedule with our lifestyle. Ideas are forming; none are worth mentioning.

■ ■ ■

02 July 2013
#15
Ecclesiastes 4:9-12
0520

Dear VI,

It has been a few days between letters, but that doesn't mean I have not written. Actually, I have been writing more than usual in my own journal, attempting to find guidance regarding the future of our family. I have felt burdened about the state of this world you are preparing to enter. I think as a man begins to consider the world from a father's perspective, everything begins looking bleaker. Every new dad must, at some point, think, "If things are this bad now, how much worse will it be when my child gets to be my age?" It is a depressing train of thought.

My situation at work is making its mark as well. Something has to give because I am really struggling. I will spare you the details. I have been doing my best to dig in and search for wisdom through meeting with the Lord and studying His Word. I am no scholar—far from it. My time spent with my nose in the Bible is a struggle in obedience fueled by the desire to grow into a better man. If I were to call myself anything, it would be "driven" and even that is a stretch.

Putting my thoughts on paper has always helped with organization; prayer is also key, but talking with God-fearing people is what I want to write about today. Having friends that are on the same page is critical. Friends from all walks of life are good, but with whom do you fellowship? Who keeps you accountable? With whom do you share your meals? Who can you ask for prayer? If I were to ask you what kind of people make up your primary group of friends, how would you respond?

Jesus had all sorts of friends, admirers, and followers. He ate dinner in the homes of the rejected, saved the son of a soldier, met with a lady at a well, and was invited to and attended at least one wedding.

Tens of thousands of people from all walks of life followed Jesus everywhere!

In all situations, He was able to have a positive impact on those He came into contact with, but what did He always do after? He went and regrouped in the presence of His Father and His disciples. He fellowshipped, prayed, relaxed, hung out, talked things over with His primary group. Many believe that within that primary group, He had a best friend named John. Establishing this intimate group of disciples was the first thing Jesus did when starting His ministry. That tells me it is an important part of a solid foundation. My best friend within my primary group is your mom. She is the human friend I can go to with anything, and I am positive I will be welcomed with honesty and love. (And yes, she feels the same about me.) I pray God brings these types of people into your life as well.

Until then, I guess your dad will have to do,

V


■ ■ ■


05 July 2013
#16
Psalm 8:4-5
1000

Dear VI,

A routine is hard to find when the Fourth of July lands smack dab in the middle of an already whacky week. Wednesday, your mom and I spent four excruciating hours in a class called "Baby Boot Camp." We both came away thinking the class was an exercise in enduring torture silently rather than helpful, but that is because your family is a unique breed.

Between Navy boot camp, six months in corpsman school, nine months in Navy optician school, two weeks of orientation, my job itself, and the hours of training I sit through weekly, my insides can be screaming in anguish while my flesh remains still. I have perfected a flat, passive expression that can be held for extended periods of time. It is as if I am in a group, listening to a comedian and the first person to smile loses, except the opposite.

I guess the military deserves the credit, but overall, I had never given it much thought until I sat next to your mother at Baby Boot Camp. She wiggled and whispered from start to finish. She cracked jokes, dropped everything that could be dropped, and opened the world's loudest bag of M&Ms. It was classic! Force of habit had me unknowingly sitting in the position of attention while your mom snickered at a picture of a nipple (which caused her to spill the contents of her purse.) Needless to say, we left the class during the first break, deciding it best for everyone if we just figure out parenting as we go.

Instead of attending "Act Two," we went home, and I dug a big fire pit in our backyard. This is much more our style. (The pit turned out to be a serious adventure, a story worth telling someday.) I created the pit so that your mom and I could celebrate the Fourth of July through the roasting of meat over an open flame. She got her exercise lumbering around our yard looking for sticks to throw in the fire while I smoked a pipe and straightened wire clothes hangers.

Months ago, when I was unpacking the house, I found some bottle rockets I had smuggled in from Mexico after a surf trip. How could we resist lighting some bottle rockets on the Fourth of July? For a finale, we ate big bowls of frozen yogurt and watched "The Patriot." Your mother and I are very happy.

We love you,

V


■ ■ ■

07 July 2013
#17
Psalm 18:6
0553

Dear VI,

Monday is here again. How does it arrive sooner than the other days? I am sitting in my spot, sipping coffee, and struggling to mentally prepare myself. I spend daily time in the Bible. This is non-negotiable. I assume most of my letters to you will contain some bit of Scripture, but that will not always be the case. This is why I put a verse at the top of each letter. I challenge you to open up the Word and find the scripture!

Today while praying I was reminded of a situation I witnessed at church. That particular Sunday we had a time for people to come to the front of the sanctuary and pray out loud with the community of believers who make up our congregation. I remember a specific gentleman who came up and said softly into the mic, "Lord, I need help. Restore my marriage; please repair my broken family. We need You real bad."

He was an older, tired-looking man with ragged clothes, assisted by a cane and, as he shuffled by me, I admired his manliness. The world teaches that real men are void of certain emotion. A real man only displays masculine emotions like anger, pride, and a love of protein. A real man must appear self-confident but is not held responsible for a lack of self-control unless his lack of restraint causes him to display girlish emotions at which point his "man card" is put into question. Crying is unacceptable, as is disappointment, fear, and the desire to snuggle. This lie puts pressure on men to bury part of themselves deep inside for fear of the potential consequences that could come with opening up. The fear of being exposed as weak keeps men from sharing their hearts and causes them to silently curse their own spirits instead.

The longer this lie goes on, the harder it becomes to break the cycle. He hates his pain because it reminds him of his unmanliness (which is a lie, remember). However, the thought of being exposed as a fraud hurts even more. So he continues to internally beat himself up with a smile, deciding that self-loathing is better than the judgment of those he has tricked into liking him. After all, at least he has some control over hating himself.

He may seem chiseled from oak, but those emotions never go away. They sit inside and rot. They grow cold and get heavy while silently biding their time. They patiently wait for an opportunity to rear their ugly heads. What a horrible way to live! The modern man has made everyone believe he is a pillar of strength when, in fact, fear has made him a coward without knowing it. He is an adult child caught in a wicked cycle; the Enemy methodically flips the script so that the man will never mature.

This is why I admire the man at church so much. Remember this man when you are in need of help or afraid to express yourself. He did the right thing. If you are sad, angry, rundown, broken-hearted, confused, ashamed, afraid, or anything else, speak up. Surround yourself with the kinds of friends who will love you for who you are and are willing to assist you through what you are feeling. Find that primary group of friends from Letter 15. They are a great resource. Of course, you also have your crusty old Ma and Pa around too. We have your back.

You are "The Man,"

V

■ ■ ■

08 July 2013
#18
1 Peter 4:12-13
0645

Dear VI,

Your old man gets to go to work a little late because he signed up for a base basketball tournament, win-win situation! The Navy is full of chances to volunteer for various events which I take full advantage of for the following reasons: they challenge me, I meet new people, and (selfishly) because it gets me out of work. I would like to say that the last reason takes up only a sliver of the pie, but in reality, it is closer to two-thirds. Playing basketball is infinitely better than sitting at a computer. I thought it would be impossible to miss work in order to play sports, but my command not only supports it, they are "very impressed with my motivation." I guess I fooled everyone! My question is, when this is the command's stance on extracurricular activities, why doesn't the basketball team consist of a hundred people?

I want to write down my thoughts on the word *challenge*. A challenge most often occurs during one of two times. One is when a man is pursuing a goal that has the potential to give him pleasure (like your mom who, out of her desire to hold you, has accepted the nine-month challenge of carrying you). The second is when he accepts the challenge of another (like a boy who is challenged to a footrace).

In Letter 5 I described my first week of work to you along with the trials that came with learning a military job. Trials are, without a doubt, challenging, and challenges certainly bring about trials, but understand there is a difference. A *trial* is a situation you have been forced into by the decisions of those around you. A drunk driver kills a woman, and now the husband is left to endure the trial of picking up the pieces. A child grows up in a house with a heavy smoker and is diagnosed with lung cancer. The Navy decides to implement an ancient and impossibly complicated computer program, and your dad endures the trial of overcoming continuous failure and frustration. A Christian has the advantage of knowing that trials (whether it be losing a spouse or developing cancer or failure) are given to us as tools for growth. We also know that the Holy Spirit will guide us through the best route.

I love a challenge—even though I fear doing something that makes me uncomfortable. I have a *greater* fear of living a secure lifestyle while, just outside, great experiences are passing by. Have I forgotten the words while singing a solo? Yes. Have I missed the game-winning shot?

Many times. There has never been a time prior to a challenge where I have not thought, "Why did I venture outside my cozy comfort zone?" Transversely, I have never finished a challenge thinking anything other than, "I am really glad I did that."

Getting out of your comfort zone stretches you. It teaches you that it is okay to be vulnerable. Most importantly, if you are giving God glory in all you do, you cannot lose.

God is good,

V

■ ■ ■

10 July 2013
#19
Proverbs 24:5
0600

Dear VI,

As I sit here praying—and your mom stands a few yards away singing to you—I have decided it best to simply remind you to read Proverbs. (Why her melody lead me to this advice, I am not sure.) These verses are awesome for a man's everyday life. I cannot think of better wisdom to give you. Find me a Proverb that is not absolutely applicable today. Now that you know a little bit about challenges, do you accept?

Classic morning at the Bradshaw home,

V

■ ■ ■

11 July 2013
#20
Proverbs 14:1
0625

Dear VI,

Our basketball team has made the finals, which means this weathered old athlete got to sleep until 0600. I am glad I signed up for the team. I have met a lot of great people.

The tournament is being held outdoors in Florida in July. It is hot here right now—so hot that the soles of people's shoes are literally melting on the court. If you inherited the famous Lewis sweat gene, you can truly appreciate how soaking wet I have been. People say they sweat a lot but they don't. Bradshaws sweat a lot! Yesterday I pretended my sweat does not act as a repellent and allowed myself to believe I am pretty tough. After all, most of the people playing in this tournament are ten years younger than me, and I have managed to keep up.

Imagine how sheepish I felt limping in the door with my backpack full of stinky braces, only to find your mom sweeping the floor with a person living inside of her. That is toughness. Your mother's humble grit continues to give me a deeper respect for a woman's thick skin and has taught me that my ability to out-jump a teenager is not so awesome after all. We are so blessed to have such a strong woman in our lives! I have always known she was tough, but observing her carry a child is one of the roughest, most humbling, inspiring sights I have ever seen.

She spent time with a group of moms yesterday and told me that watching all of the kids play at the park gave her an overwhelming desire to hold you. She wants to smell your breath and kiss your neck. She wants to care for you. I am no medical expert, but it looks as though she will not need to wait long. When will your birthday be?

Wish me luck,

V

■ ■ ■

12 July 2013
#21
Isaiah 48:10
0507

Dear VI,

Every human being will spend seasons of his life suffering. For the Christian and non-Christian alike, there is no way around it. Therefore, it is only right that I spend a morning writing some words on the issue. The definition of the word *suffer* covers the spectrum—from feeling unhappy to being consumed with anguish. Suffering can occur either mentally or physically and can be caused by self-anguish or affliction brought on by others. In other words, if one man said he was suffering because he imagined he had stubbed his toe and another man said he was suffering because he watched his true love die, both would be correct.

My goal here is not to give you the ins and outs of the subject (I am not qualified to do so), but rather to explain why a Christian is not exempt. Many churches talk about salvation as if it is the solution to all problems. "Believe in Jesus Christ, and that dream of a two-car garage and a six-figure income will be right around the corner." That is not true! In fact, Jesus promises the opposite. Suffering is a very important part of being a Christian.

It seems to me that many non-Christians see suffering accompanying conversion and, therefore, do not convert. "Oh, no!" they say. "If I let Christ into my heart, I am going to have to face things that will cause me great suffering. I am going to have to say goodbye to people and pleasures I have been enjoying for years." They convince themselves that experiencing conviction over things they do without a second thought, or the pain that will accompany the realization that they were wrong about God, is too much to handle. Instead, they believes the lie that Christianity is nothing more than an extra-curricular activity. Granted, convincing themselves that Christ is fiction may result in a life of very little suffering, at least while they are alive.

God has chosen to refine His children by fire, which sounds harsh but is actually the best way. How else does a boy become a warrior? (Remember, our best option is to prepare and become warriors because we are at war with the world on a daily basis. Who wants to go into battle without training?) If a man knows a map inside and out but never steps outside of his home, is he an explorer? Education is only a piece of the puzzle. Christ takes our lives and thrusts it into the flames, but He does not leave it there. He removes it at the perfect time, shapes it with the proper tools, adds a little something here, removes a blemish there, then blows cool refreshing air on it, letting it settle until He decides the time is ripe to repeat the process.

Each time a Christian's life is put into the furnace of affliction, a unique experience is taking place. No two seasons of suffering are the same. Each one is a little stronger, a bit more durable and, therefore, can tolerate longer durations in the hotter coals. When a man's life seems to be on fire, he is tempted to ask, "Why?" or shout, "Please, I can't take it! This is too hot!" But a Christian knows deep down God's promise that He will never give us more than we can bear. Your Architect is a master at His craft and always knows the perfect time to pull you out and cool you off. Only a Christian can say that the breath of Christ is soothing and rejuvenating. It feels like cool bed sheets on sunburned skin. It heals the wounds and mends a man in such a way that he can look in the mirror and say what a maturing warrior might say: "Yes, I *can* see now that the fire has done me a lot of good. My Creator was right. This result *is* worth the heat."

A lot of good information in the Bible pertains to this subject of suffering. Taking a closer look is definitely worth the effort. This morning I will end with a truth: as a Christian matures into a warrior, he is able to look at his life and see that the fire he endured played a critical role in his development. As much as the thought of your suffering breaks my heart, the thought of sending my son to battle unprepared pains me more.

I will not shelter you from the suffering God sees fit for you to grow through. But my love for you forces me to suffer beside you—a responsibility I willingly and gladly accept. I am your partner,

V

■ ■ ■

15 July 2013
#22
Matthew 7:24-27
0550

Dear VI,

The weekend is never further away than this moment—your dad really struggles on Mondays! This is not an intimate peek inside of my life. Most men do not like Monday because it signifies the beginning of the work week, which always seems to crawl by at a snail's pace. While our weekends fly by faster than a fast flying bird of some kind, like a hummingbird or whatever. (See? Even my similes are horrible on Mondays!)

Oftentimes while standing on the cold tile, shaving my face and staring at my pasty reflection, I find myself devising elaborate, far-fetched excuses to get out of work. I won't embarrass myself with examples. No doubt this poor attitude would fester throughout the day if not for this time right now. Here I sit in the dark praying, reading, and writing to you. During this time, I literally feel my attitude switch. It is a miracle. Nothing short of Jesus' saying, "I see you want to succeed in My name. You came to the right place! Let's get this done."

For a man to wake up and think about his aching muscles or cramped cubicle is both natural and understandable. Most people manage to find motivation somewhere whether that be a paycheck, a promotion, a sick child, or a particular lifestyle. Others go simply because society says an adult is obligated to work. But only Christians have the opportunity to meet with the living King who alone has the power to give a man the focus needed to *completely* seize the day.

I ask God every morning for the attitude and strength to attack each day with joy in the knowledge that He included me as part of His master plan. I ask that my eyes would be wide open to every opportunity I am presented with and that I would make the best choices in regard to them all.

Most mornings I slowly open the front door and glare out into the darkness. I stare the day straight in the eye as a man might do before wrestling with a well-respected opponent. I then close my eyes and take a deep breath, directing my senses to absorb the work of their Designer. Those smells and sounds usually make me smirk. Then clothed in my new attitude, I step out to tackle my day.

Praise the Lord,

V

■ ■ ■

16 July 2013
#23
Proverbs 20:4
0553

Dear VI,

One month! That is how long I must wait until I finally watch you take that first breath of fresh hospital air. Time is weird! I cannot believe eight months have passed since your mom woke me up smiling to report she was now caring for a second heartbeat. I am sure one day we will read this letter together, and it will feel to me as if the ink should still be wet. Then before I can blink, you will be a grown man, hopefully off pursuing whatever passion God has built into you. So how is it that this month will feel like a year? I blame the anticipation. Maybe anticipation has the ability to slow down seconds, who knows?

Proverbs 20:4 encourages me to be diligent in my writing. This verse warns against becoming the type of man who is too lazy to plow his fields. Time tricks the lazy man into thinking he has endless amounts of it. Meanwhile, the seconds creep silently by. Anyone who believes time is not a factor will wake up one day realizing that is no longer the case. Harvest season has arrived. Their fields are flat.

Unlike blue eyes or freckles, becoming the sort of man who works his fields with diligence is a learned trait. I realized this morning that the responsibility of developing this trait in your life lies heavily on your parents. It seems to me that you will be entering a world full of dreamers while the doers become fewer all the time. I want you to be a doer!

Things usually crumble in one of two directions:

1) The dreaming man will lower his expectations, deciding that the goal is not worth the time needed to achieve it. He instead settles for something that allows more freedom to do what feels good at the time. This is sad because the man still has aspirations of tackling that field. He wants to do it. He believes the harvest would yield exceptional crops. But he does not like blistered hands or a sore back, so he stares at his field as it becomes increasingly weed filled and unkempt. He watches as time stealthily takes over.

2) This dreamer goes from field to field. He begins a row but once the novelty wears off, he loses interest, deciding it might be better to begin work on another field all together. His life is a series of partly sown earth. He sacrificed more time than he would have if he had simply kept to the one field, but because he never stayed in

one spot, he might be lucky to get a few sparse shrubs. (I can fall into this category when I'm not careful.)

Every Christian man's goal should be to plow in such a way that his harvest gives glory to God. The crops are something He would enjoy at a feast. The question is: what field do you get to work on? The answer is one of my favorite parts of the Christian faith. Not only does the Holy Spirit lead a man to the proper field, He will then work alongside the man. Jesus will help you with the heavy lifting and speak encouragement to you in such a way that you don't care about those aching shoulders and push forward longer than you thought possible.

Keeping all of these thoughts in mind, let me end with a sobering reality. Sometimes after hundreds of hours have been invested toward a goal (one you felt certain was approved by Christ), it may seem as though crops simply did not sprout. This is not true. A healthy field has grown—just not in the way you imagined it might. It is very likely that the growing happened within. Spiritual growth is a beautiful harvest indeed. It is a field that God finds beautiful.

But who am I to write you about growing? Eight months ago you did not exist!

V

■ ■ ■

18 July 2013
#24
Colossians 3:2
0640

Dear VI,

Bad news, I am in another orientation. I thought one was excessive, but the United States government thinks otherwise. I am guessing the word *orientation* was invented to mask three days of sitting in a freezing room on metal chairs, listening to people read slides. PowerPoint exists to provide a visual *aid;* it is not there for the presenter to read verbatim! The good news is the agony doesn't begin until 0800, which allows me time to enjoy a more leisurely morning.

We went to the doctor yesterday. I heard your beating heart, and the nurse took some measurements. She said you are long and somewhere between six and seven pounds. The whole experience was unreal. I sat there with my mouth open, filled with the humbling emotions a man gets when he catches a glimpse of how blessed he really is.

I am sometimes ashamed of myself for, one second, feeling as if I am the most blessed man on the planet, and the next, feeling sorry for myself on account of something as minor as orientation. I allow myself to be controlled by feelings that accompany a set of circumstances. The waves are good; life is perfect. My computer froze; I live in hell. I remind myself daily to be less narrow-minded. I try to keep an eternal perspective by dwelling on big-picture truths like Jesus has my very best interests in mind. Or if I never experienced a bad moment, how would I ever know when I was experiencing a good one?

Thinking like this never occurred to me until I was in my 20s (which I am still in). I can look back and see many situations where I could have done special things for others had I not been so wrapped up in my own feelings. Thinking of those instances makes me feel sick with regret. I never want you to feel that. Think big picture! Make an effort to catch a glimpse of how blessed you really are.

You are a strapping young buck,

V

P.S. When you whine about life being unfair because you have to take out the trash, I can now say, "Son, I have been telling you not to think like that since before you were born."

■ ■ ■

20 July 2013
#25
Proverbs 17:6
0700

Dear VI,

Grandpa Freeman is here! What a relief to see a familiar face! I hit the jackpot as far as in-laws are concerned. Your grandpa is a remarkable man. I beg you, son, take every opportunity to learn from him.

When he arrived, he carried an extra suitcase stuffed to capacity with clothes, blankets, and toys—all of it for you. Consider that for a moment. Your grandma, Lisa Freeman, went out and spent hard-earned Freeman cash on tiny socks and onesies. Then after carefully washing them and packing them, she gave them to your grandpa who toted that suitcase 3,000 miles to this home where they sit in your room, waiting for your arrival. There is no doubt your family loves you.

Your mom was genuinely ecstatic not only to see her daddy but with all your clothes. Her strength is amazing. Keep in mind, the military has put her in a situation where many of the special traditions a pregnant woman looks forward to cannot happen. Things she dreamed about as a girl will never come true. We cannot decorate rooms; there is no baby shower with friends and family. She is far from everyone she knows in a completely foreign city. Yet she joyfully sings to you most of the day and does her best to make our home cozy. I have never once heard her complain about your ever-growing body making her own not feel so great.

That suitcase held more than baby gear. It gave her a chance to feel like a mommy. Tears of joy were in the corners of her eyes as she methodically picked up each item, saying things like "It has a little dinosaur wearing glasses!" or "He will like such soft cloth on his skin." I hope after reading this letter, you get up and give your mom a big hug. She is our queen.

You have quite the wardrobe awaiting you,

V

■ ■ ■

22 July 2013
#26
Psalm 16:8
0550

Dear VI,

After Letter 22 (describing how my motivation to serve is a result of my time spent with God), I have spent hours marveling over how effective spending time with God is and how miserable I am when I do not. A supernatural transaction occurs when a man spends time with his Maker, but our Lord is so wonderfully practical He has given us additional cause-and-effect exercises that help transform a man's perspective. One in particular I feel is worth a few words is serving others.

Focusing on someone else forces the focus off of you. It is as simple as that. How can a man dwell on his own life when he is not thinking of his life? This groundbreaking concept is called "being unselfish," and it works great for the believer and non-believer alike. While the notion may seem elementary, it is very difficult to put into practice. Humans have selfishness so deeply etched in their sinful nature, they can actually be selfish while thinking of another. A man opens the door for a lady because he wants to check her out from behind. A son calls his mother every week so that when she dies, he is thought of fondly in her will.

These are called "selfish motives." It is nothing more than selfishness wearing a disguise. I do this all the time. The front can be very convincing. It may look exactly like the real thing, but when a man commits this sort of impression, the focus still lies 100 percent on him, which nullifies any sort of kindness he might have displayed. He is up to no good.

The proof that a truly unselfish act is a novelty can be seen in the reaction a man gets after being genuinely selfless. The recipient does not know how to respond. Instead of enjoying graciousness, they try to figure out what type of disguise the giver is wearing. What is his angle? What is in it for him? Humans see selflessness so rarely that they do not know how to react and panic instead. And of course, when someone reacts to a kind gesture with panicky skepticism, the gesture is all but ruined.

Only one Man lived a truly selfless life. In Him, Christians have a huge advantage. The only way to truly focus on others is by first focusing on history's one perfect example of selflessness. The selfless life Jesus lived must be the main focus of your own. Only then will you be able to truly think about someone other than yourself. And not only will you be able to, you will *want* to. When a man focuses on the noble life of Jesus, he will find himself looking around eagerly for someone to help. He will crave the opportunity to serve. He will want nothing more than to sacrifice his life in order to better the lives of those around him.

Proverbs 21:27,

V

■ ■ ■

DEAR VI...LOVE V    43

23 July 2013
#27
John 3:30
0545

*Saint Irenaeus: "The glory of God is man fully alive."*

Dear VI,

Today I would like to give you an example of a man whose eyes were off of himself. He was a prophet who mastered the art of focusing on the Perfect One, then through Him, to others. I am talking about John the Baptist.

Before I go further, I must mention that this man was an absolute stud. He lived in the wilderness where he ate insects and wild honey. His life revolved around baptizing and preaching about the kingdom of Heaven, the coming of the Messiah, and repentance. Whenever I read about John I wonder how I would react if I met a man who battled bee hives for nourishment and had the appearance of someone whose bed was the desert floor. I am sure he did not smell like honey, and I am positive I would not let him hold my head under water. So why did people travel for days to see him. What about him was so attractive?

In my opinion, in addition to his being unbelievably confident, loving, and consistent, people saw John as genuine. He asked nothing for his services. He was visibly happy with his lifestyle. Because his whole self was focused on God, he was truly unselfish; this unselfish nature attracted people to him. His lack of selfish motive was proof of God's presence in his life.

John was vocal about his life not being his, saying things like, "He must become greater, and I must become less." What practical wisdom for our own life! The more we replace ourselves with Jesus, the more unselfish we become, the more useful we become, and the more alive we become.

I fear the modern Christian puts an unselfish heart in the same category as being a pushover. It is important we do not get the two confused. John was no pushover. He was a man of great influence who stood strong in his beliefs. He did not become less by sitting quietly in the corner with his hands folded. Nor did he become less by allowing himself to get stepped on, and neither should any man. Becoming less means striving for perfection with your heart pointed outward. It means never letting your personal aspirations snuff out the Holy Spirit. It means helping people up, shaking hands (in victory and defeat), and sharing whatever resources can be offered. The more space our Lord occupies in our life, the more impact we can have on those around us, which is how God says we live life to the fullest.

Your mom's body is full of you,

V


■ ■ ■


24 July 2013
#28
Romans 8:6-10, Psalm 37:3
0555

Dear VI,

Your grandparents started a trend. Baby gifts of all shapes and sizes are showing up daily, including clothes, a crib, nursing towels, and a wide array of accessories I never knew existed—things we apparently cannot live without. (I am not convinced a wipe warmer is critical, but experienced moms talk as if it is gold. We will see.) Your aunt and uncle wrote us a very generous check which I find more helpful than small cuts of cloth called "tee pees." (Again, we will see.) Your mom said as soon as she accepted that you could sleep safe and sound in a bed made of towels on the floor, gifts started rolling in. This is beautifully typical.

All we truly need is Jesus. I believe this with all of my heart but still have a hard time refraining from adding the word "and…." I tend to say things like, "All I need is Jesus *and* this watch," or "All I need is Jesus *and* that surfboard." All we need is Him. That's it. I have noticed when I throw my hands up in the air and declare to the Lord that I no longer care about whatever it was that concerned me, what I really wanted follows shortly after. (It is worth mentioning that the thing I really wanted is rarely what I thought I wanted at the time.) When I am truly content with what God has given me, He seems to say, "Here you go; I can now trust you with this gift because I see it will not replace Me. I love you."

Here is the progression: God told man that, for a full life, he needs only Him. If man takes that advice and honestly looks to God for everything, God will not only deliver on His word but will bless man with additional gifts simply because He is pleased with the obedience. The catch is when a man lives out a life of seeking only Jesus, he wants nothing else. And when a man who wants nothing receives a gift, that gift will always be greater than anything he wanted. Finally, because the man's life is focused on Jesus, he knows where the gift came from and to whom the glory belongs. A perfect circle of goodness! What a wonderful system.

It seems to me God enjoys blessing Christians in such a way that He can be the only possible explanation. He wants you to know where the gift came from without having to put a tag on the box. His clever genius allows Him to do this in an unlimited combination of ways, but only a man walking in step with Him can see the abundance for what it is—such as boxes we did not ask for showing up on our porch day after day or the fact that, despite our budget, the fridge is jam-packed with healthy food. I do not think He is necessarily showing off, but there is no doubt Jesus enjoys surprising those who consider Him all they need.

You're coming home to one plush baby setup,

V

■ ■ ■

25 July 2013
#29
Philippians 4:11-13
0552

Dear VI,

Stuff keeps showing up! Last week your room contained nothing but that ocean-blue stripe. Now we are running low on space! Obviously, receiving baby gifts is new to us. I find the entire experience a little intimidating. We know God does not need to do any of this. You do not need any of this. He is giving in abundance because He loves us, and that fact is mighty humbling.

Your parents have their own stuff that could use replacement—like this orange chair we bought at Goodwill! However, while staring at it risks retinal damages, buying a new chair would mean going into debt or using finances that could be better utilized elsewhere. We are practicing the art of contentment by remembering that though the chair has forty years' worth of wear and tear, it is also cozy. When God decides the time is right for "Agent Orange" to retire, God will replace it in an awesome fashion as a reminder of His love for us. Until then, we have a nice place to sit.

Be content with all you have, keep in mind that everything from your socks to your beating heart is a gift, then sit back and watch Him take care of you in ways you would not believe were possible.

Maybe the Florida Orange will end up being your favorite spot. Anything is possible,

V

P.S. Matthew 6:33

■ ■ ■

26 July 2013
#30
2 Corinthians 4:6-7
0543


Dear VI,


And the blessings abound. Your mom just received a surprise baby shower, courtesy of co-workers I hardly know, for my wife whom they have never met. One co-worker in particular, Keisha (whom I call "the queen of optometry") is fast becoming a treasured friend and is the culprit for most of the planning. God used this woman's leadership to pack a room with the express purpose of celebrating your ever-nearing birth. We had food, cake, games, and lots of gifts (mostly diapers which, to me, are more valuable than a room full of precious metals.)

I promise the love these sailors poured out on your parents had nothing to do with me. Your dad is a Southern California boy, working beside people from the Deep South. My home state is casually referred to as "the land of fruits and nuts." Because I surf in an ocean sharks call home, I am considered crazy. Most people consider stepping into the ocean a means of suicide. Practically everything I like is lame here. And because I have never experienced the things this part of the country considers a way of life (things like off-roading, crawdad-ing or deer hunting) I am doubly un-cool.

This is why the only solution for my shipmates' spending their hard-earned money on you is Jesus. This is another area where desiring only Jesus impacts a man's life. Christians have the living God inside them at all times. If a man puts effort into nurturing that relationship with his Creator, the health of the relationship becomes evident in all facets of his life. The Holy Spirit's glorious light will be seen by those who surround the Christian man, often without that Christian man's even knowing the impact he is having.

From time to time, Christ enjoys giving a gift through those impacted by the believer (like a baby shower thrown by strangers) as a reminder of the impact He is having and to show the man his consistent devotion is bearing fruit. "Bravo Zulu" the Navy calls it. I am sure any attempt to impact my command through my own power would do nothing more than solidify my status as either a fruit or a nut. But through Christ, the Bradshaws are building a more favorable reputation. I consider your mountain of diapers to be a "Bravo Zulu" from our King.

Hurry up so I can field test these diapers,

V

■ ■ ■

29 July 2013
#31
Proverbs 20:24
0556

Dear VI,

This morning I want to pass on a visual that popped into my head while praying. Consider this a reminder that there is value in connection, but no connection is more valuable than that between man and Maker. Just as an electronic item cannot work without a power source, man cannot function without *his* Source. Without Christ, a man spends his life bouncing from place to place, trying to find purpose. His days are spent plugging himself into various outlets where he then tries to accomplish tasks with the wrong tools. A man without Christ is a blender trying to shave a head, a computer trying to make coffee, a vacuum cleaning the dishes.

Christ shows a man why he is designed in such a specific way and is then kind enough to plug him into an outlet where his precise function is desperately needed—an outlet in an environment he will thrive in. "See how you get warm in these areas here?" He will say. "This is so you can help heat food. All those pots and pans need you. They cannot perform properly without you. Now do you better understand why you were made in such a way?"

It is a beautiful thing to witness an invention churning away just as the Creator had intended,

V

P.S. Last night I set up your gift from my mom—a changing table! It is ready to function as designed. All it needs now is you!

■ ■ ■

30 July 2013
#32
Hebrews 13:5
0550

Dear VI,

The most popular work discussion is that of possession. Specifically, possessions recently bought or on the short list of things to buy. Listen to enough of this type of talk and anyone might begin his own imaginary list of must haves—items he "needs." Personally, I feel a little convicted; I have spent way too much time thinking about things I am missing instead of remembering we have much more than any human needs. My last few letters have outlined contentment, an abundance of baby gifts, and a mountain of diapers, yet I continue to confuse the word "need" with "want." I think the best way to get things back into perspective is by taking a looking at "necessity."

*Necessity*: "The fact of being required or an indispensable thing." In other words, a necessity is absolute—something a man cannot live without. (Remember: this letter is dedicated to necessities the *physical* body must have to survive. I have mentioned in previous letters, specifically 28 and 29, that all a man *really* needs is Jesus. This is in order for his life to be lived with purpose and excitement. I want this distinction to be crystal-clear. A man does not need Jesus in order for his systems to function properly. A non-Christian can have a body in peak condition, yet because his spirit is dead, his flesh and bone have no meaning. Without Christ, he is a dead man walking.)

I challenge you: make your own list of necessities. If you answer truthfully, I guarantee your list will be short. My list consists of nutrient-giving calories, water, and oxygen. If I lived outside in a cold climate, I would add "shelter" or "fire" to the list. If I lived in the desert, I would add "shade." This is where things begin to get tricky; after all, how does a man get his food? Well, he might want to buy it. In that case he will need money, but where does the man earn money? Maybe the man wants to hunt for his nutrients; does he not need a weapon and game to hunt? He could have a garden, but first he must complete the lengthy list needed to become a landowner. How would he get the seed? With what would he sow his fields?

Behind the simplest necessity lurks a list of needs. Clinging to that list lie wants, and with wants come the temptation to go overboard. I have seen men need to fish for their food and end up owning a boat, then a bigger boat, then a new garage to keep it in, and a bigger truck to haul it, then a lift and rims on the truck. What was once a peaceful hour on the shoreline with a pole is now a stressful daylong endeavor requiring gasoline, permits, and a costly list of supplies.

Necessity is wrapped in a list of needs and wants; beneath the wants lie subheadings with more needs and more wants. On it goes, the text forever shrinking. If a man loses focus of the big picture, he will end up believing he must have the things he wants but has no need for. My coworkers' lists usually include a combination of big-ticket items and doodads guaranteeing to make life just that much easier. Kits that give a vehicle more horsepower, magazines that hold a ridiculous amount of ammunition, a spray that will allow hair to get wet without destroying curls. These so-called "needs" are actually wants, and their place should be very low on the list. However, they are talked about so often and with such conviction, I find myself considering them necessities. "It is time I get myself some of that spray," I think.

As I look around our house, I know we have less than most; yet I cannot shake feeling convicted for wanting more than we need. I am not implying that having nice stuff is a sin. Only that the Bradshaw family (and most humans) become easily distracted by possessions. As the head of this household, I should know better than to desire something that has no benefit. I feel guilty. Having non-essentials forces us to adjust our priorities in such a way that doing what is best for our little family unit becomes difficult. This is the problem with *stuff*. A man can subtly become bogged down with what he owns and feel owned instead. It is tough to do what will energize the spirit when there is a kitchen full of knickknacks in need of dusting. It is hard to take off for an impromptu romantic weekend when your cash is tied up in the new couch that matches the baseboards. Having little often makes room for much, while having much often makes a man feel like a slave.

Contentment is the key to not getting carried away by the never-ending list of needs and wants. Remembering that God exceedingly abundantly meets our needs allows a man to think clearly on big-picture concepts instead of wasting time poring over the fine print. Not wanting much usually equates to not having much, and not having much gives a man the freedom to go do what is best as well as the flexibility to assist others. Isn't that what everyone should want?

I *need* to hold you,

V

■ ■ ■

01 August 2013
#33
John 9
0551

Dear VI,

In John 9:3 Jesus heals a man who has been blind from birth. Before doing so, He explains to the crowd gathered around Him that neither the sin of the blind man nor the sin of his family are responsible for his lack of sight. Jesus says this man has spent his entire life in darkness, "so that the power of God can be seen."

The notion of seemingly bad things happening to good people has always been a point of contention in Christianity. Non-believers consider this proof of the non-existence of or the cruelty of God while some Christians find it a stumbling block in their spiritual life.

Let me give you an example which helped me better understand how sin equates to birth complications in some cases, and in other cases, so-called "flawed" genetics are specifically given to people. If I see a boy with special needs, how am I to know if he was chosen by the Lord as a vessel in which to show His glory? Or how can I know if that boy's mother abused her body during pregnancy in such a way that her son was born with disabilities that would otherwise not be there? If the reason for this child's physical or mental impairments is due to his mother's selfish defilement of her body, then yes, it is the sin of his parent which has put him in such a position. This is the ripple effect of a human decision. This is what happens when free will is an option. (Do not forget that this mother could have used any number of harmful drugs and still had a perfectly healthy baby. The Lord is sovereign, and her sins against the body were not beyond the Lord's control. God is also just, and while His heart breaks for the child, He allows us to be responsible for our actions—even when those actions affect the innocent.)

While every human is unique, not all humans are created with the capability of contributing to a society in the traditional sense. That is to say, they cannot go to school, work, have a family, contribute to the economy, and start the process over for the next generation. Generally speaking, humans who are not able to do these things are diagnosed with having some sort of special needs on the grounds that their bodies and/or minds are different. People quickly write off this category of human as "broken" in some way while God looks at them as sons and daughters created precisely as He intended. The human brain is unable to imagine God's reasons for creating a person in such a way; therefore, they assume the person must be *flawed*. We presume that a girl born with a crooked spine had a problem during development. If a boy cannot learn through eight hours of sitting in a classroom, he must have a blown circuit somewhere and need medication of some kind.

These people are not poorly manufactured! Their lives have a critical function. They are a unique model very capable of functioning exactly as designed. At the core, they are able to do what we are all designed to do: glorify the Lord by loving Him and loving others, effectively worshiping Him and furthering His kingdom in the process.

Serious mental or physical complications can be far beyond the scope of human possibility, but to God, the "problem" is *not* a problem. It is simply in His hands. John Calvin says, "Man with all his shrewdness is as stupid about understanding by himself the mysteries of God, as an ass is incapable of understanding musical harmony."

I can hear people much smarter than I am telling me why my explanation of babies born in such a way is dead wrong. I can see them pointing at charts, which show studies documenting the rise in autism or the life expectancy of those born with Down syndrome. "You are telling me that God allows children to be born with no sight so that His glory can be shown?" they scream. I see myself removing my glasses and massaging the raw spot on the bridge of my nose while trying to make heads or tails of the data and feeling as if my own thoughts no longer hold any water. But then, I remember two things:

1) I am an ass trying to understand musical harmony, and
2) Suppose my interpretation is inaccurate?

Even if God has a million reasons for doing what He does and I do not know any of them, this is perfectly fine. My not knowing only means that God thinks it unnecessary for me to know. And if I try and understand His reasons for keeping me in the dark, I once again become the ass.

It is important to search for understanding, but in doing so, a man must keep in mind that his job on earth is to serve—not to know. Our obligation is to introduce the addict mother, the blind man, the crippled woman, and the hyper child to Jesus. He will take it from there.

Whatever condition you greet me in, I am certain you will be perfect,

V

■ ■ ■

02 August 2013
#34
Ephesians 5:1
0555

Dear VI,

In John 10 the blind man returns, this time after his vision has been restored. I alluded to the ripple effect created by our actions, and here is a perfect example of the ripple effect created by God's love. Jesus heals a man, that man gives the glory to God, the news spreads, believers are born, and more people are now rejoicing in Heaven. If this man had not been born blind, fewer people would be in Heaven. If the man had been born with perfect vision, I would not be writing this letter to you now.

There is a ripple effect for every action we take, be it wise, foolish, godly or wicked. Because Jesus is an all-seeing, all-knowing God, He knew the path His waves would take. He knew His death and resurrection would change the world forever. Humans do not have that luxury. For a man to witness his ripple roll along while observing who it touches almost never happens.

Being unable to witness the complete ripple effect sometimes annoys me because I selfishly want to receive credit for my good deeds. But at the same time, I am thankful that I remain ignorant to many of the destructive waves created by my poor choices. God is gracious enough to keep me from much of the pain I am sure I have caused. In addition to His graciousness, I understand if I were to see the fruit created by the instances I have obeyed the Holy Spirit, my reason for following His guidance would be driven by the desire to see all that *my* good work did so that *I* could feel satisfaction and reap the glory. My motive would not be the expansion of my Savior's empire. The Lord is wise for not allowing us to watch the journey of our decisions.

We can stand firm in the knowledge that there is a reaction for every action. What we do *will* have an impact, and if our actions are fueled by the Holy Spirit's guidance, we can be certain our ripple is in the best possible situation. It has great potential to grow and drench everything in its path. See the kid eating alone? Sit with him. Do you hear those guys bragging about the girls they have been with? Do not laugh along or sit in silence. Stand tall and let them know women are a treasure to be respected. See that struggling old gentleman? Go carry his bags. Offer your arm so he can better steady himself.

You will probably never see the impact of the action, but that is okay. If Jesus was involved, it is safe to assume that it packed a bigger punch than can be imagined!

I look forward to seeing the impact you have,

V

■ ■ ■

03 August 2013
#35
Ezekiel 36:26
0515

Dear VI,

I believe that without Christ I would have great difficulty living any sort of enjoyable existence. Earth is a tough place to live. I sometimes wonder if I would think it so tough if I did not know Jesus. Accepting Christ into my heart allowed the Holy Spirit to become part of my life. Accepting Him as my Savior means new ears, new eyes, and a heart of flesh. Becoming a Christian relieved me from some of my ignorance concerning the state of the planet. Logically, it makes sense to believe I may have been better off in my ignorance. After all, ignorance has been called "bliss" while the truth often hurts. But statements like this are some of that worldly logic God has no use for.

With knowing Christ comes feeling the faintest idea of what He might feel, which means sadness on some days and joy on others. A tiny touch of His joy can fill a man to overflowing while a quick peek at sin through His eyes can make a man sick through and through. My salvation has opened my eyes to the self-destructive tendencies of man (which hurts), but I consider that awareness a small price to pay for the joyful knowledge that the battle is won! At the end of the book the good guys win, and I am on the victorious team. Sometimes, because I am a human animal, the day-to-day grind of life is so grueling I start thinking I can't go on. I focus on the evil that seems to live everywhere, and the result is overwhelming.

This evil is the result of the Devil's relentless, hard work. His job title is twofold. The first is a simple numbers game. He wants to win souls, and minimize Heaven's occupancy while maximizing Hell's population. But once a person meets Jesus, his soul goes off the market. The Enemy's first priority has failed and now he must turn his attention to the second goal which is to ensure those who are Heaven-bound never develop into the warriors God has always intended they become.

The Devil knows that one Christian man living to his full potential can destroy decades of hard work. He knows that all the time spent developing vices and regrets can (with Christ) transform into a testimony that will result in souls saved rather than condemned. The name of the game becomes minimizing spiritual growth, making sure Christian babies do not wean and adolescents backslide into infancy. A mature Christian is terrifying to the darkness.

Why God allows these evil spiritual beings to be a part of our lives is a testament to His clever design. In a mind-boggling twist of irony, battling with the Devil is a critical tool on the path to maturity. We become warriors by winning battles, by overcoming temptations, by growing through trials. The Enemy's efforts to keep us weak are often the very things that make us strong. God even uses the times we lose the battle with sin as a teaching tool to make us wiser. Consider this: how effective would a soldier be if everything was sunshine and puppy tails? What kind of a person would you be if each day was a series of preplanned events unfolding just as they should? We would all be pudgy, uncallused boys who struggle to open a Coke can and unravel at the smallest inconvenience. God gives us the tools, and if we give Him the effort, the Devil's tricks will backfire.

It is perfectly healthy for a man to throw up his hands and scream, "Why does everything have to be so difficult?" It is normal to want a break from what Paul calls, "the battle with the cosmic powers over this present darkness, against the spiritual forces of evil." But we are God's warriors, so when we are in the midst of battle, we must fight!

I hope I spend my life fighting beside you,

V

P.S. The alternative to fighting is running. Cowards run.

■ ■ ■

05 August 2013
#36
Ecclesiastes 4:10
0555

Dear VI,

Your due date is not until August 20, but by the looks of things, you could be here any second. Your mom (whose body is constantly hurting) says despite her pain she is not anxious for your arrival because you "still need to get all that good stuff in there." I would not exactly call that a medical diagnosis, but she has a gift of saying things in such a way that retort is impossible. How can anyone argue with that?

We continue our efforts to build relationships with like-minded people. We went to a church BBQ yesterday and have decided that our efforts were well received. We hung out with a few young parents. They were upbeat, and their children were not monsters. One man smelled his child's poopy diaper, then said, "Watch this." He proceeded to walk over to his wife and say, "Our son really wanted to give his mommy a hug." Two minutes later she too smelled the soiled diaper and got to work changing it. I could really learn a lot of practical wisdom from this family!

Neither of us felt like driving an hour to spend a sticky summer afternoon with people we did not really know, but we are glad we did. Life is about relationship. How could we ever develop relationships if we sat at home? It is important to take advantage of every opportunity to develop relationships. The chance of victory increases with each brother we can stand beside.

I look forward to standing beside you,

V

■ ■ ■

06 August 2013
#37
Deuteronomy 6:5
0619

Dear VI,

I don't have a lot of time today. I lost the fight with the snooze button, which forced me to modify my morning routine. I really enjoy writing to you. I am 37 letters deep and get great joy knowing that God has big plans for every word. I enjoy writing to you so much that I considered not reading the Bible in order to allow myself more writing time. But NO!

This is a slippery slope, a slope that I myself have skated down more times than I can count. One day of rearranging priorities leads to another, and before I know it, my Bible is a coaster covered in blankets of dust, and Jesus is an old acquaintance with whom I have pleasant, but distant, memories. No! No! No! I want everything in my day to be drenched with Christ, especially my letters to you.

Time spent together leads to accuracy and intimacy while time spent apart leads to assumption and generalizations. This is true with all relationships—not just Jesus. Not meeting with our King would bleed through into my words. My letters would be neither accurate nor helpful, which would defeat the very purpose of writing them! Never let your time with Christ fall lower than Number One on the priority list.

All credit for any helpful words belong to Christ,

V

■ ■ ■

08 August 2013
#38
Job 11:5
0556

Dear VI,

When wanting to write about wisdom, I find myself trapped in a delicate situation. According to I Corinthians 8:2, "Anyone who claims they know all the answers does not know very much." While Proverbs 17:28 reminds men, "Even a fool is counted wise when he shuts his lips…." Because of these verses and others like them, I feel led to give the following disclaimer: I do not know all of the answers. My first inclination is to imitate the man who fools the masses by skipping this subject all together.

Look at Proverbs 1:7, which reads, "The fear of the LORD is the beginning of wisdom…," and Proverbs 16:16, "How much better to get wisdom than gold…." These two verses lead me to believe wisdom is more valuable than the earth's most valuable elements, and the key to opening the treasure chest is through fearing the Lord. Once this is understood, the question becomes: what does it mean to *fear* the Lord?

The Bible considers a wise man to be a very mighty warrior. As your father, my role is to do my best in helping you become such a man. With I Corinthians 8:2 in mind, my goal here is to help you better understand this idea of fearing God. To begin with, forget what you think this word means. The world has associated the word *fear* with the wrong synonyms— words like "scared," "fright," "dismay," "anxiety," "horror," and "panic." This type of fear is *not* what the Bible is referring to. In Isaiah 41:10, God instructs His people to not fear Him in this way saying, "Do not fear, for I am with you; do not be dismayed for I am your God…." God is not a monster under the bed, the conversation you don't want to have, or the test you are not ready for.

If you are old enough to read this letter, then I am sure we have read the Chronicles of Narnia together. I think Aslan is a great example of the fear we are to show God. Remember the lion Aslan (the savior of Narnia and a beautiful depiction of Christ)? Aslan is not considered safe. He is considered unsafe and good at the same time. He is described as "untamed" and as a lion who "does not like to be tied down."

Imagine walking through a savannah and meeting this wild lion. How would you react? Knowing he is a good lion, would you fear him? That is to say, would you stare at his giant paws in wonder? Would his powerful shoulder muscles make you feel as if your feet were stuck in mud? If you saw his great speed and witnessed his powerful jaws crunch the bones of his prey, would you begin to realize that you were not quite as tough as you once thought? If you answered yes to these questions, then you understand the type of fear that leads to wisdom.

I chose Aslan as an example because he is a fictional symbol that a man can begin to wrap his mind around. Our God is not fictional. Neither is He comprehendible. Our God, with His perfect balance of science and creativity, breathed into existence not only the lion, but every other beast, bird, insect, and water creature. His power is never-ending and is equal only to His love for us. All the fear we could ever show the lion is not a fraction of the fear God is owed.

Yes, He is wild and unpredictable. A life with Him will certainly be both. Our God is not tame; He is not limited to the confines of human logic. Long after we yell, "No more! This doesn't make sense!" He allows trials, persecution, and battles with the Prince of Darkness to continue. All of it is an important part of His great equation. But read carefully; *He. Is. Good.* A life with Christ is promised to be the most fulfilling and impactful existence a man could ever have. His love will pack a man's days so full of experiences, his mind could never begin to imagine the glorious adventures he will encounter.

I encourage to think all this over and meditate on Proverbs 2:3-4: "Yes, if you cry out for discernment, *and* lift up your voice for understanding, if you seek her (Wisdom) as silver, *and* search for her as for hidden treasures then you will understand the fear of the Lord."

A man understands what it means to fear the Lord through investigation. Do this so that you may become a man rich with wisdom,

V

P.S. Our God is called the "Lion of Judah" (Revelation 5:5).

■ ■ ■

10 August 2013
#39
Matthew 28:19
0547

Dear VI,

Just 10 more days! I have written to you regarding the importance of developing a primary group of friends and want to report that your family has been pursuing that very goal here in our new city. Community and relationship are beginning to take root.

How did these relationships come about? First off, prayer—lots of it, but also pursuit. As much as I wish the opposite were true, I do not jump for joy when Sunday comes around. I do not cheer at the idea of a midweek 45-minute drive to small group either. I am a selfish human, which means I usually want whatever gives me pleasure at the time (even if I know that what should be done is much more important and beneficial). Like sleeping in on Sunday morning instead of worshiping my Creator.

I get riled up when I hear a man complain about being single and alone as he plays video games in his dank cave of an apartment, or when the unhealthy man complains about his body between swigs of soda. I have no right to get upset over this, as I am no better than they are.

The process is not pray, sit back, and wait. It is pray, listen, obey. Prayer without effort is lip service to the Almighty. I imagine this foolish act insults Him. If a man brings anything to God in prayer, he must be ready (upon receiving direction) to act. Prayer is only part of the equation. Jesus is not a genie in a bottle. How foolish it would be for your parents to pray for a primary group, then pass up the opportunity to build relationship with godly people!

If you desire anything at all, I urge you to bring it before the Lord. Then if you feel like the Holy Spirit has given you some wisdom (keeping in mind that His response may take time, and the answer may be "no"), pursue it.

Now get out of that womb!

V

■ ■ ■

11 August 2013
#40
Colossians 3:23
0548

Dear VI,

At the close of my first month of work, I brought home an award for my efforts. I present this award to you as proof that the Lord's strength is alive and is being noticed by those with whom I work. My attitude and work ethic is a gift from the Lord—a gift I receive after meeting with Him each morning. All of my previous jobs would usually unravel as follows: first, I would be hard on myself for my lack of enthusiasm. Next, I would blame my employer for not making his establishment more accommodating to my personality. Finally, I would either quit or get fired.

Even growing up with a father who worked hard every day to allow my mom to stay home with my sister and me did not instill any real work ethic. It took Stan Myers, my good friend and mentor, enlightening me with the words, "Too bad, so sad, you still have a Savior to represent." Only then did I understand if I were to find joy in my work, I had better start representing God, the only true source of joy.

I could get to work a little late with scuffed boots before doing as little as possible then ducking out a bit early. My coworkers do that all the time. (Without my quiet times, I would probably do the same.) What a poor representation that would be! What kind of a Christian, a husband, or a father would I be if I moped around in a wrinkled uniform?

Someday you will express how much you do not want to go to school, or do chores, or go to practice. When that time comes, know that my heart will be breaking for you, but do not be surprised if I repeat what Stan said to me: "Tough"!

When it is time to work, a Christian man must give nothing less than 100 percent effort. Our Creator deserves our all. Off I go to try and do just that,

V

■ ■ ■

12 August 2013
#41
Isaiah 44:2
0552

Dear VI,

This last weekend (11 and 12 August) had the potential to be the last pre-parent weekend your mom and I ever had. Man, was I pumped when that reality set in! If you are not late, I will get to spend all future weekends with my own precious son. I am so excited, I can hardly concentrate on anything else.

Yesterday, in anticipation of your arrival, I spent a good amount of time cleaning my car and smoking my pipe (a pipe passed down to me from Lewis III), and figuring out the car seat situation. There is no way fatherhood is as challenging as that car seat. It had me thoroughly confused, but after a few dozen tries your chariot awaits. The whole experience had me feeling fatherly and full of purpose, which is a sentiment I could really get used to. I also got a nice visual as to your actual size. You are tiny! My fat thumbs can hardly press your little belt buckle.

Witnessing every stage of pregnancy has been a powerful affirmation of the reality of God. A single cell to the need for a car seat is, to me, another proof of the Architect's existence. I will continue to marvel at God as He finishes the final touches needed before you put that car seat to use.

You are coming home in a 2006 Silver Honda Element with roof racks. How did you get so lucky?

V

∎ ∎ ∎

13 August 2013
#42
Psalm 50:10-12
0554

Dear VI,

I woke up at 0510 this morning and shaved my face. Then I put on my uniform, laced up my boots, and tiptoed to the kitchen to find your mom reading the Word. I was making a genuine effort to keep quiet (I went so far as to hold my breath while walking into the bathroom), and all the while she was not even in the room!

Upon seeing my surprised look, she expressed feeling symptoms of early labor. Neither of us knows for sure (especially not me), so I am following your mom's example and staying as relaxed as possible. We read Psalm 50 together, then spent some time praying for the wisdom to best handle the situation. Mostly we prayed for your arrival to be safe and uncomplicated.

The idea that we might meet today excites me so much I am having to focus on my breathing. The honor of being your dad is making me all teary. Our Father in Heaven has given me the opportunity to rear you up. The kicker is I do not have any clue about parenting, and still God has given me the chance. He believes I have what it takes.

I can best be described as an ignorant but enthusiastic servant,

V

■ ■ ■

14 August 2013
#43
0530
1 Timothy 2:1-3

Dear VI,

False alarm! You are still safe and snug in your womb. All is well except
for my emotions which have been on a real roller coaster over the last 24
hours! After three sleepless nights, your mom is finally snoozing soundly
in the gigantic mountain of pillows that occupies our bed. We started ac-
quiring pillows to accommodate her changing body, and the experiment
has since spun wildly out of control. (Apparently this is not uncommon.)
Now she sleeps with eight pillows of various sizes and two additional pillows called "wedges." "The poor man's hospital bed," we call it. All the
while, my own pillow is no thicker than a dishrag! I have learned to sleep
with one cheek hovering over the edge of the mattress, and my shoulder
on top of the night stand. I still sleep like a dead man. Only when my
alarm goes off do I discover I have lost total feeling in my entire right side.
While shaving, I can clearly see the pattern of our nightstand embossed in
the backside of my arm!

Enough of my complaining. Today things seem to be back to business as usual. I read John 11, the story of Jesus raising his friend Lazarus
from the dead. I consider this to be Christ's most obvious attempt to show
people He is the Messiah. In verse 4, He tells His disciples the plan. He
then allows Lazarus to die and stay dead long enough for everyone to have
no doubts concerning his condition. Eventually the stone is rolled away
and Jesus, surrounded by people, says, "Father, thank you for hearing me.
You always hear me, but I said it out loud for the sake of all these people
standing here, so that they will believe you sent me." Then he restores the
decomposing corpse of Lazarus into a fully functioning human.

I imagine Jesus trying to explain to God why so many of the people He was around never made it up to Heaven. "Remember the Lazarus
miracle?" I picture Him saying with His head in His hands. "I mean how

did that not get everyone following Me?" (I know that situation is outrageously theologically unsound, but it is early, and I am still a little punchy.)

The fact is, people see God clearly every day but still do not believe. I have witnessed people experience God's love and literally say, "I know God is the only solution, but I am still not convinced." I have personally heard men say things like, "There is no way; this is a coincidence," then pay God no mind.

This philosophy frustrates me, but (infinitely worse) breaks the heart of God, Who paid the ultimate price for their salvation. Amazingly, Jesus will continue to patiently pursue until a man dies or acknowledges Christ as his Savior. On the day Jesus receives that person's heart, He will joyously transform his life into a cleverly fashioned tool which will further His kingdom. That person's history will become a testimony. If Jesus extended His grace to me, I must follow Christ's example by pursuing in love just as He does—over and over again, even when the situation seems impossible. He is consistent; He will never call off the pursuit, and because of this, we must try our hardest to do likewise.

Four days until your birthday, I HOPE!

V

■ ■ ■

15 August 2013
#44
0523
Matthew 18:20

Dear VI,

Yesterday was one of *those* days. I assume you have no idea what I mean by that. I hope many years pass before you experience this flavor of day. The demonstrative pronoun "those" normally does not carry much weight, but when it is thrown into the sentence like, "Yesterday was one of *those* days," the meaning takes new shape and meaning. It is a way for a man to tell people that the specific day in question almost got the best of him, and he would prefer not to talk about it.

It was something about standing in line at Subway—the assembly line and the uniformity. I felt like an animal being herded into a pen for a brand and an oat bag. This is not what made the day one of *those* days, but it was the straw that nearly broke me.

After work, small group was the last thing I felt like attending, but deep down, I knew there was nothing better I could do. A friend of mine once told me his family was always at each other's throats on Sunday mornings over issues that they would normally not think twice about. He said in those moments he would keep reminding himself, "Get through those church doors." Yesterday, I thought along those same lines. I could have had two broken legs and would have army-crawled through the door.

Every man will experience days where he feels the dark world, making an extra push to break him by applying pressure in an attempt to get him doing something other than what he ought. The world breaks a man's back, then offers painkillers in the hope they will deter him from going to the hospital where real help can be provided. The Lord allows this scenario to happen. He believes that man can make the trip to the hospital and will be stronger in the future because of it.

When I walked through the small group host's door, I felt all that applied pressure dissipate—as if the residence strictly prohibited worldly garbage from entering the premises. I saw your mom holding her beach ball of a tummy and laughing with a friend, and I knew I had made it through the narrows. The world had done its best to keep me away, but I had made it to my primary group where love and rejuvenation were in control.

I love you so much, son,

V

■ ■ ■

16 August 2013
#45
Matthew 14:23, Mark 1:35
0547

Dear VI,

Several of my previous letters have detailed the various reasons why a primary group is critical for a man's overall health. In yesterday's letter, I used small group as one example of its value. Today I want to touch on the opposite by explaining the importance of spending time alone. You know I try to do this discipline daily. I am right now. Think of how rare it is to experience real silence. Even now as I sit here writing to you alone, I can hear our faithful old refrigerator chugging away. The idea is to get background noise to a bare minimum in order to more clearly focus on the Holy Spirit's voice.

He does not shout; He speaks at the perfect volume, leaving the listener to adjust his life in order to hear. It is difficult to have an intimate conversation on a cell phone at a busy restaurant, right? Jesus walked away from His disciples in order to pray alone. Likewise, a Christian man must put himself in an environment without distractions in order to give God his undivided attention. A man should avoid asking "What did You say, God? My radio was on; I didn't quite catch that." In the same way, how can a relationship grow when the people never meet one-on-one? How does a man respond to a voice he cannot hear?

It is Friday, and hopefully your birthday!

V

■ ■ ■

18 August 2013
#46
Psalm 27:14
0559

Dear VI,

I thought for sure today's letter would be one describing our first meeting. You must be awful cozy in that womb. You have made no real effort
to escape. I don't feel impatient; rather, I am in a constant state of high
anticipation, which is exhausting. It's like you will feel the night before
Christmas or on the eve of the release of a movie you have been dying to see. Imagine waking up on Christmas morning to the news that
this particular Christmas has been delayed but will be held as scheduled
sometime in the very near future. That is how I feel.

   On Friday, your mom's sister, Rachel, gave birth to a baby girl—your
new cousin, Brianna. You now have three girl cousins, which is exactly
what I have. In celebration of your cousin's safe arrival, I assembled your
crib, only to find out you won't be needing it for at least three months.
Apparently, something called a *bassinet* will serve as a "pre-bed." (When I
first heard about this contraption, I got it confused with "bayonet," which
is a knife soldiers could affix to their rifle during a time when men got
close enough in battle to use such a weapon. I wasn't about to let you sleep
on that!)

   I am experiencing a lesson in God's perfect timing. You are full-term
and healthy enough to safely enter the world, but for some reason, God has
decided it is not time to pull the trigger. The Lord has had your birth slated
in His schedule since the beginning of creation. I keep suppressing the urge
to remind Him that my wife is pregnant and suggest to the Architect, "I
think it's time for my son to come out"—as if I have half a clue about timing, and God's timeline is nonsensical. During seasons like these, I remind

myself He is God, and I am not. Christmas is when He says—not one second before.

We are so excited to meet you,

V

■ ■ ■

20 August 2013
#47
Proverbs 1:5
1017

Dear VI,

Today I am writing to you from the front porch. I feel like "the bottom of a hobo's shoe." (People say that a lot here in the South.) I am sure there is a worse time I could be sick, but I can't think of one. Your mom could go into labor any second, and I can hardly keep my eyes open. Of course, she is taking great care of me, spending what I consider to be way too much time on her mighty swollen feet. She is also battling a condition called "pup rash," which itches like poison ivy and likes making its home inside the stretch marks of an expectant mother's tummy. I will repeat myself until I run out of ink: your mom is an inspirationally strong woman.

Once more I find myself wanting to explain to the Lord that His timing is off. "This is no time for a trial. Being healthy makes far more sense." When we get down to brass tacks, the *why* is none of my concern. Why (after years of going without so much as a runny nose) am I sick? I may never know, and if that is the case, so be it. He is King; I am not—end of story. I pray, however, that in this particular instance, God will reveal why I am ill so you and I might learn and grow in our faith. Let's see what happens…

You are healthy, and that is all that matters,

V

■ ■ ■

21 August 2013
#48
Luke 12:27-28
0613

Dear VI,

Still sick! If anything, I am worse than yesterday. There is no such thing as "calling in sick" in the military so, to prove my illness, I have to report to the Navy clinic, which just happens to be where I work, and be seen by a doctor. So here I am up and in uniform, eating an apple with peanut butter between sips of coffee. My limited breakfast reminds me of stories both sets of your grandparents have told me about their humble first years of marriage. Because you will be brought up in a single income military family, I think it is important for you to understand and respect the value of a modest upbringing. That is to say, you need to recognize we do not have as much as the average American family thinks they need. We eat healthy basic food, we do not have a television, and I cannot remember the last time either of your parents bought new clothes. We are not stingy—only committed to living within our means, which frankly is not a whole lot at this point.

I do struggle with my contentment. It's difficult to work hard day after day with the knowledge that the woman I love is at home with Cheerios and tap water. A man can make himself believe his work entitles him to certain comforts, but the reality is even the air in his lungs is a gift. When

I lose focus on Christ, I start believing the illusion that my investment should be yielding a higher return.

Overall, though, I can confidently say your family has learned to be abundantly happy with what we have. Your mom and I spend a whole lot of time clinking our water mugs and laughing over plates of scrambled eggs. It does not get much better than that. If you can learn not to allow your possessions to dictate your attitude, you will begin to notice two things:

1) The things that many people might consider normal (like going to restaurants) will become very exciting. If your mom and I go to the movie theater, we savor every moment, enjoy the credits, slowly chew every popcorn morsel.
2) You will find yourself in a consistent attitude of thankfulness. You will think things like, "Wow, this machine keeps my food cold. Amazing!"

Have peace in the knowledge that God has provided more than we need because He loves us. Make an effort to take pleasure in *all* of His gifts.

You will soon enter a truly rich family,

V

■ ■ ■

22 August 2013
#49
Psalm 131:1
1850

Dear VI,

In Letter 47 I told you I would be praying that God reveals to us why I got sick when I did and why you are so late. The doctor thinks my sickness is due to fatigue. My immune system could not keep up with the demand on so little rest. Imagine if you had arrived on the date the doctor predicted. You would have been four days old when my immune system decided to take a dump which would have been very dangerous to *your* health!

Also, because of my reputation as a hard worker, my chain of command basically ordered me to stay home: "Sleep and take care of your family, Bradshaw." We have been watching movies and eating watermelon for two days! The bags under my eyes are beginning to fade, but infinitely more important is the opportunity my sickness gave your mom and me to spend time together. This interval has been a refreshing gift from God. Every parent I have ever spoken to is quick to inform me that your arrival will mark the end of these lazy days, so your parents are soaking up every second.

Am I saying that God made me sick in order to get some much-needed rest with my wife? We will never know for sure. What I do know is if I did not start my day with Jesus, I would not give maximum effort at work. If I did not give my all, I probably would not have become sick, but the effort that brought on my illness is the same effort that prompted my command to be so generous with my time off. And if you had been born on time, this paid week of recovery would have never happened.

Two days ago, I felt like a boxer in the later rounds of a close fight. My arms were heavy; it was all I could do to keep away from the ropes. I kept repeating things like, "I've got this. Dig deep, stay sharp, stay alert." Now I feel like a fresh young athlete bouncing toward his challenger, confident and excited to take on his opponent who does not stand a chance. Make of that what you will!

All glory be to God,

V

P.S. If I had not asked Jesus in Letter 48 to reveal why I was sick, would this have ever occurred to me? Would this letter exist?

■ ■ ■

23 August 2013
#50
Psalm 126:2
2245


Dear VI,


Contractions, fluid, the whole nine yards… How could I have not thought it was game time? We buttoned down the house, packed the bag, and got a hospital bed. I am sure you've guessed because today is *not* your birthday: it was a false alarm. But it was also an unforgettable experience.

What made it so wild was having nothing unfold as I had pictured. I blame movies for what I imagined labor would be like. I pictured sprinting to the car with two suitcases in each hand. (We only had one bag.) Of course, I forgot to zip one of those bags, and baby paraphernalia spilled all over the lawn. "Here we go! This is it!" I yell while driving like a maniac to the hospital. We argued about directions while your mom sat beside me with her feet propped up on my dashboard, which had now become a makeshift pair of stirrups.

In reality, I carried only one small backpack, which I made sure was securely zipped. As a last meal, we drove through Chick-Fil-A, and we laughed a lot. We were in the frame of mind where exhaustion cooperates with giddy, making everything we said comedic gold. We arrived at the hospital, and your mom could not walk. I gave her a wheelchair ride down the hall complete with wheelies. This is how your family does things!

While stationed in Virginia, I became friends with a man named Samuel Oddodonko who gets credit for the following wise statement: "Imagine what you want and the best way to go about getting it. Now understand that is almost certainly not how it is going to happen. Understand that it is probably not even what you really want." Essentially, what Samuel means is that humans do not actually know what is best for them. This idea seemed unfair at first. I can think of times when I felt very certain the things I wanted would have been best for me. I then consider where I would be right now if I had received everything I wanted in the way I had imagined, and the equation falls apart.

This concept has helped me better go with the flow, which is why I was not crushed when we sat in the car laughing and eating chicken. My only thought was, "Wow! You cannot write this stuff." It has been a long day, my boy, but I could not go to sleep without filling you in on the adventure.

See you in the morning, I hope!

V

■ ■ ■

27 August 2013
#51
Galatians 4:19
1350

Dear VI,

Well, power is found in brevity, so I will write slowly and choose my words wisely. The Lord has revealed mighty things to me. I can confidently say my life is changed forever. As I sit watching you sleep soundly on your mother's chest, I am in awe. I thought I had felt this feeling before, but now I understand I had never come close to touching this emotion. *Awe* is the feeling a man gets when something so incredible happens, his brain does not know what response to give, so instead it stands fast. Time stops. No adrenaline, no excitement, everything sounds pleasant but distant. He is alert and at peace with the moment, but the wonder is more than his body can process. In front of me, my family is sleeping, and I sit staring, spellbound. I bet all the philosophers who think they know so much about the meaning of life didn't watch their child enter the world.

I never knew pain until witnessing your mom endure contractions. I stood beside her crying; my heart broke. I would have done anything to relieve her of the hurt. The best I could do was to make sure I looked her in the eyes while she gritted and screamed. We would lock eyes, and I would remind her I was not going anywhere.

I never knew fear until you came into this world with your umbilical cord wrapped three times around your neck. You were wet, purple, and silent. I felt the unique combination of fear and panic experienced only by a parent who can only sit and watch his child in danger. Some 30 seconds later, when the doctors finally got you breathing, awe broadsided me. I raised my hands above my head and let out a tear-choked scream of joy. I then picked you up as if you were made of thin crystal and carried you over to meet your mom— the selfless warrior who had carried you these last nine months.

It was here that I felt pride. I witnessed your mom, naked, bleeding, and more exhausted than I can imagine, somehow muster the strength to kiss your forehead and guide you toward her chest. She, of course, was starving, but the only thing on her mind was making sure you got that all-important first meal. She kept mumbling, "What did we do? How is this possible?" Her example of love was my undoing. I stood at the foot of the bed, staring at my family and weeping.

A lot has happened since 26 August 2013 at 0903, a day that will henceforth be recognized as your birthday! Visitors, baths, farts, shots, and much more. (Notice sleep is not yet on that list of events!) I will do my best to recount every one of those special moments. I now finish this letter feeling as if I have grown light-years as a man. God was in the room when you were born. I saw Him clearly as you entered His world. I am forever changed. Thank you, son.

Game on,

V

■ ■ ■

28 August 2013
#52
Acts 2:42-47
0900

Dear V,

My boy, my boy, my precious boy, you are home at last! After three days in the hospital, you have finally entered your palace. I have sat in this spot many times praying for your development, your brain, your systems, your limbs. Now I can lay my hand on your chest and pray, "Thank You, God, for this baby boy!" You are healthy and strong. You are alert and beautiful. I think you look a lot like your mom (which is a good thing), but mostly you look like a baby, which is accurate, but kind of a copout—like calling a masterpiece "a painting."

I have been stripping you down to your diaper and laying you on my bare chest so we can better chat about some of my favorite topics, including how our King loves you, and the ocean. Your mom is asleep for the first time in four days. No matter how tired she gets, when it is feeding time, she is at your side lightning quick. Because she is still recovering, most things move pretty slowly. It is taking her 10 minutes to go potty, but when you fuss ("have needs" as she calls it), your mom is there kissing your cheeks, getting you cozy, making sure you are the perfect temperature.

You know that we have no family here in Florida. I now understand how beneficial a couple of grandmas could be in our present situation. Both of your parents are puttering on fumes, and your mom is also recovering from the trauma of having a human being come out of her. I would not mind another woman here—especially one who reared either myself or your mom. We have no routine or anything that might resemble a system. How can we? The manual was thrown into the fire long ago. The name of the game is "Keep Your Footing." People have been parenting newborns for a long time, so it must be possible, right? Our bodies are being forced to go further than they would like but never for a moment think we aren't enjoying the experience.

In lieu of grandmas, our church has come through in fine style. We had not been home for more than two hours when the doorbell rang. I opened the door to a bunch of food and flowers being shoved in my face. Cash is especially tight at the moment, but thanks to this Christ-centered community, our noisy old fridge is fuller than I have ever seen it. This is Christ. This is the kind of family you will grow up in.

Now excuse me while I go eat something,

V

P.S. I continue to pray about our living situation. It is clear something has to change. We are standing by for guidance.

■ ■ ■

31 August 2013
#53
Psalm 34:1-3
1106

Dear VI,

There is no lack of excitement around here, that much is certain. Yesterday, we went back to the hospital for your two-day checkup. The nurse looked you over with a strange expression before finally saying, "He is literally one of the healthiest children I have ever seen."

Ours has been a true adventure. We have no concept of day or night. We have no clue when eating might be a good idea. I don't even remember what sleeping feels like. Last night at 0300 you were wide-awake, so we spent some time together, which gave your mom the rare opportunity to take a shower. I stupidly attempted to read you the story of Lazarus in John 10, but you were in no mood for stories. I then farted which, based on the smile it produced, seemed to spark your interest.

Just then your mom announced from the bathroom, "My breast milk is gushing everywhere." I know this story might seem crude, but it does an excellent job of summing up the general feel of our home at the moment.

Throughout my life, I have been quick to call on the Lord during tough times, but I do not praise Him as I should when times are good. Drawing near to God when things are tough is almost an instinct. My foolish knee-jerk reaction to a trial is to bargain with the Almighty: "Lord, if You stop my stomach pain, I will spend more time reading the Word." Why is it when a man receives a great gift (like my getting you), he either allows himself to believe he is somehow responsible or focuses on the areas that could make the deal that much sweeter (like my getting more sleep)? This I would like to change.

The Bible demands, "Praise the Lord for He is good," so that is exactly what your family is going to do. Who cares if our house is a mess? Who cares how tired we are? We have you!

All glory, honor, and praise be to the Lord,

V

■ ■ ■

01 September 2013
#54
Psalm 18:2
1013

Dear VI,

What a sight to see you and Grandma Freeman meet for the first time! I was Johnny-on-the-spot with the camera and got a great first encounter photo. How wonderful to have family in the house! The whole place feels homier. You and the ladies are currently sleeping, so I am taking a moment to get my quiet time in.

Quiet time always seems to be first to go when life gets busy. I have told you in the past that my time with God is non-negotiable, but sadly, that is not always the case. How idiotic it is to cut the most important order of business first! But historically, that is what seems to happen. "O, Lord, help me. Lead and protect my family. Also I have a full day ahead of me, so I will be canceling our morning meeting." What sort of man does that? How can anyone expect a relationship to grow that way?

Sleep instead of quiet time, television instead of exercise, debt instead of frugal living. When a man stops an activity, he is never able to pick up where he left off. If a man stops exercising, isn't he exceptionally sore and discouraged when getting back to the gym? Is he not weaker? Do his lungs not scream sooner? If the dishes sit in the sink for a few days, are they not much harder to clean? The gunk on the pan takes twice as long as it would have had it been cleaned right away. Let some dust collect on your Bible and then crack it open; is it not more difficult to detect the subtle movement of the Holy Spirit? *Everything* needs maintenance. This is mandatory for every invention, skill, and relationship. (The only thing that does not need some sort of upkeep is God's creation. I do not see a tree in need of an overhaul or a sunrise in need of a tune up. His design is perfect.) Maintaining something is like pushing a boulder up a hill; the going is slow and laborious, but letting that boulder go will quickly undo a lot of hard work.

The other side of the coin is obsessing over every nook and cranny in your life. This is the perfect recipe for an unhappy existence heading speedily down the road to burnout. Some maintenance is simply not as important as others—like my mowing the lawn. I know our lawn must be mowed, but I also know that Saturday morning will bring with it the chance to surf, which will be a huge boost to my general well-being. I will mow the lawn this Saturday. It will simply have to wait until later in the afternoon. Yes, this does mean the boulder is rolling down the hill; the grass will be that much longer and require more work, but sometimes that is acceptable.

All of this begins with Christ. If you meet with Him, He will give you the wisdom needed to prioritize what rocks are most important to throw your shoulder against and which ones can roll a bit. Our Savior is the Rock. Never let Him roll downhill.

Much love, my boy,

V

P.S. One day I will happily hand my lawn-mowing "stone" to you!

■ ■ ■

03 September 2013
#55
Ecclesiastes 3:1-8
0730

Dear VI,

One thing you are sure to learn quickly about your father is his desire for physical activity. This has been true my entire life. It makes sense that after 29 years of this, a reputation has developed. I cannot tell you the amount of times I have introduced myself and heard the following statement: "Lewis Bradshaw? Aren't you the guy who always wants to go do something?"

Your mom finds this attractive, which alone is reason enough to cherish her forever. How blessed I am to have a wife who loves her husband's longing to go play outside! But this reputation of mine always catches me off guard, and my first reaction is embarrassment, like I spend all day making mud pies in the backyard. I imagine everyone thinks I am an immature child.

But no, every man should still crave running around, wrestling, playing catch, going a little deeper in the woods, walking where there is no trail. Man was born in the wild, and born with him is an ever-present adventure bug. Today, I want to introduce you to this metaphorical insect.

For some men, this bug is pulverized while still in its infancy by things like video games, overprotective parents, and medication. Whack, whack, whack! These young boys never have a chance to push themselves. They never find out a skinned knee is not a tragedy but a badge of honor. Instead, they grow up with a feeling of uneasiness.

Older men (I know many who fall into this category) accidentally crush their own adventure bug. Idols, like sex, substance, or pursuit of a hefty pay-check, enter the picture. I have friends with the bug still alive and kicking, yet years of beating it into submission has rendered it mangled. Why would a man crave spending time battling against the elements when a flight of stairs leaves him winded? It is hard for a man to pursue adventure when he cannot go 24 hours without a drink or mounds of debt have him chained to his job.

Some men have the opposite problem, and I am one of them. I have developed a bug so strong it has lead me around by the nose most of my life. I have lost more than one job because my adventure bug got the best of me. Sometimes I considered sacrificing a sunny day for my job sacrile-gious, so I quit. Other times I would simply stop showing up. When I was 24, I moved to Northern Uganda without ever telling my employer. This was very foolish and unmanly.

The goal is finding a balance. I know that after sitting at work all day, I will go crazy if I do not get my heart rate up. I get cranky, I am short with your mother, I get bitter at my meager salary. However, I also understand there are obligations in the role of husband and father, which trump my desire to grab my skateboard and find a hill, even if that activity will lift my spirits. Maybe I skate on our street or go chop some wood for a while. It is possible to keep that adventure bug satisfied while temporarily on a leash, and a wise man knows how to do that. (I am still learning.)

You will never need to wonder if your old man wants to go outside and play with you,

V

■ ■ ■

06 September 2013
#56
Acts 4:29
0800

Dear VI,

I have reread my last letter to you and meditated on why it is I spend one second concerning myself with the opinions of others. Why does my reputation as "active" give me a twang of shame? Why am I frazzled by the images others conjure? I know I am a normal, healthy male with natural male desires, yet I worry about how others view me.

I see now the ancient, subtle, and effective trick played on me by the Enemy. If a man lets his guard down, the Enemy will slowly seep into his brain until he finds himself embarrassed about the character traits given to him by God, while at the same time lusting for worldly traits he can never obtain. I have spent much of my life believing I was designed with a flaw, not solely based on my body's need to move, either. I had a mustache in seventh grade, I like listening to jazz, I think *Napoleon Dynamite* is a stupid movie, I find scantily clad women unattractive, and choral music makes me cry. So much of my life was spent keeping these and many more feelings buried inside because I was too busy believing the Enemy's lies. Because I believed these lies, I not only hated myself, but I lied to others so they would not think I was made wrong.

Be strong against that lie! We are obligated to embrace our design and accept those godly traits our Creator built into us. We must not torture ourselves into making our actions look similar to those around us. The first time I saw you was through ultrasound. You were no bigger than my pinky. Even then you were one of a kind. You are perfectly made. Embrace your blueprint, then use the traits, talents, and skills given to you to further the kingdom of your Designer.

Never be ashamed of who you are,

V

■ ■ ■

08 September 2013
#57
Ecclesiastes 3:18
11:00

Dear VI,

Let's dig deeper into how a man can lose his spirit for adventure. Again, I would like to elaborate on what I addressed in Letter 56. What is it exactly that puts a person's adventure bug on life support? We live in a world that can be ugly to a man who does not fit the mold.

I alluded to the horrible feeling of rejection, which is only one of the many tools used by the world to mangle a man's spirit. Have you ever considered *convenience* to be a crutch? Do you realize a human can go through the course of an average day without ever lifting a finger? There are machines for everything—credit cards, drive-thrus, swipe and receive, push and purchase. A man can easily be persuaded to chase this life of convenience, only to find himself stuck in what I defined in Letter 11 as the "sedentary lifestyle," which basically means a lifestyle that exerts very little energy. Cruelly, when a person finds himself in this unhealthy cycle, he is then given a negative label—lazy, a couch potato, fat, or a sloth. The world tempts people into living a destructive lifestyle then curses them for doing so.

In the name of advancement, the human body has been forced into a position of serious hardship. *We are animals!* We are hunters. We are gatherers. Our teeth are made to cut and mash. Our muscles are made to lift and protect. Everything our bodies need to run as finely-tuned machines has been given to us in abundance by nature.

But who has the time to sow a garden? How can a man fish for dinner when he is glued to a computer 50 hours a week? Besides, even if he had the time, he could not do it; he would miss his favorite show. Today's men are put in a bind. Outside of the increasingly difficult and expensive endeavor of buying his own land, a man must adapt to this modern sedentary age.

Here at the Bradshaw estate, we have developed a kind of hybrid lifestyle—sitting at a computer each day and carrying sandbags around the block each night. In the same way a man can take vitamins to bridge the gap in the nutrition he no longer gets with a modern diet, I do things like flipping a tire in order to make up for the physical activity I am unable to do each day.

Once upon a time, a man and his family would die if he did not use his body as God intended. He had no options: he either hunted or they starved. Either he dug a well or died of thirst. If he did not build a home, his family would have no safe place to rest their heads. Now he must be increasingly creative if he wishes to keep his instincts in any sort of shape. The male's animalistic senses are fading at the hands of convenience because his body is no longer up to the challenge.

I continue to pray about a lifestyle which would afford more time to nurture our spirits. I want to rear you in such a way that your instincts thrive. In order for this to happen, we will need God's creative solutions.

Please understand, I appreciate convenience. I enjoy dining out and shopping online. I own a smartphone and an electric heater. Modern living can quickly become a crutch, but it is not evil. My aim is to show you that we are created with certain special instincts, and unless we make a conscious effort to exercise those things, they will become lost or forgotten.

Never forget our Savior did not sit on a throne being served. He was an educated carpenter,

V

∎ ∎ ∎

09 September 2013
#58
Acts 4:32-35
0551

Dear VI,

After two weeks of paternal leave, I am back in my uniform, sitting in my spot, getting ready to reunite with the grind. The only difference is you, sound asleep in the next room. I feel as if I am living the stereotypical American dream. Here I am working in the Navy. I have a house, two cars, a gorgeous wife, and now an overwhelmingly beautiful son. My little world is cookie-cutter and predictable just as it should be. Right? While I am grateful for these blessings, my overarching feeling is that of nervousness. I am not interested in stability.

Our family would jump at the chance to live out of a suitcase in Africa. I have an uneasiness that this situation is limiting our potential. I certainly do not want to rear you with a limited world view. Now, as I look at all we own sitting lifeless in our cool, dark house, I see great wisdom in the apostles' decision to give away everything they own. A man who owns nothing is most available.

I am becoming frighteningly in love with you, my boy,

V

■ ■ ■

10 September 2013
#59
Ecclesiastes 9:10
0719

Dear VI,

Because of my utter failure during the last advancement cycle, I have signed up for a one-week class, which will hopefully help boost my test score. The good news is I don't have to be there until 0815! The bad news is that the class is eight hours long. Sixty other restless sailors and I sit listening to instructors who, like the steel chairs, leave me stiff and uncomfortable. Then I come home and study for a couple more hours. My test is in 10 days! I have been studying every day for months, but now, with the test in sight, I am really buckling down. Advancement means increased pay for the same work and opens up the door to more leadership opportunity. I want both.

Many lonely hours are always involved on the road to a goal. Last night was not bad, though. I studied flashcards with you on my lap, then we watched some Monday Night Football, week one. (Eagles v. Redskins). You made little noises and stared at me the whole time, but I still consider this our first football game together.

I am off to try and learn. I love you!

V

■ ■ ■

12 September 2013
#60
Psalm 1
0719

Dear VI,

I just read Psalm 1 to you and your mom. I feel very blessed to be part of this simple family, but adapting to my new role as daddy is anything but simple! An old saying claims parenthood is a full-time job, and I am finding that adage to be true. However, if you consider the fact that your mom and dad have made every new parental blunder imaginable, I have been logging considerable overtime.

Even after all of the new parent errors and the new baby curveballs, we love this new occupation. What a great adventure it is to grow a family! The house is a mess and your parents are exhausted, but by the grace of God, you are eating well and sleeping soundly. You are being looked after with maximum effort—not experience and certainly not skill—but effort. At this point, effort is all we have.

I am always fighting with feelings of doubt or worry, anger or frustration. It is easy to get caught up in what else needs to be done instead of focusing on the task at hand. These feelings and a million more seem to multiply exponentially when hunger and fatigue are thrown into the equation. I get irritable over little unavoidable things. I meditate on thoughts that should never have entered my brain. I desire selfish situations, then curse the people who stop it from happening.

God knows I am going to blow it. He knows it is only a matter of time before I sin again. Christ lived a perfect life before me because He knew it was impossible for me to do it on my own. What He does require is effort—whether that's rearing a child, the language I use, how I treat women, my work ethic, or my relationship with the Holy Spirit. When

God looks in a man's heart and sees genuine effort, He will be a proud Father.

I am a proud father,

V

■ ■ ■

16 September 2013
#61
Proverbs 30
0554

Dear VI,

I apologize for the length of time between letters. Life is so full, it is hard to imagine two weeks have passed. I can say, without exaggeration, that I hardly have the time, strength, or energy to construct a decent sentence.

Today I read Proverbs 30. The chapter starts out with King Agur saying, "I am weary, O God. I am weary and worn out." Then he goes on to give some other descriptions, which lead me to believe he too was once a new parent.

You and I are getting along nicely so far. You really love getting a bath, riding in the car, and time outdoors. Each evening when I get home from work, we go for family walks; I smile as you stare up enchanted by the trees lining our street. You are exceptionally alert. The hours you spend lifting your head and looking at your precious little hands have taught me many lessons in contentment. I am very proud of you, son. You are a special young buck! (I am not just saying that because I am your dad.)

Being responsible for your wellbeing and the endless amount of gear that goes where you go has completely changed my life. It is rare when life simultaneously changes both drastically and quickly. Such a change has left me scrambling to keep my priorities in the right order. I am discovering if I do not keep carful track of the important things (quiet time, church, healthy living, encouraging your mom), they start to get nudged from the picture.

Proverbs 30:2 reads, "I am too stupid to be human," which again makes me think King Agur was writing to his firstborn from his kitchen table. It is all about keeping those feet churning and putting forth effort while keeping your eyes on the prize.

Today is a "slap-some-cold-water-on-your-face" kind of a day,

V

■ ■ ■

17 September 2013
#62
Isaiah 40:29
0557

Dear VI,

There is a reason why a lack of rest is sometimes referred to as "the great equalizer." There is a reason why in boot camp or any sort of Special Forces training, the first thing to go is sleep. Fatigue puts strain on character. It gives those observing a chance to see what the man in question is made of. Sleep is a luxury that can be stolen, and when it is, character is exposed. Transversely, fatigue gives a man the opportunity to prove how serious he is about the goal in question. Everyone says he wants to be a Navy Seal, but when Hell Week comes and sleep is taken away for an entire week, the vast majority of recruits quit. Lack of sleep reveals commitment.

Exhaustion also tempts a man to strip away whatever is nonessential to his survival. He begins thinking things like, "Instead of doing laundry, I am sure I can find some socks that are not too dirty," or "It has only been three days since I showered; I can just roll on extra deodorant or bathe my clothes in Febreeze." As fatigue tightens its grip, priorities that make an almost immediate impact on your quality of life become compromised, like going to McDonald's instead of cooking a quality meal or replacing prayer with a couple whacks of the snooze button. Eventually he is left with the priorities that cannot be compromised. Unless I want to go to prison, I cannot give up on my military commitment. It is impossible to ignore you when you are crying.

Through the lens of fatigue, a man quickly discovers what must be done regardless of how he feels. It is here that he is given an important choice—to complete the task with either a good attitude or a poor one. The job will be done regardless, but his effectiveness hinges on that decision.

God is using your innocent needs to test and grow your parents. I am blessed to get the daily opportunity to prove how serious I am about being your dad. It is an awesome challenge. Now that the rubber has hit the road, will I continue to write? Will I continue to find a way for us to spend days outdoors? Will I continue to live as I know I should?

With the Lord's help, yes,

V

■ ■ ■

18 September 2013
#63
James 4:10
0520

Dear VI,

Boy! You kept me up all night! I have no idea why, but you cried like someone whose legs were being sawed off. Last night introduced me to a new emotion. It is the feeling a man gets when sympathy is paired with confusion only to be thrown in a blender with a handful of helplessness. I bathed in this recipe when it was just you and me in the wee hours of the morning (3 hours ago!).

Today I wonder how people survive without the strength of Jesus. I cannot imagine the destructive emotions I would be harvesting if not for my relationship with Christ. I am leaning on Him so hard, my feet are hardly touching the ground. How wonderful it is to have a Savior who carries our load!

I would not have traded our time last night for anything,

V

■ ■ ■

24 September 2013
#64
Psalm 18:2
0555

Dear VI,

Lewis IV (your grandpa) was here up until yesterday, and before that, your Grandma Freeman spent 10 days with us. Now I will be doing some traveling of my own. I leave tomorrow to go back home to Southern California to watch my mom get married. Soon she will be known as "Grandma O'Connor." That new name will take me some getting used to.

It is unbelievable to watch the growing relationship between you and your mother. She has been given a special fight that can only be fueled by her love for her child. Life-changing chemical alterations happen when a woman becomes a mother. I can see the motherly instinct blossoming inside of her just the way God designed it. Witnessing the transition is powerful. Lately, she spends much of the day carrying you around our little home, softly humming hymns to you. She is meticulous when tending to your needs. She is thoughtful and intentional in her every action. And God help the spider or mosquito that comes near you! She is a ferocious mamma bear.

You continue to challenge us by insisting we do our best to adjust to this new life—a life that will never again resemble how things were. I am having difficulty coping with the fact that I cannot help. Tomorrow you will be one month old. You do not need me at all. When you wake up at 0230 (which in turn wakes everyone up), your mom slips out of bed to feed you. I used to get up with her only to sit by her side fast asleep. What kind of help is that?

"You know, you could get me a glass of water if you want." She asks for water fairly often, but I would wager she is not even thirsty! I think she simply wants me to feel like I am participating. This is one of the things a man is never told about prior to becoming a father. During a father's rookie months, he is close to useless. The most helpful thing he can do is try not to touch anything.

When comparing today to our pre-child days, I marvel at how virtually everything has been transformed, but I also see small glimpses of great potential. At the moment, our lives feel like a place with no discernable climate. Every day is a total guessing game, and I keep asking, "What is going on around here?"

In the center of the chaos, our Rock continues to be as solid as ever. He is using this transition as an important tool to grow us. I feel as if my life was thrown into a blender, but while He is sympathetic toward my feelings, He would not view the situation as chaotic. He is in control. This whole season is an exercise that can teach me to keep my eye on the prize, my Anchor, my Rock, my Fortress, my Stronghold.

I am going to go get your mom some water,

V

■ ■ ■

27 September 2013
#65
Isaiah 55:9
0750

Dear VI,

I am out on the West Coast to attend my mom's wedding. It feels refreshing to be back in Southern California, but without my family it is difficult to relax. One minute I am eyeball deep in being a daddy and military business. Then, 24 hours later, I am thousands of miles away with nothing but time. The transition has me all jittery.

This West Coast time has me up way before the rest of the house, which gives me the opportunity to write a long overdue letter. I am in the home of my very dear friend Brent. I find it strange being here because the last place I can remember him living was on my couch in college, then in a van, then with his parents. His work ethic and musicianship has landed him with a well-known band, and from the looks of it, things are going well. I cannot tell you how happy I am for him. In addition to years of priceless friendship, Brent played a key role in saving your parents' marriage. He stood close by me through a very rough season and never wavered in his support. He gave me his ears when I needed them, his wisdom only when I asked, and his love constantly. Please ask me for the details someday. He was asleep when I arrived last night. I'm about to go tackle his lazy butt and drag him to breakfast. I can't wait to see him!

Three other musicians and a butler live here too. I have a precious history with each of them (except the butler); however, if you put us side by side you would never believe we are friends. These men have the look and swagger you might expect from a reputable LA musician. What they lack in body weight and skin tone, they make up for in hair product and designer boots. I could not pull this look off if my life depended on it. Maybe if I transplanted some chest hair onto my head and cut myself down the middle, but that seems like too much work.

One thing we do have in common is our love for music. Once upon a time, these guys performed my compositions, making it possible for me to finish my music degree. I used to help Brent with his theory homework. Sitting here in his beautiful home complete with a room full of top of the line musical equipment (and a butler!), I find myself tempted to ask, *what if?* What if I had a butler instead of government assistance? This question flies in the face of Letter 58 which laid out my desire for our family to live out of a suitcase in Africa, but that's my point: A man is easily swayed. He is like a boat without an anchor. He is at the mercy of the tide.

The life we live is based off of my Anchor's instructions. This has not always been the case, but my relationship with Christ now is such that if He instructs me to put my passion for music on hold, then so be it. If He decided I should spend my life scrubbing floors, then so be it. And if I am called to war, then I will pack my medic bag and march. I will do this because I believe my Anchor has plans for the Bradshaws, which I cannot fathom or understand. His plans I could never make on my own, drifting anchorless in an endless sea. A man's options consist of either pursuing "what-if" scenarios or committing to God's will, but it is impossible to do both. Trust me, I have tried.

Committing to our King's plan is not always easy—not at all! It involves a faith and willingness to put aside ALL passions for a season or possibly forever. For me, it meant saying "goodbye" to the people, places, and things I considered to be what made me tick—the Pacific Ocean, my guitar, my three skinny-jeans-wearing brothers fast asleep in the rooms above me. I stubbornly held on to these things for years after I knew the Lord was telling me to let go, and because of my attitude all areas of my life suffered. The thought of no longer experiencing what I loved outweighed my desire to follow the will of our Lord.

I would like to say that those days are behind me, but the truth is, they never are. Twelve hours after reuniting with my friends, I find myself wanting a butler. I will continue to falter for the rest of my life, but I can say with a clear conscious that I am doing my best to lead our family in whatever direction my Anchor has planned. It will be amazing to look back on this letter and see the changes that have taken place.

May the Lord forever be the Anchor of our home,

V

■ ■ ■

03 October 2013
#66
Ecclesiastes 3:1
0607

Dear VI,

Well, I am home, back to the grind I go. I have made a note never to go back to work the day after leave. "I need a vacation after that vacation" as they say.

During your mom's pregnancy I heard the advice, "Keep your eyes open; they grow up quick" no less than a million times. Like a fool I blew it off, thinking this was simply one of those bits of input old people say, but now I see there is a lot of wisdom in those words. After a week touring my old stomping grounds, I have returned to find you a different child. You are bigger and stronger, with lighter hair and brighter eyes. If this is how raising you is going to be, I had better quickly learn to live without blinking!

I long to embrace every second of your life. Since the day of your birth, I consistently hear people say, "Once he hits a certain age, you're going to wish he was still your precious little baby." I think I am going to take those words more seriously.

I love you every minute,

V

■ ■ ■

07 October 2013
#67
Psalm 138:8
0602

Dear VI,

I am getting increasingly more enjoyment from writing. It has become a habit, a hobby, and a passion. I keep a notepad handy to help remember tidbits that happen throughout the day, and this practice has brought to my attention how many amazing moments slip through the cracks of memory.

Last night for example, your mom was in your room, massaging the bubbles out of your gut. When you finally passed man-sized gas, she exclaimed, "Hallelujah!" During this "event," I was sitting in the other room, simultaneously watching Sunday Night Football and polishing off an entire rotisserie chicken with my bare hands.

This is a great example of a precious memory that does double duty by both making me smile and summing up an evening in the current life of the Bradshaw family. What if I had never written it down? The world would never know. My eating chicken to the aroma of your bowels would by no means be considered "life-altering," but now that you know it happened, can you imagine life without it?

God gives us every day with a purpose, and while it would be unrealistic and foolish to try and find the deeper meaning in every little "jot and tittle," it is equally foolish to classify an entire day of life as "a work day" or "a school day." It is best to stay alert; you never know what adventure God might have in store around the next bend.

Remember this: Someday when I ask you "What did you do today?" or "What did you learn at school?" it will never be acceptable to respond, "Nothing,"

V

■ ■ ■

09 October 2013
#68
Joshua 1:8
0557

Dear VI,

I just finished reading 2 Corinthians. I have read this book dozens of times; each page is littered with notes and highlights from years past. Yet as I read this familiar text again, I am left asking myself, "How do I always forget this stuff?" The answer is simple. Bluntly put, I am simple.

Today while praying, I was given a basic, but powerful, illustration: being a human is like pouring water into a cracked mug. No doubt the mug has sentimental value, proven by the chipped rim and worn colors. Neither is it so damaged that it can no longer serve its function, but the little crack has begun to leave a ring on the tabletop. If you fill it up and leave the room, you might return to find the mug half-full, and your beverage slowly dribbling onto the floor. Things are getting serious, but your commitment to this mug leaves you no option but to either stand by with a pitcher and a towel or walk away and let your cup run dry.

This leaky vessel is like a man's memory. The dripping beverage symbolizes what happens to the information that enters it. A man could be earth's most diligent pourer. He could spend his life hovering over his cup with an eyedropper. He could sop up the water with a towel and wring it back into the cup. He could try endless combinations of costly patch jobs. Regardless of any measures taken, eventually that water will find its way out of the cup.

Ask a man what happens to his physique when he stops exercising. Ask a college graduate what was on his final exams. Ask a musician to blow the dust off his instrument and play as he once did. Ask a former high school athlete to compete like he did in his heyday. I could not tell you three percent of the 500 flash cards I memorized for the exam, and that was only two weeks ago! And what about relationships? What happens at a reunion when a bunch of people who spent years together

DEAR VI...LOVE V  101

reunite? I cannot remember the last names of friends I surfed with every day for years! (I can see how you might wonder if your dad is the only one with the cracked cup! Mine may be more leaky than most, but I find I am not the only one.)

Relearning is equally or more important as learning. A brilliant man with the ability to read a book then recite it back to you verbatim would eventually begin to forget its contents. Over time he would begin to use broader phrases to sum up the material. After years he may only be able to recall the general theme. Eventually (as the water has all but left the cup), he will no doubt say, "That sounds familiar. Who wrote that?"

My cousin is a brilliant surgeon. Her degree required her to spend 15 years completely dedicated to her craft. Yet when I call her, I often hear a professor lecturing in the background. I used to text her hoping we might meet up, but she would usually decline saying, "I am studying for a case tomorrow." She has never once filled her cup to the brim and declared, "I finally got that doctor thing figured out." She will be learning and reviewing until she retires.

Christians never retire. We run the race until the moment we slide into our graves, dirty and battered. Only then will we be able to give a much-needed sigh of relief. We must continue to fill that filthy, leaking vessel of ours—not when it is nearly empty, but consistently, so there is no doubt its contents contain a healthy volume of fluid.

Another blessing that has come from these letters is my ability to fill my cup by going back and reminding myself of all that has happened these last few months. For memory's sake, I will end with another story involving the colon. Last night while I was getting you ready for a bath, you pooped on my arm and then gave me a big toothless grin.

That's my boy,

V

■ ■ ■

10 October 2013
#69
2 Corinthians 4:13
0551

Dear VI,

I just followed my own advice and reread yesterday's letter. Then (inspired by my own words), I also reread 2 Corinthians, and wouldn't you know it, I relearned something. This proves that I am always right.

You are starting to develop your own unique language, a series of "goos" and "gaws" strung together in one-of-a-kind combinations. Your mom responds as if your words have profound meaning. "Really?" she says. "That is so interesting!" I have no idea what you are saying, but each sound is made with zeal which I respect. Your parents are blinded by love. We hang on your every syllable.

It is not easy for a Christian man to proclaim his beliefs with the kind of tenacity you have been displaying. Claiming to be a Christian creates a breeding ground for controversy because a Christian's convictions are becoming increasingly unpopular views to hold. Telling someone I am a Christian causes them to assume that I am the same as the guy in the car with the Jesus sticker that cut them off or the Christian husband who treats his wife like a servant. Or the pastor on the news who is spending life in prison for perverted wickedness.

Identifying as a Christian gives people some accurate insight into my views on certain hot-button issues. I have no problem with people knowing my position on abortion or homosexuality. However, I am never given the opportunity to explain myself and that assumed knowledge causes people to draw a line in the sand. I find my side shrinking while the criticism of the other side continues to grow louder and more hostile.

It is unfortunate (not to mention ironic) that once a man's faith is known, a non-believer will automatically assume the Christian is judging him when, in fact, the Christian is the one being judged. Because it is automatically assumed that the Christian is judgmental, the non-believer henceforth views him as a hypocrite (which in itself is hypocritical). Now the Christian is unfairly starting off on the wrong foot. Proclaiming Christ invites persecution, which no one in his right mind wishes to bring upon himself, especially when he interacts with those people on a daily basis.

A few weeks ago I was invited to a strip club birthday party. I respectfully declined this invitation by saying I was flattered but not interested. My response prompted an interrogation. Had I ever seen a stripper? This became one of those moments I had to choose which side of the line to stand on. Either proclaim my faith or deny my Maker. I chose the former and said "no." Their initial reaction was the same look of wonder I imagine I had when you came into the world. Here I am sitting in a chair with five young men staring at me like I had just emerged from a cave where I had spent my life with my eyes closed and my fingers in my ears. You can imagine my discomfort.

I suppressed the urge to get defensive. I wanted to flip the question on them by asking if they had ever done something I knew they had not done. Things like bungee jumped naked over the Nile River, but I knew that route would spoil my opportunity to represent Christ. Instead, I held my tongue. I had chosen whose side to be on; now I had to stick to my guns.

After a lengthy awkward silence, I was asked why I had denied myself such a pleasure. "I am sure that seeing those women would destroy the way I look at my wife," I said. I was satisfied with my response because I knew I had nothing to do with those words jumping out of my mouth. The response was short, confident, and most importantly, it was true. The Holy Spirit showed up as He always does when one of His followers is in a jam. Confirmation that the Holy Spirit had given me those words was evident in the lack of response from those who heard me. I was teased and called names which more or less translated to "judgmental prude."

One man said, "Ain't nothing better than waking up smelling like a hoe's thong."

I really did not mind their responses until something horrible was said about Jesus, at which point I snapped. Getting an inch from this man's nose, I explained that kind of talk would not end well for him. Again the room went silent. We stood toe to toe, each waiting for the other to make a move. Eventually this man, who severely outranks me, took a step back, squeezed my hand, and while shaking it, explained how much he respected me for standing firm in my beliefs.

Things were fine for a while. I lived my life, and they lived theirs. We still talked daily and played sports. Yesterday, sticking to my side of the line bore some fruit. With tears in his eyes, the very man I stood toe to toe with came into my office and told me his marriage is falling apart. The eyes that once held my own with a fierce glare were now tear-filled and desperate.

If I had previously wavered in my beliefs, I would never have had the opportunity to talk to this broken man about God's wonderful design. It is unimaginable to consider that the reason the Holy Spirit gave me the response He did at the time that He did was so this man would know the value I put on marriage, which would then prompt him to confide in me concerning his own. This sort of outcome would not have been possible without a living, active, all-knowing Spirit.

2 Corinthians 4:13 reads, "I believed, so I spoke." If the Holy Spirit prompts us, we must be bold and speak. Only our Savior knows what the result will be, but we can be sure that if He is involved, good will come of it.

Stand tall and stay true,

V

■ ■ ■

11 October 2013
#70
2 Corinthians 5
0604

Dear VI,

It is finally beginning to cool down. I guess Floridians are right; there are seasons in Jacksonville. I have not spent enough time outdoors this last week, and my pasty-looking skin proves it. I look like I live in a bomb shelter. Yet again, I plead that the Lord affords us a living situation which will allow our family to spend more time in Creation.

Last night your mom read 2 Corinthians 5 to me. Its contents lay out the differences between our physical and spiritual bodies. As usual, these Scriptures came at the perfect moment. I had just finished complaining about the state of my physical body. I have not been easy on this frame, and the years of wear and tear are beginning to catch up.

I have a little scrapbook of newspaper articles documenting my accolades in high school. One title reads, "He has the heart of a lion." Another full-page article describes how filthy my jersey was after a loss. The headline is a quote from the opposing team's coach, "That guy just kept getting up. I would trade my team for one of him." Pasted between these old articles are pictures of me skateboarding off the roof of a house, surfing big waves in shallow water, and other activities that remind me why my knees hurt.

I am 28 years old and walk with a limp, but I would never trade my experiences for a fresh body. I have earned every one of my aches. I know the events that caused them played a huge role in my development. When a man goes through something that may cause pain or sets his jaw and jumps despite his nerves, *only then* can he discover he has what it takes to endure the battle and emerge victorious. This is critical.

A man's body is made to be used, not preserved. Our Creator chose a remarkably sturdy design. He created the flower. We could have been made with the same delicacy. God is a Master in every medium. He has proven His ability to design extremely fragile things perfectly. When constructing man, He chose a much more rugged approach. The body is capable of enormous strain. It responds positively to manual labor. It has systems in place which allow the body to grind through extremely taxing circumstances for long periods of time. I am proof of our body's durability.

I never want you to worry about these annoying aches of mine. I have made plenty of poor choices in my life, but pushing the boundaries of my body is not one of them. I am decades away from being knocked out. And besides, I could be in a wheelchair with my hands tied behind my back and still never miss the opportunity to whoop ya in a wrestling match!

I love you, buddy,

V

■ ■ ■

14 October 2013
#71
1 Timothy 4:8
0956

Dear VI,

One of the benefits of government employment is getting Columbus Day off. I woke up at 0930 and now sit here enjoying a late morning devotion. I have some tunes going, but not so loud as to drown out the beautiful sound of your mom talking to you during your bath.

Yesterday's letter explained why your old man sometimes gets up with a groan but also to teach you the value in pushing your body's limits. Today, I want to introduce the more important practice of pushing yourself spiritually.

In 2 Corinthians 6:3-13, there is a section entitled, "Paul's Hardships." The text lists some of the afflictions he endured in the name of Jesus. The lengthy list includes beatings, imprisonment, starvation, more than one shipwreck, and severe sleep deprivation. Do you think Paul had some nerves before going into a busy town and essentially telling the area's most powerful men that their way of life was wrong? Do you think he liked telling strangers they could not get into Heaven on their own? He knew there could be painful consequences, but his relationship with the Holy Spirit was such that he stood tall and obeyed God despite the punishment his body might endure. And because of his obedience he was, without question, the most successful missionary in the history of the world. Every day he pushed himself to do the things the Spirit put on his heart. Imagine the adrenaline coursing through his veins as he raised his voice to those within earshot, knowing that doing so could lead to his body being pulverized with rocks. He was far from his comfort zone, yet he pushed to further his Savior's kingdom.

Not everyone is called to live as Paul lived, but every Christian is called to obey the still, small voice that nudges a man to do things outside of his comfort zone. Taking a deep breath and following the gentle push of the Spirit can be nerve-wracking. For me, it is far more uncomfortable than pushing my body. I find it simple to jump off a cliff and challenging to ask a stranger if I can pray for him. But how much more important is it to pray for the grieving girl? How much more valuable to eat lunch with the shy boy? You may be tired or nervous, and, more than likely, unaware of what you are getting into, but pushing your limits spiritually is how Christian men are made.

Do not hide inside your comfort zones. Push yourself,

V

■ ■ ■

15 October 2013
#72
Genesis 1:27
0446

Dear VI,

I write to you at this sickening hour because this week is the command's physical readiness weigh-in. I am a command assistant fitness leader (ACFL), which means I am partly responsible for the proper body mass

108 LEWIS SEELEY BRADSHAW V

index of 1,200 people. It is a welcome change of pace despite the early hour.

Before church last week, I was drinking tea and watching a pair of boys (probably six or seven years old) eat candy and chat like children do, when a third boy entered the room. It was clear his grandmother had dressed him. The poor boy was stuffed into a sailor suit. It was a faux dress blue uniform that must have been found in the bowels of Grandma's closet. I saw him nervously walk up to the boys, watched him say "Hello," and then watched the rest of the group pretend he did not exist! After a few seconds he realized he was on the butt end of a joke, and his face turned burgundy. Tears tried to flow, but he did not cry. He only awkwardly skipped away, which gave the group a chance to snicker at his expense. The unfortunate outfit appeared twice more. Each time he tried to mingle. Each time he was rejected.

To witness this kind of ostracizing anywhere makes my blood boil, but the fact that it happened inside a church made me nauseous with rage. I hope that situation will upset you too. Read this carefully, son. This "we-are-better-than-you" attitude displayed by these kids is not limited to young people. This flavor of cruelty continues into adulthood. If anything, it matures and becomes even more devious. Seeing it absolutely kills your mother and me. Our King calls us to love our neighbors as ourselves. An evil seed has been planted into a man's brain the second he begins to think he is superior to another. This seed will grow into a mass of thorny vines right between man and Maker until it is impossible to see Him through the entanglement. Everyone you encounter has been molded by the same Hands; they all deserve to join the conversation.

Make sure you keep a sharp eye out for the kids in the unlucky outfit,

V

∎ ∎ ∎

16 October 2013
#73
Ephesians 2
0525

Dear VI,

It is high time I write to you concerning the most beautiful part of our faith. Ephesians chapter 2: "God saved you by grace when you believed and you cannot take credit for it. It is a gift from God. Salvation is not a reward for the good things you have done so that no one can boast about it."

Throughout the winter of 2012, I worked for a very high-end construction company. A man with unlimited funds would call this company if he wanted a brand-new custom home. The company's reputation gave them the privilege of charging top dollar. All projects were finished on time, and their quality of work was exceptional. It was amazing to watch these men labor with no music, no conversation, no breaks, only extreme focus on every cut, every screw, and every swipe of a paintbrush.

I will always love these men for providing employment to a wiggly, inexperienced man like myself, but I cannot look back at that season without feeling a tinge of sadness. The fear of hell was driving their work ethic. These men were part of a community that considered belief in Christ inadequate; salvation was earned through a combination of hard work and sinless living. Throughout my months of working shoulder to shoulder with these men, I shamelessly gave each one the third degree no less than a dozen times. My fascination with their way of life was as sincere as it was obnoxious. I was also more bored then I had ever been in my life. A man can only sand baseboards in silence for so long. Out of all the information I surgically removed from the group, the saddest was this: every one of these kindhearted men believed that they were Hellbound. Sin would not relax its grip on their lives, and no amount of work or charity could offset the balance. They did not believe the Good News given by Paul, and because of this, they completely proved his point.

If salvation was earned, we would all be destined for eternal separation from our Creator. Man is not perfect. He is sinful and doomed to fail which is why salvation *must* be a gift. Let your motivation for living a godly life be derived from the love you have for Him because of the gift He gave you.

I love you, Lewis,

V

■ ■ ■

21 October 2013
#74
Jeremiah 31:25
0543

Dear VI,

One day you will experience a series of events which will jog this letter into memory. First off, the family dryer went out, which forced me to spend a whole lot of Saturday on the cold garage floor, figuring out the guts of the machine. Then it was off to "BABIESRUS" where I went cross eyed trying to understand the complicated baby registry system. (Eventually, after walking around for what seemed like hours in my greasy dryer-fixing gear, I decided to get diapers, the least fun and most important gift a new parent can receive.) When the weekend was near and the weather forecast favorable, I looked forward with great anticipation to my day off. However, my "day off" held none of the activities I had dreamed about: only traffic, crowds, fluorescent lights, limited time with you, and wounded appliances.

The sun was low when, while loading you up in the stroller, I made a spontaneous decision. I grabbed my fishing pole, my skateboard, and your mom, and took us all to a little fishing hole down the street. Your mom and I took shifts catching little bluegill with the stale bread we used for bait. I am usually pretty sharp when a change in weather is coming, so when I say it started pouring out of nowhere, I mean it—no thunder, no temperature drop, no sudden cool wind. God punched the "Dump Buckets" button, and the skies obeyed. We loaded you up and started home as fast as a recovering woman can push a stroller through the rain with a long skirt and sandals. The rain increased during the journey home, but so did our laughter. Your mom and I shuffled along absolutely cracking up. Eventually, soaked to the soul, we made it beneath the cover of our porch where I lifted back your blanket to find you fast asleep!

This story will go down in history as one of my favorites, but the point I would like you to take away is this: the stresses that accompany the life of a provider were washed away in that storm. Our time at the pond and the marathon home refocused my mind on what is truly important. I was reminded of the solid tangible stuff man gains energy from. I never kicked the dryer or cursed its inability to create heat. The day's events did not lead to my undoing. But prior to the adventure in the rain, I felt overwhelmed with the responsibility that comes with heading up a household. Standing on the porch, soaking wet, I felt like a blessed king—the leader of a thriving kingdom and an empire with a working dryer.

Never allow those feelings of obligation to blind you from the bigger picture. Always leave time to run in the rain. Embracing adventure will help you stay focused on the important stuff which, in turn, will assist you in being a happy, more effective, leader.

Six more days until next Saturday!

V

■ ■ ■

23 October 2013
#75
Hebrews 13:8
0600

Dear VI,

I have been going over Acts with a fine-toothed comb. A correlating study at church has sparked my curiosity. If there is one theme that catches my attention, it is that of change. Just a few of the changes include the development of the church, the apostles healing the sick, Saul becoming Paul, and the constant traveling of the apostles.

You, too, are changing, my son. You look bigger, stronger, and are definitely more coordinated. Your brain is a sponge. Your mom says the beauty of your development is scary, and I agree. It hurts to think of all the seconds I am missing, but I feel privileged to be the one assigned to provide for you. As much as I dream of the day I can push you into waves or have a thinking man's conversation with you, I would hate to wish away my only chance to know you as a precious baby.

Yesterday, while practicing drums for worship team, I heard the lyric, "You are everlasting, the same forever." My first thought was to reprimand the artist for his lack of creativity. Any consistent church-goer has heard some variation of this lyric a thousand times. It appears lazy when the magnificence of our Lord is described with a phrase like "He does not change," or "Our God is a good God." There is a severe lack of substance in that type of lyric.

Once I stopped unjustly condemning the musician and focused on the truth of the lyric, things were thrust into perspective. The world has been changing from the day God saw that "it was good," through the book of Acts, and continues on in the life of my precious son. My life is changing, as is everything connected and unrelated to it. The earth and all it holds changes from moment to moment. Each second is different from the last. Tears formed when realizing that my Savior is the Rock in a world made of shifting sand. And they flowed when, for a split second, I began to understand that the promises I am not worthy to receive will also never change.

His love, mercy, protection and purpose will always be present in my life. He is unmovable in a world that sways with every breath.

To help you understand how remarkable this is, I end today's letter with a challenge. Find something that is exactly the same every day.

He is the Rock we can stand firm upon,

V

P.S. Change is not bad when done in Christ. I am thankful my life is not a duplicate copy.

■ ■ ■

24 October 2013
#76
Matthew 6:24
0541

Dear VI,

It is finally a little chilly here, 46°. I know that the rest of the nation would laugh at me refer to the mid-40s as "chilly." Regardless of a man's definition of *chilly*, no man can deny that a cool night and warm wife make getting out of bed nearly impossible. I hate my alarm clock for interrupting such perfection!

We have finally established a semi-solid evening routine which unfolds like this: you, me, bottle, couch. Last night you sprawled across my lap and guzzled down four ounces of the "house white" while we watched a few innings of the World Series (Red Sox vs. Cardinals). You enjoy wrapping your little fingers in my arm hair, and I enjoy burping you.

I also enjoy watching breast milk work its magic on a tired baby. As you drink, your eyes get heavy, and your shoulders relax. By the time you are finished, you are drifting in and out of consciousness. At this point I slowly swaddle you and pray that a mighty angel will stand guard over every part of your sleeping body. Upon returning to the living room, I hold my hands high like an underdog who beat the odds. It may seem like a small victory to you, but any new parent will tell you this is the best feeling in the world. Your mom gives me a high five. We sit down to have some tea together at last. Another successful day as new parents.

Again I catch myself longing for the future. I am tempted to dream of a time we both stay up too late in order to share popcorn and watch the race for the pennant. I want my friend swaddled in the next room to be casually chatting with me. I want to make him laugh. Like I said, I am really making an effort to soak up every season we have together instead of looking into a future I can neither see nor control. A man should be immersed in either the present or eternity. But you're not making that easy.

To work I go,

V

■ ■ ■

25 October 2013
#77
Genesis 2:17
0623

Dear VI,

Today I write to you from McDonald's where I am having my quiet time before Duty. Duty—I shudder at the thought of it. The task equates to sitting at a desk from 0700-2100, answering the phones. Seventeen hours at a desk gives a man a lot of time to think. The goal is to try and think about anything other than the big clock hanging directly in front of me.

I have been reading *The Call of the Wild* these last couple weeks. It was a reward to myself after completing the test I told you about back in Letter 59. In fact, I read a few pages to you yesterday, but you did not seem very interested.

This is a dangerous book for a man to read while on duty, with his uniform crawling into all the wrong places and his immediate surroundings consisting of blinking screens, fluorescent lights, mountains of paperwork, and so on. I spend a lot of my time on duty trying to figure out how it came to this. I cannot imagine an environment further removed from that which God created.

*The Call of the Wild* describes nature's effect on man's senses similar to how I imagine Heaven. Every smell is the most fascinating, water from a stream completely quenches a thirst, the elaborate branches of a tree or the thundering power of a waterfall brings a man the best sort of chills. Nature as an energizing emotional experience.

Nowadays, men will not tread into a place without a paved path and a 50-pound rucksack containing an air mattress, water filter, flares, bug spray, GPS, and whatever else they can stuff in their bags. Fear is an epidemic causing man to cling to comfort, rely on conveniences, and murder his adventure bug. Because of this, his senses have dulled. What once made him weep now strikes the emotions brought on by a decent movie.

I mentioned these things in Letters 55 and 57, but I bring this back up today because, up until very recently, I was able to enjoy the ocean much like primitive man did when climbing up into the strong arms of a giant oak tree. The last few times I have been at the beach, I feel sedated. I harvest bitterness toward anyone with sun on his skin. I am jealous of those who get to experience the salt air daily. I hate myself for not surfing as well as I once did. I have been too hard on my adventure bug in the name of responsibility. I feel depressed and exhausted. It is as if my spirit has been trying to fight off an infection I keep trying to give it. It has not laid down or given up, but the effort is arduous. These feelings genuinely scare me.

I continue to pray for solutions. I will not be a father who writes about the majestic creation of our Lord while moping around with a bag of snacks. I recognize that my spirit must be the example. I do not believe man must choose between going on a hike with his family or power washing his driveway. The problem is I cannot think of a better idea. I will keep seeking the Lord on this issue. I simply will not tolerate the world's policy of "sticking things out until retirement" or "being tied up until my kid is out of the house." It simply makes sense not to own a lawn or a driveway or gutters or dishes. Sell the lawn mower and go to the park! Why is that not an option?

How ironic that my letter detailing how far man has strayed from creation has been written from within the walls of a McDonald's. I am off to man the phones and think through this conundrum.

To be continued,

V

■ ■ ■

27 October 2013
#78
Philippians 4:19
1035

Dear VI,

I just finished playing drums at the first of two morning church services and now sit here in the little café awaiting your arrival. You will be spending a lot of time here, from now until you turn 18, at which time you could give me the finger and never come back, but I don't expect that to happen.

In preparation for a little cookout we hosted last night, I spent the afternoon hauling rocks, bricks, and gravel to the big fire pit I dug a couple weeks prior. (I have not forgotten that I still need to recount to you the story of my creating this pit.)

It was a perfect day yesterday. Beneath a cool, blue sky, I got busy hauling and lifting. Ten minutes of bare-chested work beneath the trees in our backward left me sweaty and dirty. I had the feeling it was impossible to work too hard and that my body was capable of completing whatever task I threw at it. I had no weight restrictions or speed limits. The dirt on my hands was soap capable of washing away the stress of work. The stones I hauled to the pit replaced the stones of pressure that I had allowed to accumulate without even realizing it. How therapeutic it is for a twenty-first century man to spend time doing activities he might have done for survival a thousand years before! A simple task that takes a good amount of effort and serves an important purpose but still allows room for a man to think.

My dad used to come home with big wooden pallets and, handing me a hatchet and saw, would say, "Get to work. We need firewood for our camping trip. Make sure it gets stacked neatly, and the nails are all out." Of course, I would pout at first, but I can think back on those times now and recall experiencing the same feelings of satisfaction I felt yesterday in the backyard.

Friday, while on duty, a 60-year-old lady came limping up to my desk to punch her timecard. Everything about her was heavy—her weight, her limp, her look of utter exhaustion. In one hand she had a purse and in the other an enormous soda. "Two months and four days until I am out of this hellhole," she announced. Because I had nothing better to do, I spent a chunk of time thinking about this bitter employee. I even asked around and discovered that once upon a time she was in the military and was a star pitcher on the all-Navy softball team. "That is what happens when you work in a dark office for 30 years," a buddy told me.

Again the question, how do I make sure I am not counting down the days till I retire? Human logic says I must "put in my time" or be counted as an irresponsible man. *Lord, help the Bradshaws not only discover a way to break the cycle, allow us to be an example to a generation that believes success is a condo with an electric fireplace. Teach me a solution I can pass on to others.*

You just showed up! Let's go worship,

V

■ ■ ■

28 October 2013
#79
Genesis 1
0552

Dear VI,

Today I read about God's original act of love: Creation. I am intimately acquainted with these scriptures because of the obsession I had with disproving evolution. I loved debating creation versus evolution. I thought I was smart because I was able to reference all sorts of documents or Scripture; I was smug and arrogant.

The only thing that evolved from my fundamental toiling was a lengthy list of severed relationships. I alienated myself from people whom I genuinely liked. I made fools of people who could have really used the friendship of a God-fearing teenager. A boot of regret kicks me in the gut when I consider the fact that my righteous attitude could be responsible for people hating Jesus today. I distanced myself from people who lived differently than myself and let them know it. I would not be seen with the guy who smoked or the girl who was sleeping with her boyfriend.

What pains me most is the position I held while doing this. My efforts in sports, the ocean, and the music program gave me a good amount of recognition. Everyone knew who Lewis Bradshaw V was. I was in a perfect situation to show Christ's love, but I spent my time condemning people instead. I was influential, but I was not a good influence. My words carried weight, but I chose the wrong words.

Today when opening my Bible, I saw these words written a decade earlier: "God is creative, and He created because He loves us." The big bold letters were written shortly after I recognized how destructive my fundamentalism had been. My priorities were flip-flopped. Introducing people to Jesus by being an example of His love is infinitely more valuable than disproving how man supposedly evolved or how the flood shaped the world we live in today.

After all, the Holy Spirit is the One who convicts and transforms a man *after* that man meets Jesus.

Live His example!

V

P.S. Like I mentioned in Letter 64, I am so amazed at the love shared between you and your mother. What a blessing it is to see this special relationship thriving right before my eyes! Relationship can be seen in all areas of creation—scientifically, spiritually, and in my precious family.

■ ■ ■

29 October 2013
#80
Isaiah 53:10
0550

Dear VI,

Yesterday, your beautiful mother and I were enjoying our usual chat over tea. We sat down shortly after you hit the bassinette. We discussed your upcoming trip to the doctor and how much we dread putting you through a second round of vaccinations. The idea of a needle jammed into your chubby little thigh breaks my heart. Your mom cannot even talk about it without crying.

We reminded ourselves how important it is that we stand beside you. How having her hands and eyes locked with yours really matters. We want you to know your parents are present when you are enduring life's painful moments—from immunizations forward.

Our conversation then transitioned into what Christ did on the cross for us. If my heart aches over the thought of my son's shots, how much more must our Heavenly Father's heart have ached while watching His precious little Boy endure betrayal, mockery, floggings, and crucifixion? And all of those things were being done by the very people He was sacrificing Himself for.

God is the commander of the universe. He has a million angels standing by awaiting orders. He could have stopped it all at any point, but because He loves us, He allowed His precious Son to suffer. Nothing is more powerful then looking at the crucifixion through the lens of a parent.

Thank You, Father, for sacrificing Your Boy,

V

■ ■ ■

30 October 2013
#81
Psalm 103
0557

Dear VI,

I am amazed. You are constantly growing and moving while somehow simultaneously eluding sleep. My wits are in a haze this morning. I keep reminding myself this is all part of the "new-parent" season, and while that reminder does serve as encouragement, it does not seem to make my lids less heavy.

Sometimes when battling with this phase of exhaustion, I remind myself of men who have impacted my life. I keep a few solid men of God in my memory banks as a source of motivation on days like today.

A few years ago, while at the peak of an amateur strongman career, I was invited to an early morning men's group. I walked around at 6'2", weighing 253 pounds and had a mustache that (when waxed) nearly touched my ears. It was a ridiculous look that brought constant remarks regarding my broad shoulders or facial hair, and while I never looked for the attention, I must admit I did not hate it.

Because of my look, I was not surprised when the men at this group commented on my size, but my curiosity was piqued when they insisted I meet a man named Jerry. I soon found out that Jerry was the size of a mountain and held multiple strength records. For his sixtieth birthday, he did something like 6,000 pushups! What impressed me most about all 6'6", 320 pounds of Jerry was his complete lack of pride. He never spoke a word about strength. He never tried to one-up or compare resumes. Rather, he introduced me to his friend, who stood steadying himself on the crook of Jerry's massive forearm. His hand looked like mine would if it rested on a honey-baked ham.

Because Jerry spent most of our visit talking about his frail buddy beside him, I learned that most of that man's 100 years on earth were spent doing manual labor on an empty stomach. I learned the two of them honored a weekly meeting. Every Friday morning, they went to breakfast at the same little diner, and after the men's group, they went back to the old man's place and watched black-and-white movies.

I call this manly. Jerry's genetics and hobbies made him a giant, but his spirit did not hold a trace of arrogance. You could see his strength did not emulate from his powerful chest but came instead from his passion for Christ. God gave him an abundance of strength which he, in turn, used to help those who were in need of a firm place to steady themselves. He saw a brother he could do life with, and because he faithfully obeyed, I am using him as an example to you years later. I am drawing on this man's strength in the Lord as motivation to go out and do likewise. This is just a taste of the giant impact a man can have when he is in Christ. Jerry will probably never know the positive influence he had on the Bradshaw family, but

Christ knew all along that if Jerry would just obey, he would cause a ripple effect that would make it into the pages of a letter to my son.

Today, I feel exceptionally weak. I am sore, my mind is fatigued, and I am overall pretty grumpy. But Christ has more than enough strength to carry me through. It is time to steady myself on His big loving arm and give it my all.

I sure love you!

V

■ ■ ■

1 November 2013
#82
Ecclesiastes 5:3
0600

Dear VI,

Keeping in the vein of inspiring men, you met your Grandpa Freeman for the first time yesterday! Your grandpa continues to be a role model for me. I highly encourage you to stay close to him. Soak him up on your adventures in Oregon. His life is a great example to follow. Learn to appreciate his even keel. It flies in the face of what the world thinks men should be like.

A man might think himself a king after a positive performance review then (a few hours later) is certain that life is not worth living when he is asked to stay late. He walks on air when a pretty girl gives him a wink then shakes his fist at Heaven when she does not return his call. A mature Christian man who truly believes he is owned by Christ (men like your grandpa) tends to have a deep, quiet peace about him. He knows he is his Father's delight, which gives him contentment beautiful to behold. His home is peaceful; his family is close. An aura about him suggests he is satisfied with whatever errand his Manager may send him on. Every man can benefit from this type of attitude.

What a gift it is to have this type of man in our family,

V

■ ■ ■

04 November 2013
#83
1 Peter 4:12
0559

Dear VI,

I was lucky enough to sneak away from work in order to stand by during your second round of immunizations. Your mom held your head and whispered prayers while I held your hand and split my focus between looking you in the eye and monitoring the corpsman. The noise you made was equal parts scream, cry, and panic. It was the noise a child makes after being introduced to a pain he previously could not fathom. I am so sorry. You cried, your mom cried, and despite my best efforts, big stupid tears rolled down my cheeks.

I love watching your mom transform into Mama Bear—from compassionate lover to jealous protector. Her jaw becomes flexed, and her eyes get a look only a fool would try and stand up to. Picking you up with great purpose, she looked at the poor corpsman and said, "Give me a place where I can nurse my son!"

Once in the nursing room, you were rocked and given praise. "We are so proud of you," she said. "What a strong man you are." And so, after a few minutes of snuggling and positive affirmation, you were back to your joyful self—an upbeat bald boy with brightly colored Band-Aids, representing the battle wounds earned during an experience that left you a little tougher, a little wiser.

Like your shots, trials enter a man's life completely uninvited. One moment might find you fat and happy, and the next may have you writhing in pain. Think of the midnight phone call that steals a man from a sweet dream to inform him that his mother has passed away. Think of a man who turns a corner to find his woman embracing another man. Think of the athlete who, after endless hours mastering his craft, turns the wrong way and blows out his knee. This is where that supernatural contentment shown by Grandpa Freeman is put to the test. How we react in these situations is what defines us as men and Christians.

The examples are endless. We simply do not know when a trial might stab. I do not relish writing to you about the ever-lurking possibility of suffering, but what kind of a dad would I be if I kept such important information to myself? My aim is to inform so that you might better prepare. But outside of a "heads up" by your dad, how does a man prepare for the unimaginable? The answer is simple, but the application is life's greatest adventure. A Christian holds the incalculable advantage of personally knowing the Creator of all things. A Christian's Master is the all-knowing omniscient Alpha and Omega. Knowing Him intimately is without question the wisest preparation a man can make.

Your bandages make you look dangerous,

V

P.S. The pain felt during your shots lasted only a short period, but the benefit of those immunizations will improve the quality of the rest of your life. Be encouraged; most trials are like that too.

■ ■ ■

06 November 2013
#84
Proverbs 19:21
0558

Dear VI,

This is my favorite time of day. My wife and our son are resting peacefully while I enjoy our cool, quiet home with the Word and a warm cup of Joe. I am especially excited this morning because I get to reflect upon yesterday's adventure. I have eagerly anticipated this event for years: your first beach trip. Of course, it was nothing like I imagined it would be. If you have not yet noticed that theme developing in my letters, it's time you take note. Almost everything is never how a man supposes it should be. This is why it is best to know the Man who knows everything and to enter all situations with a heart ready to receive whatever circumstances find you.

I present to you the following comparison as proof of my above statement.

1) How I envisioned your first trip to the beach: On a warm day under blue skies, you and I would spend hours laughing and running from the incoming tide. Castles would be built in the soft white sand. Shells would be collected; birds would be fed. I pictured catching little waves with you on my back in an attempt to impress your mom who watched while lounging in her oversized beach chair.

2) Reality: It was as windy and cold a day as there has ever been in the state of Florida. In the name of adventure, we fought through the elements until we managed to find shelter behind an old set of stairs. Your mom kept most of the sand off you by swaddling you in every available towel, while every inch of our exposed skin was pelted with stinging sand. You did manage to grab one handful of sand which you proceeded to rub into your eyes. I jumped in the freezing ocean alone. Your mom used the sand as an outhouse. I snagged my elbow on a rusty nail.

While huddled behind those stairs, looking out at the windswept beach, I realized that one year ago to the day, your mom and I had just completed a ten-day cross-country trip. We drove a moving truck from Oregon to Virginia where we rented an apartment on the sound. I started optician school. And you were a twinkle in your mom's beautiful eyes.

Oftentimes it is an out-of-the-box scenario which forces a person to compare how life was with how life currently is. It takes stumbling upon an old box of photos, the passing of a loved one, rereading a letter, or enduring a stormy day at the beach. Sadly, most days don't hold moments that force reminiscing. If life was molded only by major events, many lives would never take shape. This is why life has a reputation for passing us by.

But it is the unnoticed minor events that are forever mixing into the real stuff life is made of. They appear unremarkable and are therefore quickly forgotten, but, in reality, they are the most important. The wedding day is not what makes a marriage. Choosing to get up off the couch and help dry the dishes is the real glue which makes a marriage strong. It is not the size of the diamond ring on her hand but the hands themselves as they are folded together in prayer over each other. Life is a list of endless decisions, each one capable of drawing a person one step closer or one step further away from God.

Looking back on life is an important exercise. There is great value in acknowledging where a man has journeyed from. But it is the tiny, often forgotten, daily decisions that end up determining whether a man looks back with a grateful smile or a grimace of regret. Look back often on where you have come from, and do not hold a list of expectations when looking ahead. What is the point? Things never go as you might expect and thank God! His plan always winds up working out much better.

I loved our first day at the beach,

V

■ ■ ■

07 November 2013
#85
Psalm 18:39; Ezekiel 36:26
0556

Dear VI,

Today I read Genesis 2 and 3. These chapters recount the Fall—a pivotal point in history and what I consider to be the Devil's greatest victory. In a world gripped so tightly in the jaws of sin, I enjoy thinking about the lives of Adam and Eve prior to the serpent. I imagine two young adults who possessed the type of innocence you currently have. Earth's first couple held all the emotions today's adults hold except their emotions were not at war with a sinful nature. Their anger was not derived from bitterness, their smile masked no selfishness, their sexual desire was pure and only for each other. Because they spent their days eating the most organic food, their diets were perfect. They ate what the land provided—never thinking twice about what the calories might do to their hips. They did not own any clothing or possessions. Coveting, pride, greed—these ideas did not exist. There was no preconceived expectation of what "good" was because the notion of anything other than good did not exist. Everything around them was perfect simply because "it was." No further classification was needed.

From the moment their teeth sank into that forbidden fruit until this very second, the Enemy has worked relentlessly to assure that earth and the garden bear no resemblance. I must admit, he has done an excellent job. Humanity is a long way from eating fresh fruit in the nude. We are wretches who alone do not possess the ability to live with purpose. Never again will a Christian's life on earth consist of pure fellowship in nature. It has all been tainted. He may experience seasons that faintly resemble that, but make no mistake, a Christian is built through the blood and sweat of trial and persecution soaked in the love of God and the grace of our Savior. The days of living in a garden, lounging in the cool shade of a tree, submersed in God's presence, are over.

But the news is not all bad. Our God works without ceasing to rescue the lost. He has given us the free gift of salvation by sacrificing His perfect Son on our behalf. We are no longer at the end of sin's cruel whip. God has given us salvation along with the tools needed to combat our nature and the wickedness of the world. We can now stand and shine. We can effectively fight with our God to save the lost until we are ushered home as family through golden gates—at last returning to the perfection of His presence.

Until then, we work and enjoy as best as we are able, keeping in mind that the battle is won,

V

■ ■ ■

08 November 2013
#86
John 17:16, 2 Corinthians 4:4
0553

Dear VI,

I am about to enter my first Veteran's Day as a veteran. I have failed you as a father if you are reading this without understanding that being a part of our military is extremely special. Yes, I am the one honored with the responsibility of wearing the uniform, but you and your mom deserve equal credit for committing to the lifestyle. My job may demand I go to war in the defense of our country. It may require I give my life, and I thank you for living with and supporting a career that holds such serious potential.

As much as I love the Navy, I must admit it is a dark enterprise. It has been since day one when my instructor announced that the best relationship for an enlisted man was "two girlfriends and a wife on the side." The task of standing tall in the midst of so much daily wickedness is exhausting. I find myself wanting to run in order to avoid being surrounded by ugly lifestyles—not strictly for my own sanity, but to shield you from such things.

It is reasonable to believe that the more a Christian man spends time with Jesus, the more our dark world is exposed. (If you are reading this and thinking your old man is just a big prude, you have become complacent and must reevaluate). As a man subjects himself to one thing, the opposite becomes more obvious. The veil lifts; his view is raw. This is not only true spiritually; rather, it is true for all things. If a man stands under a bright light then walks into a dark room, doesn't the darkness appear more complete? If a man gets out of a cold pool and enters a steaming spa, doesn't the heated water feel exceptionally warm?

When a man begins to see earth through the lens of truth, it is logical that he would consider fleeing to be his best option. Before you were conceived, I would tease your mom by claiming if we were to ever have children, they would be raised in a tree house deep in the forest (especially if my children were female). While isolation might appear to be a viable option, when I look at our Savior's example, I see that running is not His desire for Christians.

Like Christ, we are to be in the world but not of it. Jesus stood tall on earth and showed love without letting it corrupt Him. He put himself in the thick of it and shook the very foundations of the universe. His relationship with the Father allowed Him to do this. He did not shield Himself from that which did not agree with Him. He attacked it head on. His is the example we must follow.

Know your Savior as you would your best friend, and through His strength, you will be able to stand tall in the world and be a light to those who desperately need His love.

Happy Veterans Day,

V

■ ■ ■

14 November 2013
#87
Proverbs 6:16-19
0554

Dear VI,

I feel like a weathered penman, and why shouldn't I? I am nearing 100 letters! This is a true accomplishment considering I used to get queasy at the idea of writing a five-paragraph essay. I am noticing it takes less effort to locate the right words. More importantly, the Lord continues to keep His promise by revealing subjects and situations that are worth putting pen to paper.

As I am sure you know, your grandpa (Lewis IV) is one of the more skilled watermen the ocean has ever seen. He did an excellent job of pushing me and educating me in all things water, from spearfishing to reading the tides, knowing what the ocean floor is doing based on the way waves break, riding waves on every conceivable board in every conceivable condition, educating me on any biology that ever occupied a tide pool, and much more. The education I received makes me far more confident and competent than most 29 year olds. I feel more at home in the water than on land.

Yesterday after work, I played some racquetball then went for a swim. While finishing up, I saw four guys I work with practicing simple underwater drills. They were doing things like going to the bottom of the pool, putting on a mask, then clearing it. I can teach you to do these things proficiently at age five if you wish. I have had minimal interaction with these gentlemen, but I have become familiar with their naval careers due to their nonstop reminiscing at full volume. Each man's brief history includes quitting a special forces program, becoming a corpsman with the hopes of seeing combat with the Marines, then (in a cruel twist of fate) being stationed at the same clinic as myself where they routinely take vitals on children. Instead of kicking down doors or dragging the wounded out of flaming vehicles, these men spend their days placing thermometers beneath the arms of infants. What bitter irony! A group of muscle-bound, tobacco-chewing, tattooed sailors telling two year olds to open wide and say "Awwwwww." Honestly, they would have my sympathy if not for their incessant complaining. (I too know how it feels to spend day after day doing what feels opposite to your design and desire.)

Hindsight tells me I should have considered the character of these men before swimming over to them. My hope was our common interest might spark relationship. Things did not go as planned. Looking back I see that I may have unintentionally put manhood into question. One thing led to another, and before I knew what was happening, I had accepted a challenge to swim 50 meters underwater with no fins or mask on the grounds that they considered the feat impossible. (I knew it was possible, your grandpa and I have done this very thing a thousand times.) I drew my breath and swam the distance only to discover that they had left while I was in transit. They ditched me.

Theirs was a petty attempt at bullying, and I was probably more hurt than I should have been. I should have seen something like that coming a mile away. As it was, I held on to the side of the pool and fought back tears. I was really hurt.

When found at the receiving end of another's spite (either through observation or firsthand), my initial desire is to forget it. The water is under the bridge off the duck's back and lost forever somewhere in the pool. However, I believe this story holds multiple lessons in what not to do. Do not let your guard down when you attempt to befriend those who do not love the Lord. (Judging another person is not our job, but discernment is always wise.) Never be the reason someone feels bullied. And never swim a long distance underwater without your dad teaching you a few things first.

Be a leader,

V

∎ ∎ ∎

16 November 2013
#88
Hebrews 4:12
0911

Dear VI,

It is Saturday morning, and you are sitting beside me in complete contentment. I love this moment. No agenda, just fresh coffee, the Bible, and my beautiful son. Today, I discovered it has been 13 years to the day since I first read the book of Romans. I know this because I wrote "November 16, 2006" in my Bible. A prayer today asking for some verses to read and some content to write led me to Romans where I received both.

The Bible's contents consist of God's words being written through human beings. First Timothy says every word of the Bible is God-breathed and useful. Do you understand that the same breath which gave Adam's dusty corpse life has touched every part of Scripture? This is why a seemingly insignificant verse one day can be life-changing the next. The Word of God is alive and extremely powerful.

This entire letter experience has rekindled a real passion for the written word. Working a pen to its full potential is a gift. I wonder: Paul was very intelligent, and I am sure he was a very capable writer before meeting Jesus, but would his letters have made the same world-shaking impact had they not been inspired? The same question can be asked about all biblical authors, from the unknown author who wrote Job to the famous lyricist King David. Without God working the writing utensil, would their writings hold the same strength? I say "no."

For lack of a better word, there is a kind of magic in the Bible. How else can the same words provoke the precise response needed by the reader? One of the greatest proofs that the Holy Spirit is alive and active can be found in a Christian's life through the communication between himself and the living Word. Ask any Christian, and he will tell you that a single verse can bring him to tears one day and at another time give courage. One day a verse covered him in peace and another day triggered strong conviction. In one season, it gave him wound-healing words and in another season left him speechless. You will never hear a Christian man say, "I wish I had done the opposite of what the Bible says."

An added beauty of this wide supernatural net Scripture throws is seen when the feeling provoked matches that which is desperately needed at the moment. Yet, until that moment, the reader was unaware that feeling was precisely what was needed. A confused Christian does not read the Bible and come away with more questions. A lamenting Christian does not open up the Bible and come away feeling more depressed.

On the days I foolishly think I know what's best for me, I find myself wishing the Bible read more like a manual. I want the solution to my problem to be found in Subsection 8 of Paragraph B. That would never work. Each person is uniquely made, and therefore must have his own unique manual. The only possible solution is to have one manual that transforms to meet the individual reader in whatever scenario he is experiencing, while simultaneously having the ability to communicate with that individual. *Thank You, Lord, for giving us such a tool.*

Your adoring dad,

V

■ ■ ■

17 November 2013
#89
Philippians 4:11-13
0605

Dear VI,

I enjoy going back and revisiting my previous letters to you. I find myself thanking God for His commanding me to write them.

Today resembles yesterday: you, me, pen, paper, coffee, Bible. As I write, you are sandwiched between two epic battles—one being your left hand and the other a wicked case of the hiccups. I have confidence you will emerge victorious in both. You are an amazing child, more so than I could have imagined. Knowing that you are here while I am sitting eyeball deep in the government's healthcare system does not sit well. I continue to earnestly pray that God provides us with a lifestyle that allows me to see your smiley face more.

In addition to serious prayer, I spend most of my commute meditating on the direction best suited for the Bradshaws. I am certain our current situation must change, but beyond that everything is fogged. I know there is value in having a plan before making a big decision and even more value when the decision directly impacts others. However, I have a tendency to dissect the small stuff so thoroughly that the Holy Spirit is unable to play a lead role. I recently heard this called "paralysis by analysis." In an effort to let go of the details, I have been putting extra energy into going with the flow and being content. Last Friday night afforded a great opportunity for exactly that.

Our cupboards were fairly bare, and dinner did not look promising but, instead of fretting, your parents stayed content and got creative. With great patience, I was able to surgically remove the remaining meat off a rotisserie chicken while your mom steamed whatever remaining rice we could find. We then took our feast to the front porch and dined by candlelight. For dessert we split a beer, then I lit a pipe, and we spent hours chatting about whatever came to mind.

Because we chose contentment, our night was spent laughing under the stars in the knowledge that their Maker loves us dearly. It was a memory I would not trade for a freezer full of thick steaks. I could have easily spent the night hunched over a piece of paper, devising strategies that might better spread the food budget. It scares me to think how close I was to doing just that and how (if I had) our romantic evening would never have happened.

No doubt, there is wisdom in planning. There is value in knowing how best to put food on the table. But again let me remind you, things rarely work out as planned. Even budgets are best written with some wiggle room. A man must also find peace in the truth that he is trying his best and always allow the Holy Spirit to play a major part. "Let go and let God," as they say.

It seems you defeated both the hiccups and your hand, but the effort was exhausting because you are now fast asleep.

Sleep peacefully, my love,

V

■ ■ ■

18 November 2013
#90
Psalm 68:4
0553

Dear VI,

I owe a lot to music. It has accompanied me during many of my favorite memories and consoled me in seasons of struggle. Growing up, music was as important as going to the bathroom. My dad could not make so much as a bowl of cereal without "cranking a few tunes." I remember Jeff Beck being played at volumes that made your ears wince almost every time my dad cooked. I loved to sit at the kitchen table, smelling the food and slowly turning the pages of the CD jacket. I knew the holidays were official when my mom dusted off her baking paraphernalia and popped in the Amy Grant or Handel's *Messiah* tape. I would play drums on the counter, and she would harmonize to the choruses. I would steal cookies that were cooling, and she would chase me with a towel. How I cherish those moments!

One interest led to another, and before I knew it, I was graduating with a music degree. You already know I have taken a break from most musical activities, but I do have a couple of tunes in the works. Just yesterday I set you up on a blanket in the grass and showed you a little folk song I have been fiddling with.

Your mother and I both love the great hymns, but her passion is more instilled than mine. She grew up in a Baptist church, listening to our faith's most famous verses sung by an excellent choir. She is always humming one hymn or another—much of the time without knowing it. With your mom in the house, it is virtually impossible for you to grow up not knowing the lyrics to some of Christianity's finest art. This makes me very happy!

Our Lord created art for our pleasure. We are encouraged to enjoy, participate in, and create art of our own as a way to express our love for our Creator. It is a medium by which people can portray their thoughts and emotions when language falls short. It is special. I do not care if it is painting, sculpting, or dancing, I pray you grow up to appreciate the arts as much as I do.

*You* are a masterpiece,

V

■ ■ ■

19 November 2013
#91
1 Corinthians 9:24-27
0605

Dear VI,

It is my fault I do not have much time today. I answered "yes" to a question that has plagued man's quiet time for centuries: "Should I hit the snooze button?" I do not know why I continue to believe six more minutes is going to make any sort of a difference.

I read 1 Corinthians 9:24-27 this morning. These verses address the race of life—a mandatory marathon in which every man participates. Paul talks about his desire to win and the training he must do diligently in order to compete. "I discipline my body like an athlete, training it to do what it should."

This is an analogy I can relate to. Your dad has spent much of his life punishing his body with the goal of being the last man standing. I am no stranger to this idea of training to win. Just yesterday I spent a chunk of time squatting for an upcoming all-base powerlifting contest, then made it through the first and second rounds of a racquetball tournament.

This may sound boastful, but remember, I did not have the diligence to get out of bed and do what is most important. I am now late for work, so I will finish this letter on my lunch break.

1210: I am now sitting at the base park, inhaling some lunch and finishing what I started. You were here yesterday! My mom (Grandma O'Connor) is in town, and everyone came to eat lunch in celebration of your twelfth week of life. We got a classic photo of you sitting on my hand and laughing.

Let's talk more about a top tier athlete. Paul chose a great type of person to imitate. A true athlete is a master at breaking things down to its most basic parts. Diet, form, breathing, equipment, stretching, sleeping, strategy—all of these are parts of an athlete's daily routine. Athletes ask themselves the question, "What is the most efficient way for me to maximize my gift?" They go the extra mile to add one more kilo or shave off a fraction of a second.

The best athletes in any sport are well-rounded. However, very few of them are born with all of the tools. Along the way, they discover one area of their game is weaker than another and, if they really want to be the best, they will spend less time doing what comes easily and more time developing their weakness. Athletes must choose to either work on their weak areas or stick with what is comfortable. This decision will either make or break them. It is here that character can no longer remain hidden. When an athlete realizes that weight must be shed or gained or his defensive stance is lacking or his squat needs work or he needs to be studying more, will he change his ways in order to better his chances? Or will he continue doing what comes easily?

If he has no mobility, will he stretch more? If he has a hard time memorizing formations, will he put his nose in the playbook? One man may have a great vertical jump but lack the ability to shoot free throws, and his decision to improve his weakness may be the difference between playing under the lights in Madison Square Garden or waiting for a game at the public playground.

Paul wants to win the race, and in my humble opinion, I believe he did. The man's work ethic was beyond question. He was constantly acknowledging his weak areas and then putting in the overtime to improve. I want to be a Christian like Paul. I want to think of my relationship with Christ in the same way that an athlete thinks of his sport. I skipped a day of training today, and I am sorry, Son. I promise you I will be doing my best to improve this area of my walk.

Your work in progress,

V

∎ ∎ ∎

25 November 2013
#92
James 1:27
0500

Dear VI,

The holidays approach! In a couple of weeks, we will be on a plane ride to your mom's hometown of Silverton, Oregon. I do not look forward to flying across country with a little human on my lap, but overall, I'm feeling the dual sensation of excitement and anticipation. I long to be surrounded by the family I have not seen since leaving for boot camp.

When I introduce a stranger to you, I have noticed that person prefers to talk directly to you as if, at 13 weeks old, you are weathered to the point of receiving compliments. "Oh, what beautiful eyes you have!" However, because you can't talk, their strategy is flawed, and they realize this when wanting the answer to a question.

The most common remedy is to pass all questions to me through you. "So how old are *we* then?" as if I am your mouthpiece. I always fight the urge to answer the question with another question, "We? You want to know both of our ages?" I have grown to accept the phenomenon of people talking to a baby through the parents via the baby. I do not, however, have to like it—especially when the stranger is offering parental advice: "It seems we are a little too hot to be wearing a jacket, don't you think?"

I have also recognized what I like to call "the It factor." Most people cannot put their finger on something about you. One woman, who happened to be a stranger in the mall, had her finger thoughtfully on her lip for a few seconds and then said, "He looks advanced." With the exception of those types of ambiguous statements, most people end their visit by prophesying over your future—the one statement that could actually be said to you is instead directed at me. "He is going to be a (fill in the blank)"—heart breaker, trouble maker, rapscallion, handful, lady killer. But I see no evidence that supports these conjectures. Maybe if you were blowing kisses to girls from your car seat, I could see their point, but so far you have stuck to the basics: eat, poo, laugh, sleep, wake, cry, repeat.

I realize that this trend of peoples' interfering with your future will be carried on throughout your life, as it has mine. Because of this tendency, I want to pass on the advice James gives in chapter one, verse 27 of his self-titled letter: "Do not let the world corrupt you." One day soon, you will understand that life is one long string of choices, most without simple answers. Life is not a paint-by-numbers kit. Around that time, you will also find that those around you will have no problem offering their two cents—even if their own lives are a complete train wreck.

You know how important I consider relationship to be. I am not discouraging you from seeking the opinion of those you trust and love. I pray you have a lengthy list of mentors and close friends, but in order to choose correctly, you must develop the kind of wisdom that only comes with having a relationship with Jesus. Libraries have been filled with books detailing how to go about building this type of relationship. Feel free to read them all, but allow me to spoil the ending: *Spend time with Christ*—the good, quality kind spent with someone you love.

I know this is much easier said than done. I expect I also will be working on this very thing until I meet our King.

Let's keep on trying together,

V

■ ■ ■

26 November 2013
#93
0550
Psalm 86:5

Dear VI,

I am at the stage of sleepiness which is often accompanied by idiocy. I put my boot on the wrong foot—twice. Today, I find out if all the studying paid off. If it did, I will receive a pay raise, a symbol on my uniform, and no longer be called "Boot." While I greatly desire all three of these rewards for my labor, my nerves are shot because my not passing will prove my best is once again not good enough. I did all I could do. Was it enough?

The whole grading system is hopelessly complicated. I understand it like I understand taxes, which is to say I see the direction they are trying to go but cannot fathom a more difficult route. Logic tells me the system is idiotic, and while I do not want to take part in an idiotic system, wisdom says I must if I am to share in the best outcome.

My anxiety is caused by my trying to predict the future, but I should be drawing peace from lessons I have learned in the past. I should be remembering the romantic dinner I wrote to you about just a few days ago. I should reread letters 47 through 49 to remind myself how God worked out everything better than I could have imagined. Why is it we must constantly be reminded of our God's mercy and providence? Today, I will either rejoice in success or take solace in the fact that our God is greater.

Be back with news later,

V

■ ■ ■

27 November 2013
#94
Verse
0610

Dear VI,

Last night your mom and I sat down on the couch and wondered, "Now what?" Our greatest project was completed: you were asleep. All we wanted to do was go to bed but decided to instead seize the moment. So we split a bowl of ice cream, and I read some of your earlier letters aloud. Letter 16 mentioned my building a fire pit with the promise of finishing the story at a later date. Today is that day.

The pit is done. I actually put the finishing touches on it just this last weekend. Building a fire pit in swampy Florida is like running underwater. While it can be done, anyone can see that it is unnatural and should be avoided at all costs. It took sand from the beach, rocks from a railroad track, cinderblocks from everywhere, and the cleaning of a grill I saved from a BBQ found on the side of the road. This last weekend I came across an old brick mailbox. I must have been delirious or recently watched a western because I decided that with a little creativity, this 400-pound pile of bricks would make the perfect brick oven. Yes, the mailbox has successfully cooked chicken but, like the first draft of any invention, several quirks are in need of tweaking.

What started as a desire to roast a Fourth of July hotdog turned into a long, strenuous journey which included lifting, loading, pushing, and hauling. The process left me sweaty and sore, but not unhappy. Based on the experience absorbed during my time in construction, I should have seen this coming. A simple project is never simple.

That being said, I believe that many men start a project for the express purpose of getting themselves into a situation (hopefully a dangerous one) they must then find a solution for. I know I do. Even as it was unfolding, I looked forward to telling my woman I nearly pinned myself beneath a brick mailbox but had the strength to carry it the distance.

I was recently watching two men put a shelf together. I probably should have helped, but instead I stood there with a smirk.

"Darn thing," one said. "We're not quite plumb. Push three inches toward the stud, and that should make her flush."

All the grumbling and archaic slang was just for show. Anyone could see they were enjoying themselves. A memory—one they could call upon when deskbound at their painfully predictable jobs—was forming.

Christians are Christ's project. The difference is that every second He spends taking care of us is for *our* benefit, not His. I went to the trouble of building a fire pit for my pleasure; I did not have the fire's best interest in mind. We, as Christian men, need to understand that we are a never-ending project and then praise our Architect for His unceasing labor. We must acknowledge His helpful nature, then live by His example and become helpers—servants. As long as our hearts beat, we will never be complete, yet He patiently works away. He tweaks and trims, rebuilds after we destroy ourselves, molds and sands and transforms us into a structure He can occupy.

I look forward to hanging out by the fire with you,

V

■ ■ ■

28 November 2013
#95
1 Peter 5:8
0925

Dear VI,

Today is Thanksgiving. Welcome to your first holiday season! I know almost nothing about how a writer gets the creative juices flowing but have gathered that many writers need a "space." Some have a cottage secluded in the woods; others have their same table at a coffee shop. My space has almost exclusively been this worn living room table. Today, I have the special treat of having you lying beside me. Every once in a while, you interrupt my flow with some little bit of news you just remembered. I don't mind a bit! Your tone tells me the information is exciting, but your language is unique to you. I wait for you to finish, then respond as I might to a dear friend. You are my dear friend.

I am still a boot—no advancement for me. I wasn't as bummed as I thought I would be. I think writing on the day of the results really prepared my heart. It is as important to be gracious in defeat as it is to be ferocious in battle.

After finding out the results, I went to lunch. Because of the rain, I sat in my car and read *Robinson Crusoe* until out of nowhere you pulled up right beside me! Your mom felt led to come surprise me, and I could not have felt more blessed. Over a lunch of cheese and crackers, I filled her in on the details of my test.

Nothing makes a man feel better than his woman scratching his neck and telling him how proud she is. "This moment is just a vapor," she said, "one small opportunity for our faith to grow and recognize God has a plan." We went on to appreciate that God's plans always involve success in the end. I believe one reason He does not allow success in everything we try is simply because knowing nothing but worldly victory would make maintaining the attitude of a servant nearly impossible. His idea of success is far different and greater than our own. It involves furthering His kingdom and making disciples. It involves conditioning a man's heart during the good and the bad. It involves transforming our hearts so that we want to give more than we want to receive. How can He achieve this without subjecting us to temporary defeat? How can a man climb a mountain if there is no valley? Often God needs us in those valleys in order for His plans to take shape.

If I were to throw a fit upon finding out I did not make the grade, what kind of a representative would I be? I would be making one of two statements: either I would be proving that I am a poor ambassador to a good king or a good ambassador to a lame king. Both are bad scenarios.

How easy it is to shake your fist at the sky. I know, for I have done it a thousand times. But today on this Thanksgiving, I am thankful for you, my talkative boy. I am thankful for a wife who is proud of her husband's efforts. Most of all, I am thankful to have a Savior whose timing is precise and whose plans surpass my wildest dreams.

I was singing you an original tune called, "Gobble, gobble, gobble, it's t...t... turkey day." It has an obnoxious hook that now sits firmly snagged in my brain. Let's go celebrate a holiday together,

V

■ ■ ■

29 November 2013
#96
Romans 12:9
0943

Dear VI,

Thanksgiving morning was nostalgic for your parents. Both of us grew up with very special Thanksgiving traditions. We have always known that the military brought with it the potential of removing us from those precious traditions. So this Thanksgiving morning was spent swapping childhood stories and enjoying the fact that I am not spending the holidays deployed. I am not on a ship in the middle of the Mediterranean. I get to help mold our own Thanksgiving tradition.

Your first Thanksgiving shaped up to be one of my all-time favorites. We spent the day with friends from church. They are military, as are the other two families we got together with. We ate like kings, watched football, shared desert, and relaxed around a bonfire. After saying goodbye, we waddled out with the elastic on my shorts stretched to maximum capacity and headed to another house where we more or less repeated the process.

In both places, the fine china was out, the pie was homemade, and the decorations were beautiful, but this is not what made Thanksgiving special. I consider all of those frills as a means for setting a mood conducive to building relationships. On your first Thanksgiving, I heard testimonies, laughed at lines from old movies, compared schools, swapped parenting tips, and shared some of the things for which I am thankful. We were people in community, motivating each other in love through good works. When experiencing this sort of community, it becomes obvious that we are designed for those very situations. It is easy to believe relationship is critical to our Creator and recognize our spirits have been constructed with this specific value at its core. When a group of people are encouraging each other, everyone thrives.

One way the Enemy attacks your parents is by attempting to convince us that hanging out with other humans (especially Christians) is not important. We find ourselves thinking "I am just too sleepy" or "If I go looking like this, they will not accept me." The reason I believe these thoughts are the work of Satan is because I have never had a bad experience fellowshipping with another Christian. If relationship is at the core of the spirit, why would a man ever argue with himself about nurturing that which he was designed to do? My energy level or my outfit has never caused a problem. The Enemy has us thinking twice about doing something obviously beneficial.

Life is about relationships. Humans receive spiritual nourishment by simply being in the presence of those who love Jesus, and the Enemy hates that. He draws people together when there is temptation and pushes them apart when there's a potential for growth. Don't fall for that tactic! Life is about relationship.

Let's try and remember Letter 96 when we feel tempted to skip church,

V

■ ■ ■

01 December 2013
#97
Ecclesiastes 11:9
1145

Dear VI,

The first day of December has brought with it perfect outdoor weather. Unfortunately, inside is all runny noses and shivers. One of the babies at our Thanksgiving celebration was sick. I am no doctor, but I assume you picked up the illness by sucking on his every toy, then carried it here (to our home) where it was passed around for all to share.

Every once in a while, I have the chance to sit down and catch part of a football game. Lately, I have noticed an increase in commercials addressing retirement. An attractive silver-haired couple enjoys wine and cheese on a sailboat named *Just Retired*. They have successfully endured the torture of tending to their children, paying off a mortgage, and climbing the corporate ladder. They have made sound investments, and now it is finally their time to enjoy the fruits of a life spent doing things by the book.

Perhaps these commercials are the reason I feel so sick. I wonder about the odds of someone actually making this fantasy a reality. If I cannot plan a day at the beach, how can someone else plan 50 years into the future? I examine military personnel on a daily basis who are days from retirement.

I love asking what they are going to do after 20-plus years of service. I plan to live vicariously through their freedom, but I am always disappointed by their response. Without fail, every one of them regretfully explains why he must find another job—a pregnant teen daughter, a sick spouse, a house with a cracked foundation. I have heard a thousand reasons why their plans of drinking wine on a sailboat were foiled and replaced instead with several more decades of tough labor. My unscientific findings prove a man can plan all he wants but is unable to determine his steps; he is at the mercy of his surroundings.

The antithesis can be found in my buddy, Rob. He recognized me from a surf film I was a part of pre-military, and we have since become good friends. He smokes a lot of pot, works retail part-time, and goes to a lot of concerts. He is also in college with a full scholarship for what he calls "being gifted." Your mom and I are happy he is becoming a part of the family.

His big plan after college is to drive a van across the country and surf the west coast for a month or a year, or until he is satisfied. His girlfriend recently dumped him after asking figuratively, "When are you going to buckle down and start saving for a white boat?" To which he replied figuratively, "Listen, woman, I have not washed my hair in two months."

Living with the expectation that the future will look a certain way is futile, plain and simple. A plan without the Lord's involvement is equally vain as it too will eventually result in your destruction.

So what is the solution for a young man such as yourself? Ecclesiastes 11:9 reads, "Young people, it is wonderful to be young, enjoy every minute of it. Do everything you want to do. Take it all in. But remember you must give an account to God for everything you do. So refuse to worry, and keep your body healthy."

Get together with the Lord and form goals together. Do not poison your body, but have a lot of fun—not only while you strive to hit your targets but whenever the chance comes your way. Spontaneity is not a sin. So today, as I sit here with my nose dripping onto this paper, know that if you have the opportunity to hop in an old van and explore our wonderful nation, you have our full support—that is, as long as you take me with you!

Do not forget wisdom,

V

■ ■ ■

02 December 2013
#98
1 Corinthians 14:15
1000

Dear VI,

You might think I am urging you to pursue adventure because I am washed up. Or you may think I am reliving the glory days through you from behind a desk. Not so! I am an example of the truth behind the saying, "With great privilege comes great responsibility." My great privilege is an amazing wife and son. My great responsibility is providing for them. In this season of life, my providing for you and your mom requires me to spend my days behind a desk. This is a challenging brand of work for me, but I am so grateful for the adventure brought on by my current employment.

The journey I am on during this season of life has many objectives, most of them being lessons I need to know or ways I need to grow. I am learning to lead a growing family in a foreign state. I am learning to manage our finances with wisdom, the smoothest way to keep my family well-fed, how to keep an infant safe, and how to best set you up for a successful future. I am also experiencing how a man feels after spending years in front of a computer. I am finding that I can truly relate to a generation of men who sit at their desks with no hope of one day embarking on the adventures I am urging you to find.

I know for a fact that I will not be behind this desk forever. My enlistment ends in just a couple short years. Each day I sit down in my chair, every time my phone rings, whenever my printer jams, I gain a little more respect for the millions of men who have spent much of their lives overcoming the minutes. I pray those men know it is not too late. I would love for our family to live out a lifestyle that inspires and gives hope to those men who have sacrificed the wind in their face for food on the table.

There must be a way to have both,

V

■ ■ ■

03 December 2013
#99
Ecclesiastes 12
1034

Dear VI,

In Letter 97 we talked about youth, but when does youth end? Is it 18 years old? Is it when you have a car payment or graduate from college or work 40 hours a week? In some cultures, the consensual age for sex is 12. At age 55, Americans are given a senior citizen's discount. Is that when youth ends? Ecclesiastes 12 says, "Remember our Creator in your youth," then goes on to describe a man who has passed beyond it. Legs trembling, no teeth, mostly blind, hearing gone, a fear of falling, no sex drive. This chapter paints a grim picture of a man who has worn out his systems. How does that description make you feel?

It's interesting to look at you now perched on my right thigh, slobbering on this letter and moving everything not bolted down. You and the man described in Ecclesiastes 12 have a lot in common. Your legs cannot support your weight, you have no teeth, and your eyesight is a long way from

20/20. Yet you sit to my right—on the opposite end of the spectrum. You are three months into life, and this man in the words on my left may have three months left. I am reminded of the adage, "Once a man, twice a child."

I am sorry I do not have more answers for you. I do not know when a boy becomes a man or when a man passes into his twilight years. There are decisions and variables that go into a boy's maturation that no one can see or discern. Everyone's journey is unique. What I do know is I am dedicated to giving you all I have, passing on what I have learned, and living as an example—for as long as our Lord lets me. I hope one day through thick glasses I can see Lewis VII smacking you with my cane. I hope I can turn up my hearing aid and hear you pray over a meal I will enjoy through a straw. But I am promised none of that. Each day is a gift, so let's view it as such.

I pray you mature into a mighty man, happy to be alive, actively pursuing your passions, and hopelessly in love with our King,

V

■ ■ ■

04 December 2013
#100
Psalm 139:13-16
0545

Dear VI,

Here I sit in uniform already missing you. Yesterday between coughs, your mom said, "I like being a little sick sometimes because it forces me to get cozy with the family." That is so true. You and I have logged a lot of hours together these last few days. I made you laugh for the first time by giving an old-fashioned hog call: "SOOOOIIEE!" You rode on my shoulders for the first time. It has been awesome spending so much time with you, my little friend. Today I read through Psalm 139:13-16, which talks about our King making all of the delicate inner parts of the human body—how He complexly wove you together in isolation. Any father who looks at his child and sees anything short of a miracle is in need of a swift kick.

In my Bible beside this Psalm I wrote, "Read this with Savannah after finding out she is pregnant! 12-9-2012" (page 988 if you want to look it up). That means next week will be one year since your Architect began His construction. I am so glad I wrote down that memory. This thought brought me to tears (which you can imagine did not help with my sinus situation). I was not always in love with you. I was too busy wondering how I would manage to provide. There were moments when your mom was huge and hormonal, which equaled fun for no one. In the sleep-deprived fog of your first few days of life, I remember thinking thoughts like, "I'm not so sure this was a good idea."

Sometimes the stresses of life can skew a man's perspective. Blessings become burdens; precious gifts become undesirable. When a man finds himself entertaining this sort of view, the best thing he can do is open up the Word and pray for a swift kick of his own. This morning I am finely tuned in to appreciation for the handcrafted masterpiece that is you.

Be good for your mother today,

V

■ ■ ■

05 December 2013
#101
Ecclesiastes 11:5
0558

Dear VI,

It is a sleepy morning at the Bradshaw estate. Some mornings I sit on the edge of bed with one leg still beneath the sheets, one limb in

reality and the other in dreamland, then I count the hours until bed-
time. You slept from 2030-0430 last night. That's a new record! It also
means your mom was finally able to sleep through the night, which
makes me very happy. Her faithful care for you during the darkest
hours of night is inspiring. (It also makes my complaining that much
more pathetic.)

You want to know something? My parents considered aborting me.
Can you believe that? My mom was close but says she heard the Lord say,
"Who are you to decide who should live and who should die?" So here I
am while millions were not so lucky. Two weeks ago a friend with whom I
sometimes surf nonchalantly mentioned his girlfriend had recently had an
abortion. His rationalization was, "We are too young, man. Can you imagine me as a father?" I tried to respond lovingly, keeping in mind that there
is no reversing what had been done. I tried to ask how his girlfriend was
feeling, but instead I started to cry and yelled, "If you are going to sleep
around, man up and deal with the results! What kind of an idiot are you?!"

Obviously, we are a pro-life family and not simply because I was personally saved from the grasp of abortion. Looking at the subject objectively, a man must conclude scientifically that a fetus is alive and to stop its
heart from beating is murder. This conclusion is simple, rigid, undeniable,
existential logic. Religiously, the Bible is clear that conception, regardless
of circumstance, does not happen by mistake. I know this and have discussed the subject with many people but never have I cried during a conversation concerning abortion. It was the notion of making the choice to
destroy you that brought on the tears. The nightmare of not having you in
my life. Now that I am a father and have experienced a child's coming into
the world, the idea of choosing not to let one in is infinitely more painful
to consider.

A week later over lunch, I told this story to my friend, John, and he responded with a staggering fact: In some areas of New York, more children
are aborted than born. That is a flat-out massacre! He said streets are lined
with abortion clinics and enough clientele to meet the demand. This is
proof that our planet does not value human life. It is more concerned with

avoiding the responsibilities that accompany bringing a human into the world. People would rather murder the one thing created in God's image.

I could fill volumes with statistics: the age at which a heart begins to beat or when a human's unique fingerprint is formed. But at the end of the day, after all of the facts have been laid on the table, people are selfish and make their decisions accordingly. The weight of this topic is equal to its importance, but I do not want to spoon feed. I encourage you to do your own research, read the Bible, open the paper, check my claims and form an opinion of your own. But a question I do not recommend diving deeply into is "Why does God allow practices like abortion to take place?" A man can lose his mind trying to figure out the whys of God's plan. Ecclesiastes 11:5 reads, "Just as you cannot understand the path of the wind or the mystery of a tiny baby growing in its mother's womb, so you cannot understand the mystery of God." Sometimes that answer must suffice.

Praise the Lord,

V

■ ■ ■

07 December 2013
#102
Ephesians 5:28
1922

Dear VI,

It is Saturday night, and your mom is out getting a little break. You and I are doing our best to hold down the fort. It is a challenge taking care of you in your current sick state. I have managed to bathe you, feed you, and swaddle you in your favorite Navy blanket. Now I am enjoying a cold Oregon IPA and writing a few words while we watch the SEC Championship.

Saturday nights were not always spent this way. Prior to parenthood, your folks spent most weekend nights out. We made it a point to try a new restaurant, see a movie, or meet up with friends. It was an excellent way to shake things up, which in turn nurtured our relationship. Since you joined the mix, we recognize that marriage nurturing must take on some different forms—like your mom going to a coffee shop alone with a book and my taking a shift sucking snot from your nose.

Last night your mom and I went to a Navy Christmas party, just the two of us. I am not one to boast, but your old man knows how to clean up when he has to, and your mom is hands down the most beautiful woman in any room when she gets dolled up (*and* when she doesn't). It was our first night out in over a year. We both got a strange mixture of emotions when leaving you with a babysitter for the first time. For months, we have been adjusting to you being in our every decision, so it was strange to suddenly say, "See ya, son!" Your mom and I drove in silence for a while, battling with leaving you and awkwardly aware of how out of practice we felt. I broke the silence by breaking wind which transitioned nicely into looking back on how much growing has taken place from pregnancy to the present.

It really is important that all men do this: choose a fixed point in time and look backward. I am not using hindsight to think "I should have;" rather, I am choosing to recognize a season in life and observing how it affected the person I am today. It is like seeing the hand of God.

By the time we reached the party, we were once again firing on all cylinders. People say we are quite the "one-two punch." My size and her beauty tend to turn some heads, but add to that how much we laugh, my old-timey chivalry, and the fact that we had seats reserved for us with the officers (I do not know how that happened), and that all equaled a very special night. A night which included us going to the car half-way through so your mom could pump.

Because of my efforts raising funds for this holiday party, I was called to the front and given the gift of a *Curious George* book. I consider it evidence that everyone knows my love for you. Why else would a gift for me be a book for you? I cannot wait for us to read this together! We picked you up after midnight and, with heavy eyes, headed home. You slept the entire way. What a wonderful night!

Your parents are not total squares,

V

P.S. The highlight of my night came in the comments made about your parents' relationship. I loved to *finally* have the opportunity to show those with whom I work how epic marriage can be and to see that others felt comfortable enough to express appreciation and ask questions.

P.P.S. I have been going back and forth between you and this letter for three hours! You are so sick and fussy. Get well soon, my lad.

■ ■ ■

12 December 2013
#103
Proverbs 30:5-6
0948

Dear VI,

Your beautiful mother and I just made a shake with the remnants of the fridge and are now relaxing before church. The Christmas tunes are playing, the coffee is brewing, and you are fast asleep. Writing to you has renewed my love for the written word, which in turn has rekindled my desire to read. This all started when my obsession with music grew to include lyrics, then eventually sentences containing all of the right words. My mom and sister are both exceptional at this (far better than me), so looking back it makes sense that all the right words situated in just the right way make me feel like I just stepped from a freezing rain into a hot shower. I get the chills and think "Ahhh, that's more like it."

In college my music was what I would call "unjustifiably complicated," and others would more accurately call "problematic." I was infatuated with finding new chord progressions and unique melody lines, while simultaneously being overly critical of folk artists or anyone not using a twelve tone row matrix. This started to change in 2007 when, before graduating, my mentor and composition professor, Doctor Glancey, told me, "You have a lot of admirers and no fans." The weight of that single sentence hit me so hard that I spent the next six years unlearning everything. I turned to old country artists and famous authors. I studied hymns and folk poems.

Why do some words withstand the test of time? God gives some people the gift of saying what everyone else has been thinking but cannot express. Others can throw emotions onto notes in ways that make people sigh in relief and exclaim "Exactly!" I, like most people, do not have this gift. For some, words flow; for most it is a grind. I am exceptionally stubborn, so I do grind more than most. One way I do this is by spending plenty of time in classic books, studying lyrics, and, of course, writing these letters to you. I may not be a natural, but I have read enough to put a dent in some paper from time to time. Enough to fill a book for you (albeit at a much slower pace than a real author)!

A pastor once told me, "The written word is a dying art," and he is right. Once upon a time, business was done by hand-scripted letter. But now, thanks to email, Twitter, and the like, I am lucky to get a birthday postcard.

As usual, all this points to the Bible. Every letter in that book is gold. There is no better Author. Every sentence has purpose in the life of man. This is why you have a verse at the beginning of each letter! I get to write; you get to read. I get to practice communicating what little wisdom I have; you get to know your dad and our King. I pray this letter gives you admiration for the power in a well-written word, especially those written in God's Word.

A real man takes the time to learn how to express himself,

V

■ ■ ■

13 December 2013
#104
James 3:1-12
0600

Dear VI,

We have discussed writing, but when do I speak? Now that is a question! My mom says, "Brevity is the soul of wit," and the same can be said for language in general. Less is more. There are just a few times I have looked back and thought, "I wish I had said something" (when the Holy Spirit prompted me to speak up, but I was too chicken to do it). But the times I have put my foot in my mouth are as numerous as the hairs on my back. What you say and how it is said tells everyone in earshot what is going on between your ears. It gives insight into what you put your stock in and what values you live by. Yes, body language accounts for a big chunk of communication, as do things like eye contact. But today let's specifically discuss the tongue.

At the moment, you have so little control of your tongue you cannot help but drool. I, on the other hand, have much to say about the tongue but am keeping in mind my mom's wisdom concerning brevity; therefore, I find myself tongue-tied. Keeping in mind this is a practical letter to my son, not a college paper, I challenge you to read James 3:1-12. Then think about how you would converse with the following: a hurting female who has opened up to you, your friend who just had his heart broken, or a kid who will not leave you alone. Then conjure up your own scenario, decide how you would act, and let's discuss it. Here is a hint: the more Christ lives in you, the more wisdom, compassion, and confidence will show up in your speech.

You can't speak a lick, and you have me hanging on your every word,

V

P.S. Just because I know about tongue control does not mean I am the master of my tongue. This is a lifelong ambition for all men. The goal is daily effort.

■ ■ ■

16 December 2013
#105
Mathew 6:25
1131

Dear VI,

Heading home to you now, my boy. I am on a plane over Tennessee, having a drink bought for me by a man who now sleeps on my shoulder. I have learned he does auto port inventory and has been married for 25 years to a women from Colombia—a marriage he claims to be his "fifth and best." I have no clue what his name is. All my flights have been delayed or cancelled. I am going to land in Jacksonville sometime after 0100. How I am getting home is still a mystery! I am not about to have you and your mom get up and drive 40 minutes each way in the middle of the night. A taxi is not an option, either, as it is far too expensive and easy. This brand of uncertainty has been the theme of my entire trip. I've had days and times to be places, but the "hows" have been a delightful variable as this is where the adventure hides. I was in California to participate in a bodysurfing competition in San Diego. The food, lodging, and transportation were not planned for the express purpose of forcing myself into situations I would otherwise not experience.

On one occasion, I found myself in San Diego with six hours to kill, so I buried my backpack in the sand and reunited with the Pacific Ocean. (She greeted me with 52° water.) I swam out to a buoy and ran into a huge pod of dolphins. I literally grabbed a dolphin's fin and went for a ride. He stayed on the surface then got spooked and went deep. I held on but the water got cold, and I could not equalize the pressure in my ears, so I had to let go.

That would never have happened if I had rented a car and a hotel room. People miss out on amazing life moments because their chief focus is going from point A to point B. Yes, I am stuck in Chicago; yes, I am tired and hungry; yes, my bed sounds like Heaven, but what else is new? Poor choices did not land me here. I am not being punished in any way. So why not hunker down and see if I cannot make a memory or two? After all, our King can use me here just as much as anywhere.

I have not the foggiest idea how I will get home tonight, but you can bet your blanket it will happen, and maybe I'll even get to share Christ along the way. As much as people enjoy pretending they have control over a situation, their outcome is at the mercy of their surroundings. So why not accept that truth and embrace the adventure?

See you in a few hours,

V

■ ■ ■

18 December 2013
#106
Luke 12:15
1843

Dear VI,

I am home safe and on duty—the antithesis of adventure. I have been sitting at a desk under the hum of lights for the last 12 hours and three minutes. I have two computer screens, a phone, a cell phone, rows and rows of binders filled with tens of thousands of papers, four walkie-talkies, and instructions covering every inch of wall space. If I had two words to describe my surroundings, they would be "overwhelming clutter." It makes my brain shut off.

As you know, I work at a health clinic owned and operated by the United States Navy, a department of the most powerful fighting force the world has ever known. You would think they would have figured out an easier method. My office tells a similar story. The walls are plastered with mandatory forms, all of which must be visible and a minimum of 18 inches away from a water or electrical source. The time I spend unconfusing patients, troubleshooting computer malfunctions, leafing through gigantic binders, and organizing paper is astounding. I estimate 75 percent of my 45-hour work week is dedicated to one of those three areas.

Just like the quantity of things at work interferes with my doing my job for the Navy, worldly possessions can easily distract a man from a quality relationship with Jesus. Stuff gets in the way—no way around it. I am not suggesting we live off the land, naked and isolated (even though this is how God created the first man). Neither am I saying possessions, school, or work are wrong. In life, it is important to account for the "why" in what we own. Do I need 10 jackets? Yes or no? If yes, why? If no, then why are there so many in my closet? What everything hinges on is what a person does next after admitting he does not need something.

One of two things happens:

1) With the knowledge that the person does not need it, and in the end will be better off without it, the individual takes steps toward removing the unnecessary item from his life.
2) He justifies the item through the logical, but ridiculous, notion of "It is better to have it and not need it than need it and not have it."

Once this train of thought begins, the game is lost. The closet is closed, and the jackets rest secure until the next time the owner cannot find a hanger. The more someone chooses Option 2, the more he accumulates. The more he owns, the more his mind becomes overloaded, simultaneously clouding judgment while quashing motivation.

Comparing people's homes with this duty desk is not much of a stretch. What about a friend's room? His dad's garage? It is good and practical to look at your environment and make steps to cut through the fat. The more often this procedure is done, the easier the process is. After all, once the layers of junk are peeled back, the junk beneath comes into focus. It is easier to contemplate why you live alone but own 30 mugs when the 25 dishes that once sat in front of them have been whittled down to your favorite few.

With less stuff, you are left no choice but to make more memories,

V

■ ■ ■

19 December 2013
#107
Galatians 5:25
1109

Dear VI,

You are currently perched on my lap still groggy and warm after a nice nap. Today on day 87 of your life, you weigh a solid 13 pounds 10 ounces.

Your mom just walked into the room and said, "Our son is like a fake baby. He is so cute, it's sick!"

I bet you are wondering how I made it home from the airport. Eventually, the man who slept beside me awakened and, while rubbing his eyes, asked, "Who's picking you up from the airport?"

I explained the situation to him, unaware that the flight attendant serving drinks was also listening to our conversation. She later saw me standing on the sidewalk and offered me a ride. "My husband will take you as far as San Jose Boulevard." she said. Thirty minutes later I was walking along San Jose with my pipe, whistling praises! After a two-hour hike, I slid through our front window and, 10 seconds after that, I slid into bed and wrapped my cold hands around your mom!

When embarking on these types of whimsical adventures, always follow your gut. Listen to your instincts. Heed the direction of that "still, small voice." If you *ever* get that yucky wave of emotion (the one that begins in your stomach and travels through your body and rests at your eyes), stop whatever it is that is causing it and create a "Plan B." I would never have entered that vehicle without assessing the situation and deeming it a secure step.

Use wisdom when creating adventure. My heart cannot hold all the love I have for you,

V

■ ■ ■

20 December 2013
#108
Psalm 77:14
1226

Dear VI,

Today I am writing from the park while trying to absorb as much of this beautiful day as I can. While most of the country is shoveling snow off their driveways, Jacksonville is 75° and clear for as far as the eye can see and for many miles beyond that. I had big plans to get up early and write you a letter. I wanted to surprise your mom with breakfast in bed before I headed to work, but instead I found myself on the pot, sorting out a bad case of the squirts. I have said it once, and I will say it again: when plans actually work out, you should be surprised.

Five years ago today, I put a ring on your mom's finger. A more appropriate symbol of marriage would be a seatbelt and the instructions to keep your hands and feet inside the vehicle at all times. It has not been five years of rainbows and puppy dog tails. The first three years were awful. At one point after agreeing to separate, I was living in my car at the beach in California, while your mom was waiting tables in Oregon. My heart aches when I think of those days.

A real, genuine miracle saved our relationship. Your mother and I are absolutely willing to share every detail with you or anyone who is interested because God was the star in the story. It is not our history; it is our testimony, and testimony is one of the tools God uses to further His kingdom. This is why we are always open to talking about it. But not here, not today—not beneath this sharp blue sky. Instead, let's talk miracles.

A *miracle* is "an occurrence of something surprising *or* unexplainable by the laws of science." Notice I chose to use the word "or." I do this because, for some people, a miracle is nothing more than a pleasant surprise or experience. A clear sunrise when rain was forecasted, watching a chicken break through an egg, or a person with bad eyesight receiving his first pair of glasses. For some, these things constitute miracles and, while I do not necessarily agree, I cannot imagine telling someone that the miracle he or she just witnessed was actually common and predictable.

A miracle to me contradicts the will of earth. A miracle occurs when circumstances give only one possible option, but a second inexplicable one happens. A real miracle tends to make people uncomfortable. To the atheist, it serves as a reminder that he is not in control. I am thinking of the cancer patient who goes to an appointment and discovers the sickness has vanished. Or Lazarus' obeying orders by climbing out of the grave. Now *that* is a miracle!

The fact that your mother and I are the best of lovers and friends fits into this miracle criterion. On paper it was inconceivable, yet the Lord paved a road which took us from worlds apart to one flesh. Man saw no second possibility, yet here we are, five years in and stronger than ever.

You are blessed to grow up in a home witnessing a man and woman who genuinely have a blast together,

V

■ ■ ■

30 December 2013
#109
Colossians 3:16
0730

Dear VI,

I am writing from your grandparents' house in Silverton, Oregon. Same set up (coffee, you, Bible), just thousands of miles west. I've been dying to write, but the last few days have not allowed for much beyond necessity. I had a hunch being in an airplane with a baby wouldn't exactly be relaxing, but now I know from experience—even when the baby is as well-behaved as you were.

As stressful as it was to get here, it was worth watching you enjoy a week of firsts: your first time on a plane, your first visit to another state, seeing the church your mother and I got married in, and meeting your three cousins—two of whom are less than four months older than you!

Yesterday at church, your mom's entire side of the family was in attendance: her parents, her two siblings, their spouses and kids. The church, First Baptist of Silverton, is a very special place for your mom and me. Many of our closest friends and fondest memories have been made there. Your mom grew up in this church, and I began attending shortly after meeting her, then started the First Baptist worship team. The memories make this place special, but the people make it feel like home.

Silverton is a small farming town. Many of the families have inherited the family trade for over a century; generations are born, reared, and buried on the same acreage. It is not uncommon to see three or four generations filling a pew. Their hair gets progressively whiter as you look down the line. It is beautiful to see.

Yesterday as I looked out into the congregation of 300 or so, I recognized most families and thought of an importance they played either in my life or the life of your mom. Think about it: I showed up to this country church with sandy feet and an empty wallet because I thought your mom was a babe (I still do). Yet I can look at each of these people and think of a way they blessed me. I lived with that family, that guy got me a job, she prayed over us, they got us that wedding gift, he used to take me to play basketball. This is how God intended the church to be. In most churches, 20 percent of the people do 80 percent of the work. But thanks to business strategies and seeker-friendly sermons, many churches grow big and wealthy, yet those in attendance never experience true church. How special it is to enter a building and know that, because of the love of Christ, everyone has my back! How sweet to sing with a group of believers and never worry about voice quality!

I write all of this to you because I want this for you. I have been on many teams in a wide variety of sports and hobbies, all of which are special in their own right, but nothing comes close to being a part of the body in a healthy church. The question is, when others look around the room, identifying those who have impacted their lives, what will they say when their eyes fall upon you?

Love others while enjoying the love given to you by others,

V

P.S. If you are a part of a church whose primary concern is anything other than loving the Lord and loving others, that should raise some red flags. I am not suggesting you leave the church, but it would be wise to sit down and prayerfully consider why you are a part of that community.

■ ■ ■

01 January 2014
#110
Luke 11:22-24
1240

Dear VI,

Happy New Year! It's a slow day here at the Freeman estate. The whole family is lounging in the living room and swapping stories, a festive blend of catching up and recounting favorite memories. It is a classic Oregon winter day—foggy and cold outside, cozy and coffee-scented inside. Your grandpa and grandma love nothing more. I have a hard time with these story marathons because I strain to sit still for more than five minutes. But I am extremely thankful. I do not see a lot of this camaraderie in many other families we know.

There will come a time in life when those around you start getting married. Shortly after that, you will experience a season where many of those marriages hit a rough patch or, in some cases, fall apart completely. In the last year, I seemed to find this kind of news—adultery, divorce, abuse, death—waiting around every corner. No cozy days, no swapping stories—just various shades of hurt.

Recently I have listened to more men than I care to admit tell me the stories of their broken relationships, hoping I can help in some way. In every scenario, the problem is a pathetic lack of effort. Videogames play a prominent role in an alarming percentage of the stories, mostly because the man will not stop playing them. "Well, I cut back when she moved out," I heard one guy say. That is not effort! Effort is throwing the television out of the window. When I suggest something to this effect, I am always called *extreme*, but am I? If I asked you, "Would you rather get divorced or throw your X-Box out of the window?" how would you respond?

*Take drastic measures against sin.* Deal with foolishness harshly. Why would anyone, once he realized how destructive something is, continue to cling to it? A man cannot be held responsible for blowing himself up if he was not aware a live grenade was in his pack. But if he pulled the pin, put it in his bag and slung it on his back, whose fault is that?

Spending a day basking in the companionship of a healthy family is becoming increasingly rare, yet I can think of few things more profitable. It is truly a rejuvenating experience that leaves my face sore from laughing. I hope you grow up feeling blessed to be a part of such a healthy family situation. Make sure to pencil in days like this with your own family. Most importantly, when you meet people who did not grow up experiencing such a gift, invite them over.

You are a great baby,

V

∎ ∎ ∎

07 January 2014
#111
Luke 5:15-16
1308

Dear VI,

There are times a man can point to one specific decision in his life and be certain all his subsequent days were affected by that one choice. I just returned from a surf trip with your godfather (my best friend, Lucas Myers). It was our third adventure to the wild Oregon coast. The tradition goes as follows: surf until reaching complete hypothermic exhaustion, lock ourselves in room C4 at a $29-a-night motel, play lots of cards, smoke our pipes, and discuss the pros and cons of any life-changing choices looming in our future. For hydration, we alternate between Rainier beer and gas station coffee; for nourishment, we eat whatever. (This time it was three bags of popcorn and a can of chicken noodle soup.) This is a critical ritual for both of us, a kind of retreat before embarking on the next season. The calm before the storm. Considering that after our last trip I joined the military and he joined the mission field, you can imagine we had much to discuss.

In several upcoming letters, I will outline exactly how life will be changing, but today let's concentrate on the value of seclusion. If unchecked, life will devour every second until a man cannot tell the difference between direction and distraction. It does not have to be a mildewed motel room on the beach. It could be a tent in the backyard or a parking spot on a hill. The pace of life is ever-quickening, making it that much more imperative that a man take deliberate action toward times of solitude. Every man needs an extended period to regroup, clear his head, and be vulnerable. This should be non-negotiable. Schedule it, make it a priority. Otherwise, it will simply never happen, and you will be worse off, guaranteed.

Unplug,

V

P.S. I have written to you before about the importance of daily time spent alone with your Maker. The retreat Lucas and I just returned from shares several similarities but is different. It should be considered supplemental but should never substitute a man's daily quiet time.

■ ■ ■

08 January 2014
#112
Genesis 22
1303

Dear VI,

Today is our last day in Oregon. I think the fresh Silverton air coupled with the additional affection you have received has accelerated your growth. Infancy is over; you are a full-fledged baby boy, rolling over, laughing, putting everything you can find in your mouth. Four and a half months never passed quicker, "faster than wet turd through a tin horn," as they say in the South. Your mom is wiped out. Introducing you to the Pacific Northwest while also trying to maintain some sort of east coast schedule has left her needing a vacation more than ever. A couple of days ago we entered the "see-ya-later" part of our trip. It is an exercise the Bradshaws have unfortunately become all too familiar with. I hate it.

There was once a time when your mother and I lived in an apartment just down the road. Ours was a cozy place in a great location, and both of your parents held steady enough jobs. Family, friends, and church were always close at hand. Life was a predictable blend of comfort and practicality. As we once again say goodbye to those we love, I cannot help but ask myself, "Why did we walk away from this life?"

In reflecting on this, I happened upon Genesis 22, the story of Abraham being told to sacrifice his son. I am sure you are unfamiliar with this story, so forgive me for playing the spoiler. Abraham obeys! Not until I entered fatherhood did I understand how absolute Abraham's obedience was. The thought of killing you makes me physically sick. But that is my answer to why I said farewell to the cozy Oregon life and got on a plane to boot camp: obedience.

Obedience is why the Bradshaws became a military family. I had a million questions regarding the Navy, questions that went either unanswered or were not explained thoroughly enough to satisfy. Abraham went through the same situation in verse 2: God said, "Take your son to the land of Moriah and offer him on one of the mountains of which I will tell you." God could have said, "Walk 500 yards up that third mountain to your right, raise the knife and, right before you do it, I will put another sacrifice in the thickets behind you." In the same way, He could have informed me that I would wind up being an optician in Florida, but He didn't. (Trust me, I asked.)

The Lord likes to use a kind of ambiguity that forces a man to lean on Him and exercise his faith muscle. Much like He did when instructing us to join the Navy, the Holy Spirit recently suggested a bold, new adventure; with great fear, against all human logic, and with many unanswered questions, your mom and I are ready to obey. Tomorrow I will fill you in on the few details I know. But today as you read this letter, ask yourself, "What would God have to ask me to do that I would reply 'No' to?"

I'm excited,

V

∎ ∎ ∎

09 January 2014
#113
John 14:31
1240

Dear VI,

The last leg home finds three raggedy old Bradshaws stuffed in a little puddle jumper. You have done amazingly which contradicts all baby plane stereotypes. Upon seeing you, all passengers give a look that translates to "Great! I always get stuck beside the baby." These looks irritate me until I remember that I think exactly the same way when I see a baby on a plane.

We are selling it all and moving into a fifth wheel! There, I said it! I have wanted to tell you since September when this all started. Driving around base one day, I noticed an RV park and felt an overwhelming need to check it out. I learned that almost everyone there is retired military. They travel from base to base and park to park, enjoying their golden years. These are the special few who made it to a legitimate retirement, but instead of buying a white sailboat, they bought a motor home. American flags and cute little signs that say things like "Home is where you park it" are everywhere. Then I saw an empty space and felt everything "click." I understood that I was looking at the most ideal property for the Bradshaw family. As usual, my first response was to argue through a series of logical excuses:

- I'm just thinking this because I sit in an office all day.
- RVs are a horrible investment.
- These people are retired and well-off.
- Savannah would never go for it.

No matter what reasoning I threw at it, the resolve grew stronger. Butterflies took over the pit of my stomach. I decided to try the idea on your mom who, to my absolute shock, was entirely supportive—a fact which in itself is a miracle from God. There were no questions of space, no safety concerns; she simply said, "I feel peace about it; let's take a deeper look." You would think that our friends (or at least our parents) would point out some red flags, but the general consensus has been "Sounds like a good fit."

Oftentimes while praying over this matter, I was directed to refrain from pulling any triggers until after I spent time with Lucas at the coast. I am impressed with myself for keeping my mouth shut about it for so long. But that is why I have waited until now to share the plan with you, my precious boy. Choosing to embark on an adventure of this magnitude is no small matter, and I have my fair share of nerves. The next steps are going to require heaps of faith and miracles. I know almost nothing about the process but am committed to it nonetheless. Let's see how this thing plays out.

Get ready to rough it smoothly,

V

■ ■ ■

11 January 2014
#114
Philippians 4:19
2328

Dear VI,

It's late; I am wiped. It is nice to be home, but everything looks different now that we will be moving in less than eight weeks. Endless searching has narrowed our options down to two trailers. Both are similar, 39 feet, brand-new, and much nicer than anything your mom and I have ever lived in before. We are leaning toward the one in Ohio, and if it is still available on Monday, I will put down a deposit.

I say "deposit" like I've got actual money to throw down, but we both know that is not true. For this I must rely on a credit card, which I hate! This is reason one of many areas where faith is playing a huge role in and during this transition. On paper this is financially impossible. We are currently in the process of selling *everything*—cars, my drum set, your changing table, television, couch, art. You name it, and it is being listed on Craigslist or going on our front lawn.

Basically we need about $7,000 to appear. Where will that come from? My peace lies in the truth that God would not ask me to do this only to abandon me without the means to accomplish the task. While I see winning the lottery as a viable option, we both know that is rarely how our Lord operates. He chooses to reveal His power to provide by letting things go down to the wire. He does things in ways I would define as "creatively abstract" so that all fingers *must* point toward Him. I promise in an effort to strengthen our faith and dependence on Him, future letters will contain stories of God's amazing provision over this family. Tomorrow, my car goes on the market. Let's see what happens!

I love you, my friend VI,

V

■ ■ ■

12 January 2014
#115
John 15:15
0900

Dear VI,

I consider a nickname to be anything other than that which is printed on a birth certificate. I recently read that a nickname plays an important role in a man's life. Obtaining a nickname is oftentimes considered to be a rite of passage, an evidence of acceptance. On the other hand, parenting books recommend the opposite. They suggest calling you strictly by your birth name in order for you to better understand we are communicating with you. If that is true, it is likely you are never going to realize you are being talked to.

My dad recently said that concocting nicknames is part of the Bradshaws' genetic makeup, and it is true. This family is notorious for our nicknaming ability! I am surprised I know who I am today! This partially stems from my dad and me growing up in the ocean where, for some reason in the culture of watermen, everything is called something else. But there is the bigger issue of Bradshaw family gatherings. Legend has it that because there were always three people named Lewis in the room, someone had the idea of nicknaming my Grandpa, Lewis III, *Brad* which is short for "Bradshaw" but also happens to be the actual name of his brother. Despite this nickname working against the goal of clarification, it managed to stick, making it necessary to introduce secondary and tertiary tiers of nicknames to several people, including my favorite, "Grandpa Doo-Doo." Big Buck, Noo-Noo, Little Lew, Fiver, Bucka-Lew, and Lewie Lankster, are only a few of my names thrown around at the Bradshaw family gatherings. I have dozens of nicknames, and you are on pace for just as many. I've called you "Buddy" since the womb. More recently, "Big Man" has become popular as has "Monkey" and your American Indian name: "Poops on His Back."

But what about our identity in Christ? What do we go by in God's family? I am sure a Google search would reveal more nicknames than a whole army of Bradshaws could create. *A branch of the true vine, a temple of the Holy Spirit, new creature, sheep, lamb, child of God* is a short list of possible nicknames for the believer. The list goes on, and I challenge you to compile your own list. If nicknames equate to acceptance, it is safe to say Christians have been recognized as part of the family of God.

In John 15:15, Jesus uses my favorite nickname: "friend." I was once a slave, but I am now a friend. Because He is Lord and Master, it would not be out of line for me to be called nothing more than "servant," but that is not the sort of relationship God is after. He genuinely loves us! By calling me friend, the persona of God laughing as He lashes His slaves with a whip of fire cannot stand. People cling to this view of Christ because it gives them an excuse to spite God and pursue the cravings of their flesh. But no, I am God's friend, and He is mine. Try and wrap your brain around that blessing!

I love you, "Sweet Lewie,"

V

P.S. Our Lord has assembled His own respectable list of names. Isaiah 9:6 is a good place to find a couple of them.

■ ■ ■

13 January 2014
#116
Philippians 2:8
0540

Dear VI,

I have been spending too much time devising a complicated mission statement explaining why I have decided to move my family out of a comfortable home and into a fifth wheel. "Steps toward maximizing family adventure while eliminating possessions." People regard me highly enough not to openly call me an idiot, but just barely, so I feel like our move needs justification. Lucas called the transition "the perfect opportunity to point to the glory to God." He is spot on. I am weak and therefore am having trouble choosing "simple obedience" as a satisfactory answer. I have the urge to chart graphs and develop a list of worldly reasons why the move is beneficial.

Yesterday at church, your parents went to their knees at the altar and prayed that we would consider obedience to be sufficient justification. I explained to the Lord that the moves I am about to make have potential to set us back for many years if the particulars are gone about the wrong way. In answer, I felt the Lord say, "However you decide to do it, I will use you." Why is this true?

Sometimes our Lord gives His children a direct order. An example is God telling Noah to build the ark, or God's instructions for the building of the ark of the covenant. To disobey such an order is a blatant sin. Other times the Holy Spirit nudges a man in a certain direction and allows him to use wisdom during the decision-making process. Do I take a loan out? What type of truck should I look for? How do I inform my landlord we are breaking the lease? I can look to the sky and plead, "Oh, my God, what do I do with my old yearbooks?" and He could give a direct answer. (On occasion, He does. See Matthew 17:27.) But in my experience, He gives a command then lets the believer exercise wisdom in many of the decisions along the way. Traditionally, it seems the Lord enjoys allowing a Christian man to use his wits along the road of obedience. Why else would God's directions so rarely come with a step-by-step instruction manual? Who knows more about building a shelf—the man who followed the Ikea leaflet, or the man who took saws, rulers, levelers, and nails to a felled tree? If a man is in Christ and if his goals are in sync with that of his Master's, he simply cannot go wrong when doing what he thinks is wisest. What peace that gives the man who has God's will as his highest priority!

Today I put our couch, television, and some art up for sale,

V

■ ■ ■

14 January 2014
#117
Proverbs 20:4
0554

Dear VI,

Your discomfort gives me reason to believe you have some teeth trying to poke through! Every time I turn around, I hear the question, "Has he cut a tooth?" I am not sure why everyone insists on using the archaic language. I, for one, am not a big fan of this phrase. It sounds morbid. Growth always seems to hurt—be it muscle, knowledge, or teeth. However, prior to becoming a victim of male-pattern baldness, I do not remember hair growth causing pain.

Your parents are certainly growing right now. I am being stretched and pulled in such a way that if I do not keep up with the demand, I will tear. The same can be said for your mom. The list of details continues to grow while the details already listed seem to have sprouted subheadings.

Every great accomplishment is invariably accompanied by many lonely hours, sifting through the unpleasant stuff. I am trying to exercise wisdom, shuffling one foot in front of the other, attempting to stay organized, and trying to keep positive. However, while sitting on the kitchen floor surrounded by boxes and trying to decide which spatula to keep, it is hard to imagine the end goal. I cannot conceive that somewhere beyond the horizon, I'll be lounging on my new trailer sofa with a cold drink and *Surfer's Journal*. Soon, but not yet. Here, as we wade through the muck toward the horizon, is where the maturation process occurs. Your mom and dad are committed to utilizing the circumstances in which we find ourselves. We are putting our heads down, wrapping our arms around each other, and pressing on as best we can. We may rip, but we will not tear.

Working hard in the moment for memories in the future,

V

■ ■ ■

15 January 2014
#118
Matthew 6:21
0545

Dear VI,

Yesterday went ages longer than I like. My eyes are literally closing right now. I am still bitter at my obnoxious alarm for jolting me from such a sound sleep. (You are not the alarm I am referring to. Even if you were, I do not have the proper "equipment" to turn you off. Your sweet mom with her food-producing body is the one who faithfully gets up in the sleepy hours. Unlike me, she never complains or delays. Do not forget that!) No, the alarm I am referring to is my stupid phone. Its relentless vibration tells me, "Get up! Pray! Write! You have an appointment with the Lord!" It is great advice, but I do not want great advice. What I want and value in that fog of weakness is five more minutes of sleep.

It does not take an intimate relationship with someone in order to learn something about his or her values. Yesterday I was lifting with a guy who told me he averages three or four hours of sleep a night because he "gets sucked into the realm of video games." Little value on rest, high value on Xbox. I recently met a man who, regardless of his financial situation, spends $40 on a weekly haircut and $10 a day on beer and tobacco. Little value on financial stability, high value on appearance and catching a buzz. Not all values are linked to destructive character traits; some can be innocent quirks. I knew a girl in college who did not own a television so that she could spend more hours reading comics. She placed little value in television, and valued reading comic books.

Our shift into this new lifestyle gives me the opportunity to prove where my values lie. I have written to you many times, stressing the importance of aligning our values with those of the Lord's (things like obedience, effort, and serving others). I have also written to you detailing some of my own values, personal interests, and activities (nature, campfires, the ocean, time together, freedom to find adventures). We have the chance not to just tell you but show you what we consider valuable. All I know for certain is that which I believe. How can I show you what I find valuable if I bring you up in a way I do not value?

During this huge life shift, I am trying my best to consider the end to be more valuable than the beginning and patience more valuable than pride,

V

P.S. Let it be known that the new trailer is not a burden. Your mother and I are ecstatic about this change. It's going to be an amazing adventure!

■ ■ ■

16 January 2014
#119
James 1:6
0531

Dear VI,

Last week I won "Sailor of the Quarter" out of all the clinics in Florida and Georgia. The award goes to the junior sailor who has had the greatest influence on his command, which basically means I am more involved and have impacted my department through attitude, character, and military bearing. Today, I go in front of a board of chiefs in my dress blue uniform where I have to try and answer questions pulled from any number of subjects. While this is an honor and was a goal of mine, I keep thinking, "Why did I try for this?" This always happens. I train, outwork those around me, then when the rubber hits the road, I want to puke and run far away.

Monday in my basketball league, I made a shot and got fouled. Time was running out; a free throw would tie the game. As I walked to the line and dried off my hands, all I could think was, "This is easy, no problem. Why do I put myself in these situations?" Same goes for lifting, performing music, speaking in public, you name it. The possibility of alternative scenarios seeps into my brain, and I feel the acid of doubt eroding my confidence. What if I blow it? What if I put up an air ball? What if I forget my lines? Possible negative outcomes are what make it a risk, and risks are not limited to competitions or time in the spotlight.

Plenty of times during your mom's pregnancy, I wondered, "What where we thinking?" Her unpredictable hormones and constant pain did not exactly remind me of rainbow daisies and puppy noses. Then there were the potential medical complications like her death during labor or your coming out with mental or physical complications.

The fear of not knowing the outcome is what leads to doubt. If I knew the shot would fall, I would be fine. If I knew I was going to rock this board, I would not feel nauseous right now. If I knew you would be my son, I would have been doing a jig during your birth instead of wiping my nose on your mom's hand. But in the doubt, we look to God, which is the very thing He desires! Where is the faith development in knowing the future? What reason would you have for relying on God's perfect plan and pursuing the Savior if you knew what was going to happen? There would be much more, "*I* can do this." And much less, "Lord, I need your strength to do this."

Besides, where is the adventure in knowing how a situation turns out? Isn't it more exciting to watch a movie without knowing how it will end? Whether the topic is shooting hoops or moving homes, our Lord wants us to replace that feeling of doubt with dependence on Him. I made the free throw,

V

■ ■ ■

18 January 2014
#120
Psalm 9:10
2105


Dear VI,


What a week! I just got home from standing watch, which would more accurately be called "sitting and staring." I am home at last, devouring chicken legs and catching up with you and the King. Your mom is over on the couch with a glass of wine and a heating pad. I can see her melting into the fabric with a smile. This is definitely not the night on the town we enjoyed during our pre-child days, but I would trade all that for you every time—no questions asked. Three years ago, your mom and I thought, "We will never be one of those boring couples who sit at home and go to bed at 2100." How that foolish little tune has changed! Twenty minutes ago, I looked at your mom and asked if it was time for night-nights!

Why is this? Change happens after thinking has changed. And experiencing parenthood has dramatically changed my thinking. In general, experience is history's greatest teacher. This is why it is rare (but wise) for people to learn from other's mistakes. They need the experience. I see this at work every day. "Sir, you are a diabetic; you cannot eat that candy bar or wear those contacts." Until he experiences the consequences of high glucose through loss of limb or blindness, nothing will change. Even if I had no legs and corneal scarring, it would make no difference because it is not *his* lost leg or wounds on the surface of *his* eyes. A person needs the realization brought on by experience. Unfortunately, peoples' bad experiences affect them more than the positive ones. People do not learn a lot through experiencing an all-expenses paid vacation or a backrub. But a heart attack gets the obese man to change his diet, a DUI gets an alcoholic to AA, the death of a loved one gets an atheist to church. I am as guilty of this as anyone. No less than 1000 experienced mothers warned me of the exhaustion that comes with parenthood, and every time, I responded, "I'm sure it's not that bad."

There is much good and bad to learn in every experience, but there is also something to be said for learning from others—"Letting others pay your dumb tax," as I recently heard it called. If I had listened to those who had already experienced parenthood, I would likely have better prepared myself for this new season. As much as I am enjoying it, I must admit we are learning a lot of this parenting stuff the hard way. Avoid "the hard way" whenever you can.

I love you,

V

■ ■ ■

19 January 2014
#121
Luke 2
0914

Dear VI,

I got home this morning to find you on the living room floor, eating your blanket. I could not have asked for a better welcome. I've been on the floor wrestling with you, and now we sit in my chair together with paper and pen. Six weeks ago, I could hold you while I wrote, and you would shift your gaze back and forth between me and the pen. Now you are sitting on my lap, trying to grab my pen and whatever else your grubby little hands can reach. Your development is scary—not that I am complaining! The more durable you become, the larger a role I can play.

In Letter 64 I mentioned how completely useless I once felt. Through much of pregnancy and infancy, the father's role consists of the occasional cameo. You were once blind and starving. Through God's beautiful design, you were born with an innate knowledge of your mom's smell, sounds, and skin. You knew who she was instantly. You knew she held your nourishment. You knew she would keep you safe. And she did all that and more while also recovering from the trauma of human extraction.

Meanwhile, the dad is stuck in the middle. This less attractive animal who cannot sit still and occasionally asks questions like, "Want some chips? Hope that helps." Thankfully, we are nearing the end of that season now. Your mother's body has healed nicely, and you are growing relentlessly in every possible way. You are longer, stronger, heavier, and smarter, with a flash of personality here, and a sit up there. In a month, we will begin supplementing nursing with real food! A new chapter, a new way of thinking accompanied by new obstacles and lessons to learn.

I love thinking about Jesus experiencing your current season of life. Like you, there was a time when He was unable to crawl. There is a section in Luke chapter 2 where pre-teen Jesus worried His parents by not telling them where He was. I love that Jesus knows what it is like to be twelve! Unlike the Enemy, our Lord has firsthand experience as a human. He knows what anger feels like; He experienced fear, starvation, exhaustion, joy. He got His first whisker; His voice cracked. Because God became man, we can be confident that He truly does know exactly how we feel.

Let's go outside and play,

V

■ ■ ■

20 January 2014
#122
Luke 8:21
1035

Dear VI,

Thanks to one of the greatest men in American history, Martin Luther King, Jr., I have the day off work. Because of his work, I had a dream that would not have happened if my alarm had been set. You have been dreaming too! So much in fact, your mom slept through the night, which for her is a dream come true. Lots of dreaming going on today.

Now to reality. In early December, your mom said, "Lewis, you need to invite the guy who changed my oil to the Christmas Eve service." She went on to explain his name is Travis, and God had put him on her heart. This describes your mother in a nutshell. She has no interest in sports or games. Her loves are nature, *Reader's Digest*, and everyone she comes into contact with. When I ask about her day, I usually end up listening to someone else's day, be it a friend she talked with on the phone or someone she passed by on her walk. Experience has taught me that your mom has a gift and to take her suggestions seriously, so to Travis we went. I got an oil change and invited him and his family to church. He replied he could not make it but maybe some other time. I was not surprised. I receive this response often after inviting someone to church. I shook his hand, said "Thank you," and figured the relationship would end there. So when Savannah received a call from Travis a couple of days later saying, "I need church; my whole family will be there Sunday," I was shocked.

Sure enough Travis, his fiancé, and their three kids were there! Travis cried most of the service and eventually gave his life to the Lord. After church, we went out to lunch where I was blown away by his family's testimony and his comment, "Today literally changed my life."

Back in Letter 34, I wrote you detailing the ripple effect created by a man's actions and how most often we do not see the impact our actions have on a person's life. This experience with Travis is a rare exception, thanks be to God. Look what came from obeying the nudges of the Holy Spirit. How easy it would have been to simply not get my oil changed! I could easily have avoided a potentially awkward situation. I would be none the wiser. I probably would have forgotten about him altogether. It breaks my heart to think of all the opportunities I have let slip through the cracks by not acting upon the Holy Spirit's direction. I pray this experience serves as a reminder to you and me that the Lord uses our actions to make a difference even when we do not see how. I am interested to see how the new relationship between Travis and myself plays out.

To God be the glory,

V

P.S. If you want to hear the voice of God, listen to your wife!

■ ■ ■

21 January 2014
#123
Isaiah 43:18
1941

Dear VI,

It's amazing the amount of stuff a human accumulates over the course of his life. Seeing all the junk, I feel a little disgusted with myself. The last few weeks have been spent painstakingly looking at an ever-lengthening, increasingly daunting list. It seems like every time we cross something off the list, two more projects appear. I thought we were in the deep stuff then, but now I see we were in the kiddie pool. I have begun to wrestle the garage into submission so that it might serve as a bay to organize what to sell and what to keep. I gave it my all for several hours and feel as if nothing was accomplished. Round 1: Lewis 0, Garage 1.

I would remove the lid to a box, sigh deeply, and then with great will-power, empty items that have moved from my childhood bedroom, to college, to apartments in California and Oregon, to storage, to Virginia, and now to Florida.

An additional pang of difficulty showed up unsuspected: I found it emotionally difficult to deal with the nostalgia that accompanied the stuff. Much of the boxes' contents contained souvenirs from a wonderful and terrible time in my life. The trophies, awards, letters from girls, souvenirs from travels, gifts from my first girlfriend, and albums full of pictures with friends I had forgotten about all reminded me of the best and worst of times. Each item triggered memories I had not visited in a long time, like playing football under the lights in the mud or the talk that ended in heartbreak. The boxes did not hold photos and plaques; they held issues I would not have had to address if I had kept the lid on. I resolved to signifi-cantly downsize by allowing myself one small box which I look forward to showing to you one day; the rest hit the bottom of the dumpster with an unsatisfying thud.

It is a strange sensation to look at posters reading "Lewis is the MVP of my life" sitting beside a big bag of dirty diapers. It makes a man think. How can both items be going to the same place? Will I eventually wind up in the same spot as those diapers? This downsizing is much harder than I thought it would be. But with each empty box, I feel a little freer, and my determination to finish this transition is slowly winning out.

Your diapers stink,

V

■ ■ ■

22 January 2014
#124
Matthew 6
0557

Dear VI,

I have been really bothered about how emotional I got in the garage. For the last two weeks, I have been putting every stick of our furniture we own on Craigslist without a second thought. Someone might buy our couch tonight. This prompted your mom to ask the logical question, "But where will we sit?"

"I don't know," I said, "put blankets on the floor." That is my general feeling about stuff. The cash in hand represents progress and a check off the list, which to me is far more valuable than a couch.

Then today my head cleared as I read Matthew 6 which speaks about storing up treasures in Heaven vs. on earth. Those boxes full of moldy trinkets were my earthly treasures. Like I said, they contained trophies and medals from a time my body did not hurt. They held letters from a girl who, at the time, made me feel like I was 10 feet tall, pictures of summers where all I did was go back and forth between sand and ocean with friends I have not seen in a decade. Verse 21 reads, "Wherever your treasure is, there your heart will be also." I realize now that oftentimes I don't dream about summer days, surfing, and sports, but rather *those* sunny days and *those* sports. A man only has one light, and if it is shining on the past, it casts a gloomy haze on the future. This is a situation where I needed the experience to arrive at the realization. It took me watching the treasure enter the trash before I could say goodbye. I am learning that watching Travis give his life to the Lord is far more valuable than my wrestling trophy and, therefore, should be what I desire.

Service over stuff,

V

■ ■ ■

188 LEWIS SEELEY BRADSHAW V

24 January 2014
#125
Ecclesiastes 3
0601


Dear VI,

There is an adage that goes "When it rains, it pours." Well, boy, it is dump-
ing now. It has been a week of huge events piled on top of the busyness
that accompanies a normal work week. I am at a critical point in my training for a power-lifting contest, I am giving a presentation to our commanding officer, and I am in charge of a clinic-wide blood drive that has
taken *way* more time than it should (like those things always seem to). And
things are selling! In the last couple of days, your mom and I have looked
at each other a dozen times and said, "Are we really doing this?" There
was something about selling the couch that made it all a reality—like we
were on a boat and pushed away from the dock.

Well, yesterday we finally got a grand tour of our new home. It is
amazing! During the tour, I could not help but notice how pathetically
"American" I am. For example, there is not enough room for a crib, so
your bed will be a fold-out couch in a spacious and comfortable loft,
but thoughts like "This is not proper for a baby" kept making their
way through my head. When I was in Africa, I noticed that babies slept
on an old sheet in the dirt without a second thought. I complained the
sink was low before considering it provides better water pressure than
many people's showers. Not to mention the water is filtered and has
the option to be either hot or cold. These are first-world problems, like
anxiety over which iPhone best represents me as a person or complaining that Netflix does not have any good movies. I am not suggesting
that being picky is always bad. But a healthy dose of perspective goes
a very long way.

If selling our couch is like pushing off the dock, signing papers is like
seeing the last sliver of land disappear on the horizon. That is what will
happen today. We will sign with confidence and become the proud owners

of a giant fifth wheel. We will stand tall in the knowledge that the Lord is with us. Then we will go to our new home, get on our knees and praise God for this blessing. He has given us a home and the first task is to give it back to Him. Our home will be His temple; our home will be a place from which to minister. I am so excited to use this blessing as a tool to bless others.

I have no idea how to work it, but we will cross that bridge when we come to it. For now let's rejoice!

V

■ ■ ■

25 January 2014
#126
Psalm 119:105
0953

Dear VI,

I have this thing where I try not to let people know when I am exhausted. This started in college where sleep deprivation is almost a requirement. I got tired of people responding, "I'm tired," after being asked how they were doing. What bothered me was their reason for saying it. Their objective was to gain my sympathy but, with me, they had no such luck. Instead I'd ask "Why?" then roll my eyes at the predictable answers. "I was playing PlayStation." "I was watching *Lost*." "I was trying to drink a gallon of milk in an hour." "I was at the bar." I don't have much patience for people complaining about a very avoidable situation. The answer "I was spooning with the toilet because I have the flu" would get my charity. "We were making blue flames" would not.

Because claiming sleep deprivation in college was an epidemic, I get particularly annoyed with that situation. However, my attitude toward those who play on the sympathy of others in order to help fix their mistakes is not limited to complaining about sleep. That is called *manipulation*. If a human's choices have forced his life into a bottleneck, he must admit his fault and repent.

"My wife kicked me out, and now I don't even have a pillow to rest my head on" is a story given by a man who wants help but will not change.

"I am homeless because I cheated on my wife. Can you please help me?" is the story given by a man who owns his mistake. A statement like this shows a lack of pride and a willingness to change. As Christians, we are obligated to lend a hand in this situation.

I keep all of this in mind as I rehash the event that unfolded yesterday. I was sitting at the bank in my car looking over our down payment check and eating carrots when a grubby teenager knocked on my window and asked for a ride. It seemed he and his pregnant girlfriend were living on the streets. They were on their way to meet a friend at Olive Garden and would miss the appointment if they traveled on foot. I sat for a second, imagining your mom on a long walk while pregnant with you, and then agreed to give them a lift.

On the way there, the conversation consisted of several rounds of one complaint followed by a question. "Last night some guy got us a motel room, but the bed sucked. Can I use your phone? Yeah, she is pregnant; it was a mistake because the stupid birth control should have lasted longer. Can I smoke in here?" As we drove along, we passed the RV dealership where I saw our new home being waxed—sparkling in the sun like a beacon of hope.

I realized in that moment, if not for the words of the Bible, my life would look a lot different—quite possibly very similar to the lives of the people sitting in my back seat. Girls, drugs, theft, attitude, work, my parents...all of those areas of my life have had seasons of extreme instability. I have been one word away from making a seriously life-altering choice. Curiosity or desire has had me a hair from destruction on innumerable occasions. This is precisely why every one of my letters to you contains Scripture. The Lord's Word is your sword in battle; it is the answer to getting away from those dangerous traps. It is our

Owner's Manual. Write its words on your heart, and you will have mornings where you will wake up and praise God you didn't go through with some regrettable choice.

After hearing about someone buying this couple McDonalds, which they were not in the mood for, and me wasting my time lecturing the young man on taking some responsibility instead of being a wimpy victim, I pulled into the restaurant where, instead of offering his thanks, this grungy 15-year-old looked at me and said, "You look really tired, homie." Thanks.

I love you,

V

■ ■ ■

26 January 2014
#127
James 4:17
0941

Dear VI,

As I am sure you have noticed (and probably have pointed out innumerable times), I am not immune to bad decisions. I just reread my last letter again, and the entire time, I could hear the future you asking, "What, Dad? You think you are perfect?" Yes, that is disrespectful, but it is exactly what I would ask my dad. The joke is on you, however, because I already admit I am majorly flawed. Nice try!

A couple of poor choices can change your life forever. And often the change comes as a consequence for going through with something that ought not to have been done. But keep in mind that the same can go for the opposite. It is equally as foolish not to do what you know you ought to do. Some of these examples are obvious: not doing your homework, not paying that parking ticket, not fixing the leaking roof. When a decision is made not to do something of this sort, a clear-cut fallout can be linked with the decision: a poor grade, late fees, or a flooded living room. However, in other situations choosing to disobey by avoiding a task may not lead to any tangible consequence, especially when it comes to the gentle prodding of the Holy Spirit. It is hard for a man to think, "If only I had done such and such..." because he does not know that doing such and such would have really made a difference in the grand scheme of his current situation.

How would my life be worse off if I had never talked to Travis? What would result from your not opening the door for that lady? What might happen if you choose to walk by the kid who spilled his milk instead of helping him clean it up? Probably nothing.

But James 4:17 reads, "If anyone, then, knows the good they ought to do and doesn't do it, it is sin for them." People like to say that hindsight is 20/20, meaning that an individual has the ability to look at his personal past and find the point where it all went wrong. They think if they had just made one little tweak, all subsequent events would have unraveled differently. This is not so.

It is best to think of life as a painting where the broad brush strokes and minute details are of equal importance. The world likes to think of life as a journey where some parts of the road are more critical than others. Some regions are flat and soft underfoot while other parts are steep and slick. But with Christ, each choice is part of a bigger picture; the moss and jagged cliffs are equal. Just because the decision maker may never be personally affected by not praying for that friend in need, that does not mean there is no repercussion. In fact, the only thing a Christian knows for sure is that whenever the Holy Spirit is involved, there is greater purpose behind the action— even if it is invisible to us.

Think of it this way: you are standing at the edge of a pond, holding your favorite stone. The water surface looks like liquid glass. The reflection shows the surrounding trees upside down. As you look out and admire its perfection, a still, pleasant voice says, "Throw your stone into the lake." What do you do? If you decide against it, you can continue to admire this perfect picture and keep your favorite stone. Things are fine as they are. But the voice nudges again, and you decide to obey. So you throw the rock, and it skips one, two, three, four, five...all the way across until finally resting in the shallows on the opposite bank. As it dances along, perfect circles begin to rise from the surface. The concentric rings grow steadily bigger and begin to mingle with each other until the entire pond is moving perfectly to a rhythm you cannot hear but feel thumping somewhere deep. Instantly, you know you made the right choice. The still lake was dull compared to the show before you, and you decide your favorite rock was a small price for the experience. Eventually, the performance is done and you walk away changed, the lake having displayed a side of creation you never thought possible. The experience will seep into everything you do from that point on. And to think, you could have put that rock in your pocket, headed for home, and lived the rest of your days ignorant to what could have been.

Throw the rock,

V

■ ■ ■

27 January 2014
#128
Psalm 138:3
0554

Dear VI,

While organizing pictures yesterday, I stumbled upon a few of you at two weeks old. The change is unbelievable! Besides your being three times your birth weight and eight inches longer, your face has taken on some of the features that will last your entire life. You have one dimple when you smile; your eyes are almond-shaped just like your mom's. I imagine you at age 20, giving me a grin and my catching a glimpse of that same dimple hiding behind your whiskers. Your daddy is hopelessly in love with you.

Last night your mom made me go to the movie version of one of my favorite books. The true story of four Navy Seals whose mission goes very wrong. I walked out of the theater with a deeper understanding of how lame my job as an optician really is—a feat I previously thought was impossible. I am not alone in my thinking. Ninety-nine percent of sailors hold a grudge against their recruiters. Recruiting offices are dens of deception full of dive gear, guns, quotes from John Paul Jones, and life-size cutouts of men in camouflage singlehandedly ready to take on American enemies, both foreign and domestic. The *real* Navy is full of sweeping, carbon copies, urine samples, and computer malfunctions. At least *my* Navy is.

Today I got out of bed, cursing my recruiter for putting me in such a position until Psalm 138:8 told me to stop being a victim. "The Lord will work out His plans for my life." This verse is commonly misinterpreted as a blank check, then used as proof that God does not exist when a man's dreams do not come true. The bounced check is waved in the air while the man screams, "I wanted to be a singer, and You didn't do it!" In reality, God's plans for me are different than my own; He is in the business of working out *His* plans, which are promised to be drastically different and far better than anything a man's feeble brain can conjure up.

The point of refinement is to transform a man's plans into God's plans. From thinking, *I want to be an artist* into, *Lord, if it's Your will, I would love to glorify You through a career in the arts.* This is where I am at: in a season of aligning my plans with those of Christ so that I can function as I was designed to, instead of how I think I should.

Unlike your facial features which are taking shape without any assistance from you, my dreams taking on the shape of God's plan requires serious work on my part. I can choose to kick and scream, which will affect the degree to which I am refined—but never to my advantage. Or I can chose the wisest option and let go of thoughts like

*My job is terrible, and I hate my recruiter,* lay my plans at the Lord's feet, then utilize the circumstances in which I find myself and the people around me.

This is how a man achieves contentment,

V

■ ■ ■

29 January 2014
#129
Romans 15:13
0545

Dear VI,

Yesterday evening we had the opportunity to hang out, and I discovered I can officially throw you! This feat to me is on par with your graduating from college. I could not be more proud. You're strong and durable. What's more, you laughed and screamed in excitement. We had a blast playing together. It was a sneak preview of coming attractions. The excitement in our home is not limited to our guy time. Yesterday I sold our television, my drum set, some weights, and a fish tank. It is game time under this roof, and things are moving quick. Your mom captured the general feeling of exhaustion and eagerness perfectly last night when, while eating a spoonful of peanut butter, she made up a song with the lyrics, "Insert calories in body."

God's faithfulness has been so humbling. From the first time I drove through the RV park until today, His presence is obvious. We have seen people saved, big checks randomly appear in the mail, items I considered trash sold at amazing prices, and the price of our new home drop to an amount we can afford. All of this is God saying, "You're going to trust in Me? Well, check out what I can do!"

I do not understand it. I cannot comprehend it. But neither can I deny or assign credit elsewhere. I am seeing tangible miracles take place under our roof. What a blessing it is to be a part of His plan!

Got to keep grinding,

V

■ ■ ■

31 January 2014
#130
Psalm 55:22, Galatians 6:2
0550

Dear VI,

In the book *The Call of the Wild,* there is a chapter where a team of sled dogs are forging through wild Alaska. The year is 1903, and the team of dogs are in totally uncharted forest. The book details the transformation of a spoiled St. Bernard who is stolen and sold to be part of a dogsled team of explorers in search of gold. These dogs go 100 percent every single day for months on end. It is not their masters' whips that drive them but the love of their purpose. Even in the most hopeless circumstances, they do not stop. Even when their feet are worn to the bone, they keep moving.

At one point the lead dog, who has stomach cancer, has become so weak that his loving masters try to remove him from the lead into a position requiring less strain. The dog does not allow it! He keeps barking and pulling and trying to prove that he can handle his role. He refuses to die in any position other than the lead. The masters respect this dog's faithfulness and allow his efforts to go on for hours. The dog is coughing up blood, fainting, has no strength left, but his head continues to face forward, his every muscle straining. He knows his role and will not let it be taken away until he collapses and breathes his last.

The book exposes how soft men have become; at least that's what I took away from it. The St. Bernard goes from sleeping by the fire in a rich man's chair to fighting bears. His fat is exchanged for tight muscle formed out of necessity rather than for vanity. His coat is glossy and perfect—thanks to his new diet of fish and wild foods. The story makes me think a thousand things. Like Native Americans chasing down buffalo in their bare feet and men I know who complain about their love handles but cannot do one pushup.

But I digress. This idea of going hard in the reins until you just can't (and I mean literally cannot, as in you are dead) is a beautiful analogy of our walk with Christ. Being a warrior at all times, watching our tongue, looking out for those in need, and turning to the Spirit. The difference is we are not pulling our Master along. We are free from whip and harness. In fact, our Master commands that we "cast our burdens upon Him." And Paul says, "Share each other's burdens, and in this way we obey the law of Christ." What a beautiful picture! We are not one dog pulling our Master's burdens; rather, we are a team, a network, serving side by side, working hard for our Master out of gratitude for His taking our burdens in exchange for a real purpose. Collapsing in our graves dirty and broken, ready for our glorified body at last. Man should think of his life as a picture, but one in no need of preservation. He is to be used like the beast he is, whether on the battlefield or in the classroom, in the pulpit or in the coal mines.

The Bible goes on to encourage us by incentivizing with "At just the right time, we will reap a harvest of blessing if we do not give up." (Make sure to note the words *at just the right time* and *if* when reading the verse.) With all you do, go hard and make sure God is your Master. When you live this way, you cannot go wrong.

I'm going to go answer phones as best I can,

V

■ ■ ■

01 February 2014
#131
Proverbs 7:2
0800

Dear VI,

Last night with no furniture and no television, your mom and I partied hard, which is to say we ate veggies and breakfast sausage on the floor, listened to Sufjan Stevens, and read the first of these letters aloud to each other. I was reminded of how sure we were that you would grow up in this house. I reminisced on the exhaustion that comes with a fresh human. I laughed at the memories that, if not for these letters, would be lost forever. I was blessed while remembering my wife's dedication and unwavering commitment to being your mom and the queen of our little kingdom. It pains me to think of the events that never made it to paper, but I am so thankful we at least have some in the history books. These letters have taught me the importance of recording family memories.

My nose is back in the advancement book. What a bitter grindstone it is! A lot of what I am studying is like listening to a song I have heard and once knew, but can't quite put my finger on who wrote it. The fact that it sounds familiar is a good sign. At least I am not totally up a creek! For a Christian man, the Bible should never take the form of a pleasant, but distant, melody like my corpsman manual is currently. During the process of moving, I have gone through things that date back further than my first series of letters to you. I have 12 years' worth of journals and letters. I found it fascinating to read some of the things I put down years ago. In 2008, when your mom and I were first married, I wrote the following excerpt:

> The list of things that demands a percentage of my paycheck goes past the paper, off the table, and out the door. Toward the end of the month, I find myself developing plans to sell it all, buy some old RV, and take off with the wife. Alas (yes, I did use the word *alas*), money, children, insurance, it is all a trap made to keep a man in the rat race.

It never works. The system is broken. I swore it would never get me, but it has!

There is a whole series of these long chains of important thoughts that made it to print. They bring back memories that have always been in my brain but had no key with which to access them. What a wonderful reference! What a helpful tool!

In order to avoid ever needing a key to unlock Scripture, it is so important to be in God's Word daily. Never let the words of Christ get lost in the depths; we need quick access to them at all times. We need to have them handy so that when the pressure is on, you can find and use them smartly. A corpsman can pack and unpack his medical bag in the dark. He can find anything at any time. He spends countless hours packing and inventorying so that when he is in battle and his Marine is wounded, he has the highest probability of saving that man's life. He is prepared. The thought, "What did I do with that gauze?" never runs through his mind. This is how a man needs to be with his King's commands.

Keep your sword sharp,

V

■ ■ ■

1 February 2014
#132
Ephesians 6
1430

Dear VI,

So how does one keep his sword sharp? Go to a bookstore, and you will find hundreds of ways how in books like *Formulas for a Spiritual Walk* or *Closer to Christ Quickly*. The next aisle over, you can find books with the same title. The only difference is the spiritual words are replaced with whatever subject suits your fancy, like *Formulas for a Healthy Diet* or *Say Goodbye to Debt Quickly.*

The fact is, keeping a sharp sword is a lot like exercise; there are a million ways to go about it, but every way must have a few common denominators. For example, Google how to do 100 pushups, and you will find endless routes to achieve the same goal. Some say give maximum effort daily while others say never max out, but all of them suggest stretching and increased protein intake. You see? One man may read each morning while another may read at night while hanging upside down. Very different approaches but both are studying the Word, and that's what counts. First Corinthians 3:11 reads, "No one can lay another foundation than the one we already have— Jesus Christ." As long as He is the foundation on which we stand during this sharpening process, the details can be left to your own discretion.

Wisdom and creativity are highly encouraged,

V

■ ■ ■

02 February 2014
#133
Ephesians 5:4
1003

Dear VI,

Welcome to the first Sunday of February, better known as Super Bowl Sunday (Seahawks vs. Broncos). After church, we are going over to Travis' house for the big game. This is the man whom we invited to church a while back and have since become close friends with. Travis is an ex-Navy damage controlman, one of the roughest rates a sailor can have. He was also a Chief, which means he was tough enough to be the respected leader of a hard group of rough men. Being his friend is a humbling experience. I am a lowly hospitalman who leafs through medical records in between sips of coffee. I have no idea what a ship is like. I know his rate considers mine the softest of the soft, but recently he shot me this text: "I've been leading men since age 17, but now I am being led to true manhood by you." My jaw sat on the top of my foot when I read that message.

I am not sure what Travis likes more—his chief's anchors or the Seattle Seahawks. His loyalty is mild compared to many Seattle fans who are notorious for being completely obnoxious and very, very loud. Their stadium holds the world record for decibels. Last week Travis' fiancé and I were discussing his team being in the Super Bowl, when she said, "You should come watch it, so he doesn't cuss." As you can guess, this comment caught me totally off guard. Why would my presence make a man, especially this man, feel as if he ought to be on his best behavior? Does my religion convict him? Is he afraid of offending me? Is cussing a sin? Remember, I work in the Navy. Profanity is part of the culture. "Cursing like a sailor" is a big point of pride.

In trying to figure out all of this, I read 1 Corinthians 10:23-33. In these verses Paul talks about the same idea but relates it to food. He explains we are allowed to do anything but not everything is beneficial. Back then food was a huge point of contention. Do you eat pork? What was this animal used for prior to occupying your plate? Paul says, "You may eat any meat sold in the marketplace; however, if someone else is eating with you and is offended by your meat choice, do not eat it." The pleasure produced by the meal is not worth it. What is seemingly harmless to some people (things like eating pig or dropping a four-letter word) could turn another person completely off to the gospel. C. S. Lewis hit it dead center when saying, "The human without scruples should always give in to the human with scruples."

This is why I do not cuss. I do not want to misrepresent God. I want to avoid any habits which, over the years, will burrow deep into my character like profanity has in Travis. He is why the Bible repeatedly warns about controlling the tongue. I know he does not want his children to swear. He knows he is being hypocritical. And I know the more time he spends at church, the more desire and motivation he will have to get past it. My role is not to make him feel bad but rather to stay connected, leave room for grace, and encourage him to keep pursuing Christ. I do not want a man to act any way other than himself

202 LEWIS SEELEY BRADSHAW V

when around me. I want him to transform into the man God has designed him to be, and hopefully I can stand beside him and be useful in the process.

Will I ever need to wash your mouth out with soap?

V

■ ■ ■

03 February 2014
#134
2 Corinthians 2:16
0550

Dear VI,

Breaking a habit is never easy. Any man who is serious enough to adjust a 30-year cycle should always be praised and respected. Christ has been called "the great stumbling block." He brings to light self-destructive practices and forces people to choose between them and Him. He makes a man ask "Do I continue what I have known all my life, or acknowledge what I know is wicked and start over again?" What will it be, the Creator of the universe or a routine? You would think the decision is a no-brainer when, in fact, it is one of the most difficult choices a man must make. People cling to what they know for dear life even if it is destroying them, purely because it is tangible, reliable, and does not require faith. Many people choose to live a meaningless life, knowing full well that the choice means spending eternity apart from God. It takes courage to admit to a messy existence because shame and consequence may follow. The mask is off; who knows what might come next.

To put it mildly, the world calls men who need help "weak" and, unfortunately, it is not uncommon for spouses to do the same. Many women are turned off by the notion of a man's admitting he does not have his act together. My lifestyle has gotten me into serious debt, I drink too much, I hate my body. Too often the female's response will be some variation of "Well, don't whine to me about it! Be a man!" Men are supposed to be pillars of strength and seeking help for body image issues does not fit that criterion. But it should! Consider the apostle Paul. Prior to Christ, he was a man famous for his piety and persecution of Christians, and then he encountered God and ran toward Him, establishing Christianity throughout the known world and writing most of the New Testament.

When a man meets Christ, many of his old ways begin to be seen through a new lens—a sharper lens that puts a proper focus on stumbling blocks and exposes them for what they are. Here he either waves "so long" to the old life and runs the other way or continues to stumble along. Choosing to run toward Christ is choosing to run toward full potential as a man, a husband, a father, and a leader. But beware, this is no easy transition (read Letter 21 on refinement by fire), and it certainly does not come overnight. Choosing relationship with God is embarking on an adventure that does not end until eternity. When considering all of this, the idea can appear daunting, but keep two things in mind: 1) God does not demand perfection, only effort, and 2) He will never forsake those who desire Him. Run into your Father's arms.

It is easy to judge a wayward man, but don't do it! You are no better; I am no better,

V

■ ■ ■

04 February 2014
#135
Psalm 127:3-5
0550

Dear VI,

I need to take an intermission from these heavy life lessons and celebrate the amazing person you are. It is good for a man to put aside the shovel and reflect on the soil. Monday, after putting either a giant "keep" or "sell" sticker on every item in our house, we all went to the beach and hit it good! It has been so busy around our home that, until Monday, a beach session seemed impossible. No doubt God has us in mind when sticking a warm, windless day into the dead of winter. Your mom and I played lots of Frisbee while you watched from the sidelines. I surfed, and you and I identified shells together. The time together was so refreshing. It took all I had to keep from daydreaming about a time where you will be walking and talking and playing Frisbee with us.

That night, as most nights before you hit the pillow, I gave you a bath. It is kind of our man-time tradition. Sometimes you kick water, and I yell, "Show that water who's boss!" which you find hilarious. And other times you just stare up at me while I tell you about my day or sing you a song. I always carry you naked to the bath on my shoulder and put your bottom by your mom's face, asking if she ordered the "Moons Over My Hammy." It's important to both your parents that your body receives excellent care, and while she does this all day while I am at work, it means a lot that I bathe you, making sure your skin is clean, your areas are rash-free and your hair is washed.

You are a young warrior; of this fact I have no doubt. You can be exhausted with a blowout diaper and sand in your mouth and eyes and never say a negative thing. You are highly, almost strangely, alert and aware of your surroundings. I often think your only worry is missing something.

You also laugh at everything, which makes everyone in earshot laugh as well. You are such a great example. Thanks, son!

I admire you,

V

■ ■ ■

05 February 2014
#136
1 Peter 5:7-8
1923

Dear VI,

I just finished our nightly wash tradition. Now your mom is feeding you before we call it quits for the evening. You sat up for close to seven seconds this evening. It was awesome! My days are still full. In an effort to make our hospital more financially viable, the Navy is increasing enrollment, with means more patients but no more staff. Anyone who looks at our workload can see everything is redlined, but the referrals keep coming. Extended hours and diminishing morale is inevitable. Also, we were ordered to park a mile away. Joke's on them though, the RV park with its view of the river is closer than the staff parking lot. I am going to buy a beach cruiser with a big basket.

That is a taste of some of the stuff I am dealing with at work right now. Nothing catastrophic, just a bunch of minor things teetering on top of each other. Sometimes when the phone is ringing, my computer is frozen, people are walking into my office unannounced with questions, CNN is blaring, and the lights are flickering, my eyes begin to water, and I want to rip the phone out of the wall and use it to smash whatever keeps making that beeping noise. Of course, I don't. I remind myself that this is not all there is. It is my temporary mission.

Outside of work, I have a long list of blessings, including an amazing family, church, sports, the sun, and a steady income. Sure, my desk is made for a third grader. Sure, I am on a very cutting weight for an upcoming lifting contest. And yes, our house looks like a tornado went through it, and there is a rotting animal very well hidden in our garage.

Life is stressful; I am having trouble fighting off anxiety. If you think I sit with you on my lap all day and write, think again! These letters come shortly before or after being swept away into a stressful whirlwind. During the commute home, I am routinely finding myself in the midst of some sort of laugh-cry episode while wondering, "What just happened, and how can I manage to do it again?"

I realize, based on the bubbly tones of many of my letters, that you might think I do not feel the pressure. You might wonder if your dad ever gets that tightness in his chest or lies awake, staring at the ceiling. I do. Casting anxiety upon the Lord does not mean that there is nothing to be anxious about. Because I have complete faith in our Great Savior, there is a thick rope of peace wrapped around my trash bag full of dread, but that does not mean I live a stress-free life. I will continue to battle. I will go on doing my best on this journey of a lifetime, and I will go through seasons of great strain along the way, which is absolutely okay. God is greater. He will see I get through safely.

If He thinks I have what it takes, then I do. Simple as that,

V

P.S. Some of my daily stress has been brought on by my own folly (the lifting contest, for example). I decided to participate in that before consulting your mom or the Lord. This spontaneous decision now involves others who would be crushed if I backed out. I decided that since I have committed, I will therefore see it through to the end. But the next time I have the opportunity to add additional activities to my plate, I will go about it differently!

■ ■ ■

06 February 2014
#137
1 Timothy 1:1-17
0549

Dear VI,

I just stirred agave into my coffee with the end of this pen and then wiped the pen on my uniform. Sure, that's not the most orthodox way of doing things, but who can tell me that I didn't just save myself a trip to the kitchen? One of my favorite aspects about Jesus is how unorthodox His life appeared to be. In that day, the Jews were waiting for a Messiah in the form of a majestic king, who, with a horse and sword, would kick butt, take names, and dismantle the Roman government. He was going to defeat their enemies and whip this world into shape. Then Jesus came along and loved the very people He was supposed to defeat. He was whipped by His enemies. He exchanged His horse for a donkey and His sword for a cross. No one understood that the cross was a much more effective weapon than the sword.

Our church is unorthodox in a lot of areas as well. One way can be observed in the wide variety of people groups. Many are part of a recovery group started by our pastor over 20 years ago. We have a "Bikers for Christ" small group, a BBQ club, and a lot of members who look as if they had a lot of long, hard nights but have since stepped up and said "Yes" to doing life God's way. It is inspiring.

When we drop you off at the nursery, you are greeted, kissed, and hugged by a Hispanic woman, whose body shows all the signs of a long life of working to survive—missing teeth, gnarled hands, leathery skin. If her back was straight and her knees 100 percent, she would stand about 5', 4" tall but, as it is, she might hit 5' on a good day. She has two assistants: one a middle-aged woman with Down's syndrome and the other an older gal with one leg. They all have matching church shirts and handle dozens of babies over the course of two services every Sunday so that tired parents, like your mom and I, can have a break and worship.

Son, I want you to recognize that these women are true warriors! To think of the effort it takes to get all ready for church on one leg in order to arrive early and deal with a bunch of snot-nosed infants gives me chills of respect. One of the Enemy's favorite tricks is to disguise physical characteristics by dressing them up like spiritual characteristics. If they have special needs or love handles or sing off-key or have a dandruff-plagued scalp beneath a poor comb over, then they must not be as "saved" as you. But our Father sees an eight-foot-tall soldier with an angel on each side, muscles in all of the right places, and wits fine-tuned for battle. We may hear a flat voice, but our Father hears a perfect pitch. A man needs to look past the flesh and be able to decipher what kind of a person lies within. What's going on in the heart? That's where God looks.

The Jews were lucky the Messiah did not come as they wanted. They would have been in the same boat as the most perverse—we all would. No one is righteous, not one. God, in His right-brained wisdom built His church on you and me and the least of these, the chief of all sinners, and the man who denied knowing Him. The fortune cookie point is "Don't judge a book by its cover." But more importantly, you, a handsome young man with a good family and lots of opportunity had better check yourself when thinking your situation makes you better than someone else. That is not the Holy Spirit giving you those thoughts.

Using wisdom to discern is good, judgment is not our job, and God does not love you more than anyone else,

V

■ ■ ■

07 February 2014
#138
Matthew 11:30, 1 Samuel 16:7, Jeremiah 17:10
1800

Dear VI,

I just weighed in at 232 pounds, and I now sit at home with you talking away beside me in some language I have never before heard. I can only speculate, but from the looks of things, your toy elephant has done something to earn a chewed nose and an earful.

Let me give you a word to consider: *hypocrite*. I have heard equivalent terms such as "poser," "weekend warrior," "fraud" and "wannabe." The definition of these words is roughly the same across the board: "a person who tries to deceive others into believing they are something they are not." It is the age-old result of envy binding itself to discontent. This is the guy wearing a crooked hat with enormous biceps and pencil legs. He spends three hours a day at the gym; two and a half of those hours are spent flexing in the mirror. A sailor at work owns a different $500 watch for every day of the week, drives a BMW, and is famous for blowing cash at a strip club, but his apartment is bare. He works nights folding clothes and is in terrible debt. To hear my basketball team talk, you could assume every one of them almost had a division-one basketball scholarship, but their talent tells a different story. Some have never heard of a zone defense.

One-upmanship is the poser's favorite game. If one man went 100 miles per hour in his car, the man beside him went 150. Back and forth it goes until the game ends after someone's one up is so outrageous that everyone's bluff is exposed. "Oh, yeah?! I went 400 miles per hour in my friend's Porsche!" Usually a "friend" no one has ever heard of is involved and it is he who has the variable needed to win. If you broke your hand, someone's friend got his leg cut off while practicing a sword trick.

If you think this one-upmanship stops at church, you're crazy. It may be worse at church because the posing usually pertains to how godly a person is. People lie about their godly living, people try to one-up another's spiritual life. The guy with his hands raised up looks to be singing with fervent passion but, in reality, his hangover is reacting to the noise. Ask Tom how his marriage is going and he will go on about God's abundant blessing when, in reality, he hates his wife.

It would be easy to call this one-upmanship an epidemic, but these kinds of things have been happening since the first pages of time. As long as men try to aspire to be someone they are not, instead of standing tall in who God designed them to be, the posing will continue.

One-upmanship can be physical as well as verbal. I am an E3 in the Navy, a seaman. That is close to rock bottom in terms of rank. I have never been deployed, never seen a ship, and my uniform has three ribbons, two of which everyone gets simply for joining. Many of the people with whom I work are several years younger but have been in the military much longer. They are what you might call "saltier" than myself. Their ribbons are a mask and their medals act as a kind of winning hand to any one-up challenge. They walk around steeped in authority and demand people to shine their boots or dust their desk, while making sure to weave profanity into every sentence for good measure. Understand, I am not complaining nor would I ever disrespect the uniform. I joined the military knowing I would be entering into this sort of culture, and honestly, most of the time, it's strangely humorous. Some petty officer gets real close and tells me to get a haircut when I am as bald as a button. What can I do but smile?

Seeing this type of man outside of work is unsettling—like seeing the person naked. I remember seeing one chief getting into his car with McDonald's and a 12-pack of beer one Sunday afternoon, and my heart just broke for him. He had recently accused me of being "a burnt-out old man sucking on Uncle Sam's tit." But as he drove away, I noticed his bumper sticker: "May the force be with y'all!"

The expensive watches, the sports car, the ribbons, the outrageous hair, the Twitter followers, the one-upmanship, the trophy wife, the big arms, the foul mouth, the money, the fame—every bit of it is a mask so other people do not catch a glimpse of the real situation. They are lost. Without Christ, we are all lost actors in a play. The nice car gives people a reason to argue, "I'm not lost! Look at my car; I'm successful." They may even trick themselves into believing it, but at the end of the day, that car does not answer the deep spiritual cry born into every human.

There is this belief that God will strip a sinner to the bone, beat him, and then throw him in a cold, dark room before walking away for eternity. But the exact opposite is true. Jesus is standing by, waiting to clothe people in a new superior identity. His arms are open wide as He eagerly waits for souls to embrace Him. He is all-powerful *and* all-loving. When people remove their masks and say, "Here I am, Jesus. I am tired, weak and pathetic. I cannot one-up another person. I am sick of acting," there is a celebration in Heaven, and God instantly steps in.

Have a good day, buddy,

V

■ ■ ■

09 February 2014
#139
Matthew 7:12
1718

Dear VI,

We always make an effort to recover on the Sabbath. Today, we enjoyed hotdogs in our sunny backyard and laid on a blanket for as long as you would let us.

Something has been bothering me. Oftentimes a bully points fingers and tears others down in order to distract people's focus away from him. I realized after completing yesterday's letter that the way I presented my examples could be read as my poking fun at others. And if that was the case, I might be thought of as that bully. My intention was to present obvious examples, and today I intend to ask the question: why? I do this because my heart breaks for the modern man. I aim to help, not to tease.

So why do men stand in line at the bicep machine? Why does a man desire to one-up the man beside him? What is going on? A little investigation shows that a deep hurt is usually involved; a single moment has sown havoc into the person's life. Perhaps he removed his mask to a particular woman or a group of friends, and his true self was made the object of ridicule. Or he expressed a passion for dancing only to be called a homosexual by his father. Maybe he let down his guard to someone he thought really loved him but received no encouragement at all or, in order to find someone who would love him, he had to act, talk, and dress a certain way.

Far too often, a wound has carved the mask, so our first response should be one of empathy coupled with godly discernment. Cautious compassion should be our first response. Your mom, by the way, is an excellent example of this. She is the queen of compassion, and I pray you inherit this trait. For instance, one time we were driving somewhere on a date and, while stopped at a crosswalk, an old man began slowly shuffling across the street. I just sat there, sighing out of inconvenience and selfishly wondering, "Why me?" but your mom said, "Bless his heart. He's wearing suspenders." She got out of the car and helped him cross the road. Her amazing example of selfless serving opened my eyes wide enough to see the wisdom I now write to you.

Sadly, your mom is no stranger to disappointment. This is where discernment becomes critical. Sometimes the person behind the mask is wicked, a wolf in sheep's clothing. If allowed to, he will feed on kindness, and extort time, energy, and finances until the resources run dry, at which time he disappears. This is survival of the fittest via deception.

Discernment (which is different than judgment) will not filter all the liars from those whose wounds call for your compassion, but it will help protect your heart from that particular sting that comes when you realize you've been duped. I remember hearing a pastor say, "Anyone who lives a life ministering to others is very familiar with the feeling of a knife in his back." Pain will always accompany compassion to a degree. Putting yourself in the shoes of another and feeling his pain is what causes sympathy. Our Lord Jesus was spit on by some of the very people He healed! And while anyone can see He was not deceived, He was hurt by those he ministered to. No matter how many times you have been hurt for helping, when you look upon a man who is living out life as an actor, your first step should be to remind yourself of the presence of a potential wound. And if your heart belongs to Jesus, you will have no choice but to feel sympathy toward one of God's children.

Do you know the Golden Rule?

V

■ ■ ■

11 February 2014
#140
Mark 10:45
0542

Dear VI,

There is a saying, "If it looks like a duck and quacks like a duck, then it is a duck." I have heard this line used to strengthen a case meant to justify a stereotype. "Well, he talks with a lisp and likes the color pink." Or "Well, he is African-American and seven feet tall." (This is an area I really need to work on. Every time I see that a slow driver is Asian, I look at your mom and say, "See, I told you.")

What if the tall man hates sports? To figure this out, let's look at a different "bird" adage: "Sticking feathers up your butt does not make you a chicken." Many men have stereotypes assigned to them by others and spend their lives trying to stuff their face into a mask crafted by those around him. The mask simply does not fit. I see this in the military constantly. "Yeah, my dad was a captain, so here I am." Or "All the men in our family become sailors." I never hear these comments made with excitement or pride; instead they sound hollow—like lines fed to them by someone else and backed up with a threat. They sound like a marionette on a string.

One man hates himself and is desperately trying to buck creation; the other man is submitting to that which he hates by bending to the pressure of those around him. Both men are lost. Both men are walking through their one chance at life, doing what they would rather not. Some are so lost and have been for so long that they do not even remember who they are or what they actually like.

Jesus said, "I, the Son of Man, came here not to be served but to serve others and to give my life as a ransom for many." Notice how He knows Who He is and what He is born to do. He did not say, "I *think* I came to help in some way. At least that's what My Dad says I have to do. I kind of want to try painting for a while." Son, I do not know what age you will be when you read this letter, and I do not know how many times you will read it over, but I challenge you to know your name and be confident in it. Identify what you like, how you can serve, and know the role God has given you. Your mom and I are here to support however we can. There is no need for a mask in your life.

You are Lewis Bradshaw the VI!

V

■ ■ ■

13 February 2014
#141
Acts 5:29
0552

Dear VI,

In all of this writing about men looking for image elsewhere, I suppose it is time to tell you about myself. I found my true identity during my sophomore year at Camp Cedar Crest. This is the same evening I mentioned in Letter 08. Even though I grew up in the church, it was not until the second to last night in the California mountains that the significance of the Cross clicked. My life was changed forever. The only thing I could think to do was fall to my knees and weep tears of regret, of joy, and of thankfulness. I had discovered who I was.

I will never forget leaving that room to rejoin my youth group. Everyone stared at me for a while, then my sister said, "You look a lot older for some reason." I remember the feeling of confidence flowing from me. I remember coming home, and friends whom I had known for years literally did not recognize me. I remember not caring if I locked eyes with a girl, or what I wore, or if what I said might be considered abrasive. My only concern was acting in such a way that I did not make God appear foolish.

I wish I could say that life has been all perfect since then. I would love to report that I have never wavered, but that is not true. I had a long season of body issues; when my girlfriend broke up with me I lost my hair and spent years trying on all sorts of masks. I picked up smoking. I changed the way I dressed at least a dozen times. It would take another book to list all of the masks I wore. When I was in Christ, I was confident. I heard people say things like, "It's fun going to a restaurant with you because people think you own it," or "When you talk to me, I get nervous." When I was not, I felt vulnerable and tried to set people up to give me compliments: "So what do you think of this shirt?"

I have ebbed and flowed, gone up and down through hills and valleys, and I have learned the following lesson: nothing is more powerful than a Christian man who has found his identity in Jesus. He has a brand of confidence that makes heads turn but never consider the possibility of pride. He will leave a mark of God's character without drawing attention to his own. He has a kind of swagger that forces people to think, "That man has something I need," rather than, "That man is full of himself." It seems to me that the modern-day Christian man is considered godly when his actions are meek and mild, and I admit there is some truth to that. An obvious proof of an indwelling of the Spirit is shown through extreme tenderness in personal dealings and in dealings with others. This does not mean submit to a nagging wife with hands folded and head down! (We touched on this when discussing John the Baptist. See Letter 27). After all, how could a man share an identity with the King of the universe and not be the best kind of secure?

The only true identity is "Child of God,"

V

P.S. Look at my life! Once this identity is found does not mean it cannot be lost. It is found and then discovered over a lifetime.

■ ■ ■

14 February 2014
#142
Hebrews 1:3
0542

Dear VI,

My mom once said, "Your stuff is only as valuable as what you can get for it at a garage sale." With our garage sale less than 24 hours away and the very chair I am sitting in labeled with a five dollar sticker, I can see her point. Our home is chaotic! Your mom has been doing an amazing job of getting things ready, but it's difficult when we are selling things we still need. Plates, for example, or the microwave. Add the fact that we both have a cold, and you are looking at a tough place to find relaxation. Last night I was heading out to my car, which has yet to sell, with my before-bed tea. How good it felt to go from our claustrophobic home outside to see the vastness of space! So instead of going to my car, I called to your mom, and together we stood looking at the Heavens, pretending to know constellations. It felt good to feel small.

Martin Luther said, "Nothing is so small, but God is still smaller; nothing so large, but God is still larger." The universe is beyond comprehension. There is nothing bigger a man can look at. But God also has a patent on the proton, the neutron, and the atom. It is impossible to imagine what that process must have looked like. A human cannot wrap his head around the fact that our God holds the entire universe in His hands. But even when these concepts are put on the table, I still find another truth even harder to comprehend: the Lord of all creation became small. He showed up on earth as a baby, grew into a man, and saved us all. He flipped the script so that He might live in us, and we might live in Heaven.

To work I go! So glad it is Friday,

V

P.S. Jars of Clay paints a beautiful picture of this idea with the lyric, "You turned on the lights and stumbled inside, with me."

■ ■ ■

16 February 2014
#143
Ephesians 3:20
0955

Dear VI,

You and I just went for a walk around the block on a beautiful Sunday morning. I am trying to apply the lesson I relearned when looking up at the stars. That lesson being, "If you have the opportunity to go outside, do it!" On our walk we saw two red-tailed hawks in a tree, looking for squirrels. As an optician, I have a newfound admiration for sharp eyes, especially when they are attached to a bird. What we can see at three feet, a hawk can see at twenty feet. If you had hawk eyes, you could move twenty paces from this letter and still read it just fine. I will never forget when our class took a close look at the intricate anatomy of the eye. My brain nearly overheated when I realized that I was using the very things I was learning about. My eyes were taking in all the eyeball information and transferring it to my brain in real time. Unbelievable!

Remember Travis and his family? He came over Friday afternoon to help post signs for the garage sale, and while we were spray-painting cardboard, he dropped a bomb. "I'm getting baptized next weekend. Ashley and I are meeting with a pastor, then getting married. Will you be my best man?" Then he just kind of smirked and shook his spray can. Obviously, I accepted! Slapping him on the back, I said "Dude, it would be an honor!" Your mom overheard the whole exchange from the garage, and in the interest of not wanting to interrupt a special guy moment, she offered me a wink-smirk combo.

At 0430 that next morning, I awoke to what sounded like a bomb, but was, in fact, a tropical storm pouring on our house at the worst possible time—just three hours before I would be driving around putting up signs under a clear starry night. Because I was gagging at the smell of my knee braces and realized no one would ever buy my car if the stench didn't leave, I had left my car windows open. Boom! "Are you kidding me?!" I yelled as I ran to my car in my underwear and closed the windows. I sat wet and lamenting on my bed when Travis called and dropped a third bomb. "Listen, I have been doing some praying and decided to just buy everything, put it in my garage, and sell it at my neighborhood garage sale this spring." Boom! After some argument, he told me to "shut up and stop stealing his joy." At that point I accepted and, after talking with your mom, we both went back to bed in peace. My last thought was how wonderful it would be not to set an alarm.

But at 0645 an alarm did go off in the form of our doorbell. I shot up and opened the door to find a dozen eager garage-salers, chomping at the bit for first dibs at our stuff. Boom! The sun was out, the garage was opened, and I spent the next 45 minutes literally throwing our possessions on the front lawn where people shamelessly whittled down the price. If an item was a dollar, the buyer offered ten cents; if I countered with 75 cents, the buyer would offer 11 cents. During each one of these haggling episodes, I was reminded, "Mom was right! My stuff is only worth what it will sell for during this garage sale." While taking a desk to a woman's car, I told her how surprised I was at the turnout. She looked at me like I was an idiot and replied, "If you post it, we will come."

As our junk became other people's junk, I decided to call Travis and tell him the deal was off and that most of our stuff was sold, but before I could, he was in my now-trodden yard, shoving 200 bucks into my hand. He told me to shut up and let him look over all *his* new stuff. I pleaded, explaining that 80 percent of it had been sold. "I'd be lucky to get 40 dollars for this," I said.

"It's worth it to know that we are doing everything we can to help you with this huge transition," he replied. Boom!

As I sit in a lawn chair in our living room writing down this account for you, I want you to remember that this all stemmed from my following the guidance given to your mom by the Holy Spirit. All I did was ask Travis to church. Do you see how God can work? Eight weeks ago Travis was a stranger; now I am to be his best man. I have told you that oftentimes we do not see what effect our efforts have. We only know there is one. I have invited many people to church, so why is this time so special? I don't know, but I am sure not complaining. The thing to take away here is that Jesus has already given us a gift—eternal life. But

His love for us is so abundant that He pours additional blessing upon His kids, blessings we could never dream of wanting, just for doing as He says, "Love Him and love others." Looking back on how yesterday unfolded I can hear God saying, "Lewis, because you are selling your stuff like I told you to, I am going to give you much more money than it is worth. That money will come from the man you invited to my church like I asked." BOOM!

I am not worthy or responsible for any of this,

V

P.S. What if the reason all this happened is so that I could write to you about it?

P.P.S. BOOM!!!

■ ■ ■

17 February 2014
#144
1 Peter 5:6, Philippians 2:3-22, Proverbs 16:18
0730

Dear VI,

I am sitting on our front lawn today using a beach chair and a TV tray as a kind of poor man's desk. It is a beautiful day, and I cannot help but wonder how many days like this I have missed sitting in front of my computer, straining my eyes against its harsh light and praying for a power outage or an electrical fire.

As you know, last weekend I finally participated in the highly anticipated tri-base power lifting contest. The posing I detailed in Letter 138 was in full display. This was not my first rodeo, so I was not surprised by the skintight shirts, grunting, and strutting. The exaggerating was pal-pable, and as I walked in with a cooler, two chairs, and a backpack full of braces and clean shirts, the mumbling began. "Look at how old those chairs are. What is he thinking—eating beforehand?" That tune changed when everyone discovered that these contests are usually eight hours long, and for some reason, the venue never provides seating. At the risk of toot-ing my own horn, I must add that your dad put a pretty solid whooping on everyone—except one man who is the reason for this letter. He also had a lawn chair, and I knew instantly he was the real deal. While every-one was one-upping, he was stretching; when they were grunting, he rode the stationary bike; and when I deadlifted 575 pounds, he came next and deadlifted 710. The most impressive part was that this man, who stood 5' 9" and weighed 270 pounds, said nothing but encouraging remarks to every lifter he talked to.

This is the way of a confident man; this is the way of a man who knows his gifts. The best musician quietly practices his scales and warms up his fingers. The basketball star shoots a lot of free throws. The scholar is not always raising his hand. Those who are truly exceptional do not need to wear a sign that reads "Look at me!" During the contest, hundreds of people were wandering around or putting their latest lifts on Facebook, but not when "The Hulk" was lifting. Every eye was fixed on him.

Whoever created the Jesus seen in children's Sunday school—the "felt-board Jesus," as I call Him—was way off. It is very likely Jesus did not have blue eyes and sandy-blond hair. He was not a shining 6' 3" Adonis. In His day, men from the Middle East were fairly short; food and sanita-tion were scarce, which means quality nutrition and personal hygiene were a luxury. Beards were also a key part of that culture, the longer the bet-ter. More than likely, his was long, dark, and scraggly. He rode a donkey, slept beneath His Heaven, and ate whatever was available. He did not yell, "Hey, everyone, look at me over here! I am the Messiah!" But whenever He spoke, people listened, so many, in fact, a world-changing revolution began and continues to this very day—the likes of which has never hap-pened before or since. You see? Be yourself, and strive to be great at what-ever it is God has called you to be. By living this way, people will have no choice but to take an interest. When your abilities have drawn people toward you, remember it is not you people are looking at, but the Holy Spirit within you. Use the opportunity to bless others.

You are my greatest blessing, son,

V

■ ■ ■

19 February 2014
#145
Psalm 92:1
0556

Dear VI,

For the last two Valentine's Days, your mom and I have gone to Chick-fil-A. The first year you joined us from within the womb, but this year you sat beside me. We call it a tradition, but I am not sure if two years merits the word *tradition*; "back-to-back" seems more accurate. I had never heard of the place until we came to the East Coast and have since learned that every time I say, "Thank you," the employees are required to respond "My pleasure." I am never more polite than when I am in that restaurant.
"Here is your water."
"Thank you."
"My pleasure."
I make sure to thank the employees for directing me toward the catsup, then ask if I can have some of the catsup, knowing full well I can have all I want and making sure to attach the appropriate appreciation: "Thank you."
"My pleasure."
It is as if we are characters in a manners book from 200 years ago.

In reality, I do make it a point to say "thank you" to people—especially the guy at the gas station or the drugstore where it is easy to imagine they are unhappy with how they spend their days. Growing up, if I found a penny on the ground, my mom would say, "What do you say to the street?" The words have been tattooed on my brain!

But *saying* thanks is different from *giving* thanks. Too often I thank God for my food like I say hello to a stranger on the street. It has become a programmed response. So programmed, in fact, it takes hearing "My pleasure" to make me aware that I said "Thank you." This is what happens when the same word is applied to the entire spectrum. I could say "thanks" to express gratitude toward the man who saved my life or the lady who refreshed my coffee. After a while, a word can become so trampled upon that no one even notices when it is right under foot. This should never be the case.

Psalm 92:1 reads, "It is good to give thanks to the LORD." This is different than thanking Him for the grub. It means taking a real moment to acknowledge that much of the planet doesn't ever get the chance to eat a delicious meal. Entire countries are starving, yet He has provided the resources for us to eat nutritious food daily. We are so blessed to have a Valentine's Day "tradition." (That is more along the line of actually giving thanks. Still pretty weak, but I am working on it.) If a man approaches life this way, he will soon find little to complain about.

*Lord, thank You for the job I am headed off to. You have answered my prayers by giving me employment that provides a debt-free lifestyle, medical benefits, and, most of all, the opportunity to be an example to many people.*

Thank you,

V

∎ ∎ ∎

21 February 2014
#146
1 Kings 3:13
1709

Dear VI,

I have been busy! I try to separate "hectic day" from "letter" but because this week is the absolute apex of our transition, I have got to keep you in the loop. As you know, we have sold almost everything—prematurely in some cases. We have no furniture, microwave, washer or dryer, but we are certainly making the best of it. I bought a 19-inch television at a pawn shop, set it up on a desk I made from scrap plywood, and for the last few nights, your mom and I have stayed up way too late watching the Olympics together. I love the Olympics!

As of today my car is gone at last and has been replaced by a 2008 Ford F350, King Ranch, crew cab, long bed, twin turbo, V8, diesel. Two months ago, I had no idea what any of that meant. I have spent end-less hours versing myself in the language of heavy-duty trucks. Being a Southern California beach kid, I was completely ignorant about all things payload, but learn I did and blessed we are. It is, hands down, the nicest vehicle we have ever owned. The fact that we have it is yet another confir-mation that we are doing God's will. "Here, take this truck. It has 1,000 times more comforts than you need—at a suspiciously low price."

The dealership is 90 minutes away, and I have been there three times this week. Last night, just us guys rode home from the dealership togeth-er. You slept most of the ride, which is totally understandable. The com-bination of a long day at a dealership and the low hum of a diesel engine made for prime sleeping conditions. We listened to music and cruised.

This weekend we move what remains into a storage unit. Next week I get the hitch installed on the truck. And finally, on Thursday, we move into our new kingdom. I know nothing about setting up a trailer. One wrong move and I could shower in urine water! But whether easy or difficult, we will learn, adapt, and overcome. We are dropping ourselves into a world of adventure. So as you sit here on my lap, relentlessly trying to grab my pen, get ready! Our lives are about to look very different.

May marriage, manhood, and most of all, Jesus Christ be shown by the lives we live,

V

■ ■ ■

22 February 2014
#147
Matthew 6:8
1849

Dear VI,

Once upon a time, I could write a letter with you sleeping along the length of my arm. Now, as I sit at my usual spot after a long day of packing and organizing, you are on the ground rolling all over the place, laughing, making noises, and looking over every few seconds to make sure I am here. Your larger-than-life personality leads strangers to categorize you as either "heartbreaker" or "handful." I don't like when people predict your future. That is for you and the Lord to decide.

You now know enough to acknowledge what you like and do not like. Wet rag in mouth is good; no wet rag is bad. The same goes for bed; if you don't want to go, you are not afraid to tell us. As of late, your favorite way of communication has been via demon birdlike shrieks. If you can imagine nails on a chalkboard piercing your eardrum with a frozen ice axe, then you get the idea. The great battle of "obey your parents because they love you" has officially begun. The war with my parents wages on; however, it has been a lost campaign since day one.

I know that the rag you crave has soap on it and putting that in your mouth will lead to a whole host of secondary problems. But you don't know anything about soap or its function, so I am scolded for saving you from a bad taste and a bellyache. I can't help but draw a parallel to our Heavenly Father. I can picture Him looking at me, rubbing the bridge of His nose, and, with a sigh of exasperation, saying, "I've told him a million times…" while I sit complaining about not getting what I want. He knows that letting me pursue what I desire will leave me sick to my stomach but because I know nothing, a consequence is not even on my radar. I kick and scream, thinking I know best when, in reality, I am completely clueless. He stopped poison from entering my body and ruining my day, and for that, I look to the Heavens and make my own demon-bird noise. He looks down thinking, "If you only knew what I saved you from."

Praise God He loves us enough not to give us what we want,

V

■ ■ ■

25 February 2014
#148
Proverbs 21:5
2029

Dear VI,

What a season! I'd estimate three-quarters of all we own is either out of our lives forever or sitting in storage. I hate everything about a storage unit, but I can't stomach the idea of getting rid of its contents. It holds our most precious family history—my scrapbook, your great-grandfather's sword, Lewis II's snare drum, and other historical artifacts that will one day belong to you. These visual aids will help you become a man proud of his heritage. Life at the moment is strangely peaceful. With so much going on, I find the quiet security to be a little eerie. Your mom is currently picking clean the bones of our rotisserie chicken in the hopes of a chicken sandwich tomorrow. (The rotisserie chicken is a Bradshaw staple, if you haven't noticed.) She just broke the silence by exclaiming, "I think I found a gizzard! Or a funny bone. I'm great at anatomy."

I just took a picture of our living room where I am currently writing. This photo is worth its thousand words, so instead of writing much more, I will simply attach it to the letter. You will see a 50-year-old card table, my chicken dinner, a large stack of flashcards, and, beneath it, the Bible and the beginning of this very letter. Our bed is gone, which is why the blankets are on the floor. That little TV on the plywood is our pawn shop "big screen," which is responsible for many a late night winter Olympic memory. That flashcard on your mom's glass of wine is to keep out the flies. On paper and photograph, our lives are as unstable as the card table but, I assure you, we are standing on the solid Rock. I feel His firm foundation among the chaos of our transition. So much uncertainty, so many questions and yet I can say that because we have made sure to stay in the palm of His strong hands, this stage has been my favorite.

I feel worked to the marrow. Moving lost today's battle, but it certainly put up a fight. My joints are so swollen, it looks as if I had golf balls implanted below my knee caps. Studying has paralyzed my brain. If I wasn't planning on typing all of these letters, I would surely have to rewrite this one; both spelling and penmanship are not even close to legible. "Not close to legible" is the best description I can muster. I rest my case. There is great joy in your house. We are all in high spirits, knowing that these strange seasons are a critical part of God's perfect plan.

Tonight I fed you yams. I swear you and I eating together made me feel like the most blessed man on earth. As Grandpa Freeman would say, "Bill Gates has nothing on us,"

V

∎ ∎ ∎

26 February 2014
#149
Philippians 4:7
0739

Dear VI,

I slept like a rock on what must have been rocks. I am as stiff as a board. The same can be said for your mom who woke up with bruised hips. In my last letter, I described a strange peace. It is important to understand that the peace that surpasses understanding is different than sedation.

This supernatural peace has taken on many forms in our western culture. I have heard many a man with a well-groomed mustache and sherbet-colored polo shirt recite "God is good, His will be done" in a tone you might expect out of a zombie. It is void of fire or conviction. They sound medicated, like the lady at McDonald's asking, "Would you like fries with that?" It is the kind of peace you might find in the sentence, "They gave him something to put him at peace before he passed away."

I have also observed the church define God's gift of peace as the kind you might find in a hippie commune: "Jesus is my co-pilot. God is love. Hemp crafts and waterbeds"—as if the Lord gives us a blank check whenever we sin, so take a hit and enjoy the good times. Really? As if we are forgiven and can now turn our attention to wickedness and a game of hacky sack. He died for our sins, so it's all good.

The peace that God gives, the kind that surpasses understanding, takes on many forms. It is your confidence during conflict, your wisdom when counseling others, your determination when pursuing your goal, and yes, it can be a downright cozy feeling—a big hug during the loss of a loved one or a slap of encouragement when all your possessions are on the lawn being sold at fifty cents a pop. God's peace is knowing that God has our back, that we are in His hands. It does not mean that our enemies do not exist or calamity is gone forever. It is not what comes when the world has stolen your desire to live. It is not an excuse to do whatever you want. It is what a soldier feels when he is in the thick of battle and knows that the victory is won. It's the kind of peace a man feels when he sees a mighty lion in the wild and knows that it is there to protect him rather than eat him.

Peace out,

V

■ ■ ■

02 March 2014
#150
Matthew 23:12; 1 Peter 5:6, James 4:10
0917

Dear VI,

My pen has been hovering above this paper for a while as I try to process the events of the last few days. I am sure future letters will reflect upon what I have learned during this transition, which we are still very much in. I am happy to report we are making a swift descent toward routine at last. Your mom says she has never felt more at home than she does here in Space 10. Thursday, February 27, was the day we pulled out of the RV dealership with our new house in tow. I had a big grin on my face until I saw what I was expected to back into. It was not so much a tight fit as it was a tricky angle, and the sight of it caused a cold sweat to run down my face. It was painfully obvious I had no shade of a clue what I was doing.

Thankfully, we had made friends with the guy from whom we had bought the RV, and he came along to help guide me in. For 20 minutes, I backed up and pulled forward. Twice he offered to do it himself, but I told him, "I need to get this. I need to see this through." Most of the residents in this RV park are retired veterans. Their schedules are wide open. An open schedule is a valuable commodity when a moron with a 40-foot fifth wheel shows up and keeps yelling things like "So when I turn the wheel left, the back end swings which way?" I provided entertainment for several spectators, all of whom felt the need to put their extremely unhelpful two cents in. "Crank her to 11 o'clock and dig a spur in. That should help grow some legs." It was touch and go for a while, but I managed to swallow my pride and eventually got us home.

Water, electric, and sewage was all hooked up, then it was back to the old house to grab our clothes and other items we were bringing with us. We still have to scrub down the house. That should get done at some point today, Lord willing.

Your mom (the Warrior Queen, as I have been calling her) has hardly eaten, slept, or showered in the last three days. You, my precious boy, have shown some real grit through several days of complete inconsistency. I can't imagine what must be going through that head of yours. You are a champion for spending so much time in the car seat while we move things from A to B and organize. You have grown impatient on several occasions, but I totally understand. If I were a teething baby (or teething adult), I would be complaining too.

What we have here is an obvious blessing from the Lord. When something like this happens, it is tempting to think, "I have arrived, this is it, we finally have it all figured out." That attitude is not a sin, but it is incredibly foolish. While God has given us this gift, He has also given us a new mission and the opportunity to bless others, and by doing this we are giving the blessing back to Him. This is contrary to the world. The worldly man points to himself and says he deserves the credit for all the great things in his life. This is a recipe for disaster every time, I promise. Pride comes before a fall, but the Bradshaws plan on staying extremely humble, and in doing so, we will stand taller than ever.

You are home now,

V

P.S. You are currently sleeping in the Pack and Play, but it takes up too much room. I am going to have to build you some sort of locked-in hammock.

■ ■ ■

03 March 2014
#151
Psalm 5:3
0614

Dear VI,

My first early morning letter written in our new home! It took me a while
to get situated, but now I am set up and deeply satisfied. These manufactured homes were not made with insulation in mind. My early mornings are
going to require great strategy and stealth. One misstep and I could wake
you up. Nothing is worse than a quiet home interrupted by a baby waking
prematurely.

Tiptoeing around the living room does not bother me a bit. We have
accepted the fact that we are now fully submerged in a completely different
style of living. A style with paper-thin walls, black tanks, doors I don't fit
through, and a shower I can't stand up in. For the first time in my life, I
am sleeping in a king-size bed and flushing a toilet with a foot lever. Our
fridge is small but fuller than ever. The dishwasher is gone, but we only
have six dishes.

Whoever was in charge of designing our home deserves an award for
space efficiency. There is far more storage than any apartment I have ever
lived in. So much so that even in 400-square feet, we have drawers and
closets that are completely bare. The layout is simple: master bedroom and
bathroom in front, all living necessities in the middle, bunkhouse (a.k.a.
your room) in the back. If we had no roof and a bird flew over our house,
it would see a man sitting at a miniature table, working on a piece of paper,
a precious child sleeping to his left, and a beautiful woman asleep on his
right.

So there you have it—a flyby of the quiet time for a man in a trailer. Off to work I go. I am pleased to report my 40-minute, bumper-to-
bumper commute has been replaced with a three-minute walk through

a nature trail. Punch me in the face if you ever hear me complain about that!

See you at lunch… I think I am going to like this,

V

■ ■ ■

06 March 2014
#152
John 3:16
0555

Dear VI,

This place is starting to look like home. I tested out the grill last night and after sitting down to our first meal at our new table, we almost fell asleep in our food. I pictured wine, laughter, and live music, but once again my imagination did not align with reality. We are beat up from the last few weeks. Traditionally (when we are not snoring in our chicken), your mom and I each say three things we are thankful for. This usually gets the ball rolling down other trails of conversation, but last night the conversation did not roll far. Most of the words drifted right by my ears without ever going in.

We did manage to spend a couple of minutes discussing a song we sang in church last Sunday,

"O How He Loves Us." While I sang this song, I wondered how much He actually does love us. Was it possible to break down God's love into laymen's terms so I might comprehend it? To my inquiries, I heard a voice in my head say clear and bold, "Would you give up your boy to be tortured and killed to save someone who hated you?" At having that question answered, the very notion of doing something as brutal to you as what Christ endured sent me to my chair weeping. I was absolutely undone.

After church my friend, Jeremy, a man of God, told me the story of his boy's going unconscious in his arms. To make a long story short, Tristan had a seizure and stopped breathing while Jeremy did CPR through uncontrollable wailing and crying out to God for help. His wife said it sounded like a man who really knows how bad he needs something. She said she did not know that type of desperation was possible.

Tristan eventually gave a cough and is now back to his beautiful self. Doctors say the seizure was brought on by a fever. I am sitting here writing this paragraph with tears in my eyes because the thought of losing you is more than I can bear. I have always known I love you but, between God's Word and Jeremy's testimony, my love has taken on a new maturity that has helped put a father's love for his son into perspective. This father now sees why parents do not let their kids go explore by themselves. I understand why my friends were forbidden from playing contact sports. I realize why parents let their 22-year-old pothead son live in the garage. Their apprehension is out of the fear of losing them, driven by the unimaginably deep love of a parent. When the depths of that love is felt as I have felt it, it is scary to think of the possibilities, both good and bad.

But I understand why blind love—love without wisdom—can hurt a boy. By not allowing him to explore or hit or became his own man, they are protecting their own hearts but hurting the child's development. And while this may be done in the name of love, it is not love at all. This is the line a parent walks. While my love for you tells me to keep you safe, it also says, "If you love him, you will let him learn, let him grow, let him progress, even if the risk is great."

This letter contains the ramblings of a new parent who is still far from the beginning of a clue. The goal of this letter is to recount for you the depth of God's love. You and I are the sinful creatures who hated him, but He loves *us* so much that He, in fact, did allow His only precious Boy to die a brutal death. I would die for you without a second thought, but allowing you to die for me is beyond my understanding.

I am going to go stare at you before I go to work,

V

■ ■ ■

07 March 2014
#153
Psalm 119:105
1630

Dear VI,

I have some alone time! It is really bizarre not to have someone within arm's length of me. You and your mom are picking up "Mimi" (Grandma Freeman) from the airport, so here I sit taking advantage of the solitude. With the exception of some pictures on the wall, all of our possessions have found themselves a home. I've got Radiohead pumping through the speakers, and all seems to be right with the world.

Every day I seem to find myself surrounded by what Proverbs would define as *folly* except the world views that behavior as exactly the opposite. You, as a man, will have to decide who is right. It is the entire world versus the supernatural Book sitting here before me. I say the world masks *pride* as "confidence," the *drunkard* as "the life of the party," and *promiscuity* as "a ladies' man."

I have noticed that it is becoming increasingly common for Christians to isolate themselves in order to avoid this type of attitude. There is a sort of "us-versus-them" mentality developing in the world. But this is not the example Jesus gave us. He ate, drank, fellowshipped, led, healed, and died for the masters of folly. So the question then becomes: how did He pull this off? There are many ways. Some are theological and shrouded in mystery, while others are practical and much more applicable to a man. All of them are important, but I think every man can benefit from reflecting upon one, in particular.

The man knew His Bible. Throughout the gospels, Jesus consistently quotes scripture, proving that He was proficient in the actual letter of the Word but was also able to recognize the types of people it referred to. He could see through the positive spin the world puts on wickedness. He knew the hypocrite, the deceiver, the man who put his faith in worldly possessions, adulterers, prideful men, and schemers. His Bible knowledge gave Him the ability to decipher good from evil, which then allowed Him to stand in the presence of evil and do good.

Let's show this world how to love,

V

■ ■ ■

08 March 2014
#154
Proverbs 5
0830

Dear VI,

What a glorious Saturday morning! All week the weather has been cold and dreary by Florida's standards, but today the sun is back in charge and, to celebrate, we are going to the beach. Yesterday I endured duty, a monthly activity described in past letters—not my least favorite thing on earth, but close. It ranks slightly lower than wiping with poison ivy. Yesterday's duty, however, proved worthwhile because of some insight God gave me on an issue I have been praying over for some time. Sex, or more specifically, a man's testes, which house one of the most powerful drugs on earth, testosterone.

It can be an awkward topic, which is why many parents never throw it on the table. My mom and dad sat me down at age nine on a Saturday morning when I was about to go skateboarding. "Do you know what sex is?" my dad asked. I then burst into tears and asked what I had done to deserve such punishment. Bewildered, he said "Nothing!" I ran outside, end of discussion. That memory stands in my mind as clear as a bell. But because that conversation never developed, I ended up finding out about sex through a combination of hanging out with older kids and some magazines my buddies and I found in the dumpster. Those experiences also left their mark on my mind. A mark I wish I could erase.

Thankfully, I took Proverbs 5 seriously and can honestly say I don't have many sexual regrets, for which I am most grateful. When I was in junior high, high school, and college, it seemed like everyone was enjoying sex, but I held my ground. I got a lot of flak, but I stood strong. I like to think that I could have had a long list of girlfriends who all wanted me, but that's just something I told myself to make me feel better.

I was as sexually frustrated a virgin as there ever was, and the battle with testosterone manifested itself into all sorts of other regrettable traits. Proof of testosterone's powerful grasp was found in the fact that I was obsessed with something I was sure to be horrible at. What man in his right mind wants to pursue a high risk activity they have never done and are guaranteed to do poorly? I remember hearing that a male elephant near females in heat has upwards of 30 times more testosterone than normal and literally sprints after those females with an elephant-sized erection. He will fight anyone, tear through anything, and possibly kill himself in the process. His mind is focused on one matter; he can only see sex. The shape, smells, noises of the female elephant were always attractive, but now they drive him literally insane with desire.

This is you; this is me. This is all men with a twig and berries. Before I say anything else, I want you to understand that when you feel ready to run through a wall after catching a whiff of a woman's perfume, you are experiencing normal, healthy, good emotions. The Enemy has done an excellent job of making sex either a meaningless, nonchalant activity or completely taboo. This deception makes today's man either a frustrated, confused, angry virgin like I was or like the young men in Proverbs who "spill the waters of their springs in public."

In the name of waiting in anticipation, I will end today's letter here. You just woke up. I am going to go make us some oatmeal,

V

■ ■ ■

09 March 2014
#155
Song of Solomon 1:2-4
1600

Dear VI,

Every time you and I hang at the beach, I get a longer preview of coming attractions. This was our first adventure where we could slap some sunscreen on you and let you roll around on a towel for a while. I have literally never seen you more excited. You were laughing and eating your towel, trying to crawl, chattering so loudly it was like you were on a roller coaster! Wow! Loopy-loop, big seashell tastes like salt, woahhhh! I know the feeling, my son. I get the same way every time. As we near the beach, I get increasingly annoyed with touristy drivers. I start tapping my foot. I've got my head out the window checking the wind, my body has primed itself for ocean entry and now sits poised, waiting for submersion. A time will come when I'll be pushing you into waves, but for now I am fulfilled by simply sitting beside you in the warm sand, listening to your little boy beach giggles. We had a perfect day at the beach together. You make me very happy.

I remember seeing some research a while back, claiming that young men experience between 12 and 25 erections a day. I think I remember that study so well because I was shocked that someone figured that out. After all, how do you track data on something like that? We may never know how the statisticians landed on those figures, but thinking back on my own life experience, I can't disagree.

For all time until the recent past, men married young, as teenagers—around the time sex has officially taken over most of their thought process, and they are experiencing three erections an hour. In addition to a shorter wait, a man's mind was more innocent due to the fact that women dressed conservatively, wearing long dresses, stockings, high collars, and baggy blouses. To enforce this kind of dress code now would be viewed as suppressing women's rights or not allowing those of the female gender to express their individuality. I agree there is some truth to that stance. However, conservative dressing was a great blessing to men because it limited the mental torture inflicted upon them. They had fewer opportunities to sin. A sexually frustrated man, even one with great self-control and armfuls of good intentions, can be a very dangerous animal. He is like a wild elephant. A man is not immune to rape, molestation, or twisted thoughts, and clothing that reveals the detailed form of the female body does not help his situation.

I just heard of a man who, in the name of "not thinking sexy thoughts" would, upon arousal, throw himself into a thorn bush. I'm sure that tactic was effective, but also foolish. When the Bible talks of dealing with sin harshly, this is not what it is referring to. God does not want people to inflict pain upon themselves. Even when the Bible explains, "If your eye causes you to stumble, gouge it out," Jesus is telling His followers to remove themselves from the source of temptation. However, in today's culture, there are very few places a man can go.

In our society, as a girl's body develops, she is encouraged via pop culture, idiot parents, or both, to flaunt her beauty under the alias of "looking cute." After all, drawing the attention of males does brings confidence, happiness, and contributes to a high self-esteem, but being an object men lust after is a horrible way to gain self-assurance. And while I believe most women do not have a clue as to the degree their body affects a sexually mature man, they are not oblivious. They comprehend that men are donkeys, and they possess the carrot.

What does this mean for you? Obviously, the odds are stacked against a man from the start. The provocative ways women dress in magazines, at school, on television, and at church are worse than at any other time in history, and the trend is not heading towards nuns' tunics. Other variables include the multibillion-dollar porn industry and the lack of support men provide each other. The outcome does not look good for the man who wants to save his heart and mind for one special woman.

There is a solution, but in order to find it, you must first throw out any idea of a formula—little tricks like looking at the ground while you walk or not watching movies, using a computer, or going outdoors. I consider these choices to be in the same vein as throwing your body into a thorn bush. Staring at your shoes is not the answer, neither is exile. God needs your presence in this world. I suggest combining knowledge, wisdom, and diligence into a pursuit of God. *It is possible* to look at a woman with deep admiration and appreciation for her beauty without letting your mind wander down lustful paths. With God, you can learn to view a woman as He does—a creature designed to be your mate, one whom man is called to serve in the most intimate, all-encompassing way. She is a sister of Christ. She is a father's little girl.

I was not like this. I was in the "little-skirt-to-my-left, walk-to-the-right" camp. I was bitter at the female race for wearing tank tops. Learn to love women as God loves them; He is their Dad just as He is yours. There will be times when you wonder why it is you seem to be the only man in the universe who treats women this way. You may wonder if this letter's contents are flawed. But trust me, I beg you! One day you will meet your wife, a female body you will get the honor to explore, love, and be vulnerable with forever. You will experience unimaginable emotions, and shame will never be one of them. When this day comes, you will experience God's greatest gift exactly as God intended, and your bride will feel the same. I promise, son, if you can win this battle, you will one day lie beside your lady unafraid and think, "Waiting was 100 percent worth it!"

Here's to open talks about God's most beautiful creation,

V

P.S. Bonus point: Treating women as our Lord would also filters out the seductive women (Proverbs 5:3-6) and attracts the quality ones (Proverbs 31).

■ ■ ■

12 March 2014
#156
Song of Solomon 4:10
0525

Dear VI,

Our home is amazing! Your mom has a real knack for creating a cozy environment. As I sit here in our kitchen/dining room/living room, I feel like a king settling into his dream kingdom. Imagining moments like this one helped keep me moving during the long journey here. Fighting through that long list has made me especially appreciative of these precious seconds in our peaceful abode. This will be a home you enjoy growing up in.

Two letters back I alluded to a couple of situations that gave me an idea as to the sexual darkness in which our world is shrouded. I have decided to share them with you.

1) I borrowed a coworker's truck, famous for having a top-of-the-line sound system, a two-story lift, and 15 television screens. It is one of the most excessive things I have ever seen. When I started

his truck, music that could be heard for miles thumped out of the speakers, and thick African-American women began stripping on every one of the 15 screens. Honestly, the whole situation was so outrageous, I actually started laughing while desperately trying to figure out how to turn off the stupid thing. (The radio face was the size of an IPad and plated in gold.) After mashing the main controls with my palm a few times, the screens finally went dead, and the music fell silent. Upon returning his keys, I mentioned he had unique taste in cinema, to which he laughed and said, "Well, yeah! I watch them coming to work for motivation." What must be going on in a man's heart for a stripper to be his motivation?

2) Shortly after that encounter, I sat at my desk, searching my soul, when another coworker stopped by to see how I was enjoying the trailer life. Before I could answer, he added, "I don't think I could do it. I mean, how do you look at porn without your wife knowing?" What must be going on in a man's heart when his priority is having enough square footage to be able to masturbate?

I see many angles to attack these illustrations. I could address the sexual abuse and slavery that the majority of women in adult films endure. I could write a series of scientific letters, detailing the addicting chemicals released in a man's brain while he is watching pornography. I could also give solid biblical examples showing the twisted spiritual warfare that makes its home during such activities. But I believe taking a quick look at the life of King Solomon is a clear and simple way of observing what pornography is capable of doing.

When Solomon was a young king, he married his love and wrote "Song of Solomon," a poem that intimately details the body of his beloved. The lyrics are dripping with the ecstasy of a young virgin who has at last laid eyes on the body of his life partner. They love every inch of each other. They are one flesh spiritually as well as physically. The book is a work of art showing the sanctity of marriage.

But Solomon did not stay faithful to his first love. The novelty wore off; he became discontent. He wanted to relive his poem again, then again, then again, until he had 700 wives from all over the world. But still he was not satisfied, so he accumulated 300 concubines, which were essentially, as one pastor called them, "stripper girlfriends." Consider Solomon's sex life. Big, little, skinny, wide, tall, short, any combination of hair, eyes, and skin. No sexual fantasy was too outrageous. He had the real-life version of what a modern man has on his smartphone.

Now fast forward to the end of Solomon's life and the book of Ecclesiastes. The young stud from Song of Solomon is now a dirty old pervert. As he is looking back on all he has accomplished, trying to grasp some meaning, I believe he spends some time reflecting upon how wonderful it was to be vulnerable with that one woman and how he allowed the desires of his flesh to lead his heart so far away from the way God designed it, only to find 1000 woman did not compare. He then writes Ecclesiastes 9:9: "Enjoy your wife."

Pornography is a multidimensional complex reality that will closely surround you throughout your entire life. It will absolutely distort the way you view a member of the opposite gender. It is the antithesis of how we are to view women. Instead of admiring a daughter of God, it will cause you to view women as objects to use and abuse in order to gratify your own selfish desires. I never want you to be with your true love while your mind flickers lustful images you watched in secret.

Pornography has the ability to turn a young king into a pervert. It can cause a man to think his days need to start with a car ride full of naked women. It can take its place on top of a man's list of priorities so much so that it factors into the layout of his home. A woman is the most captivating creation. The Grand Canyon is a muddy puddle when put beside your mom. But pornography is a twisted addiction that forces a perfect creation into sinful captivity.

I love you deeply, Lewis. My heart is to inform rather than scare, and because of this desire, I have had enormous difficulty writing this letter. My job as your father is to equip you, and skipping something as important as this subject just because it is difficult to discuss would be cowardly on my part.

When people find out that your mom is my only partner and pornography is not a part of my life, I usually hear, "Man, a big part of me really wishes I had done that."

V

P.S. Just because I know these truths does not mean I have never fallen.

■ ■ ■

14 March 2014
#157
Ephesians 6:12, James 1:2
0557

Dear VI,

I need to always keep in mind that these letters are more than just letters! They are what the Lord has commissioned me to do! They are a tool that might help further God's kingdom. I need to remember that when I am writing I feel I am in the center of God's will. It is a peaceful place to be. Every Christian man following the direction of his Father knows this peace. I would describe it to you, but it is beyond description. Obey the Lord and feel it for yourself.

I need to meditate on these facts often because most mornings I literally feel as if I am being shoved back onto the pillow. I turn off my alarm without remembering it, which is strange. Historically, I have been a very light sleeper, but lately I have been all but unconscious. When I awake at 0500, my bladder is bursting. I am sore and starving, but I lack the power to get out from beneath the sheets.

Sometimes during the night when you wake up crying and I go to you and whisper in a poor western accent, "Who's out there stumbling around in the dark?" most often the issue is your managing to get hopelessly tangled in your blanket, but the second I get you situated, you return to dreamland.

I feel like the Enemy is tucking me in in the same way each morning. I know that sounds ridiculous, but it's true; and to be honest, it kind of excites me. I consider this struggle proof that my words are greater than ink and paper. But because I have been losing the struggle lately, your letters have suffered so I need to regroup and refocus.

The Bible consistently speaks of spiritual warfare throughout the entirety of Scripture. It is impossible to believe in the Word of God without acknowledging the existence of a spiritual realm. I don't want to start down the road of angels and demons quite yet. I don't even want to elaborate on my waking-up issue. The Enemy does not deserve that much credit. Please understand that it is foolish to pretend the Devil does not exist, wise to discern what role he has in your life, and unnecessary to fear him. I have mentioned before that our God allows us to be tempted so that we might grow, but the Lord promises never to give us more than we can handle. I believe that there is more than sleepiness keeping me in bed, but the power of the Prince of Darkness is a complete joke when compared to our God. Because this is true, I have no excuse for not getting my butt out of bed!

Talk to you tomorrow morning,

V

■ ■ ■

17 March 2014
#158
Ecclesiastes 3:1-8, 1 Corinthians 14:40
0553

Dear VI,

I won the fight with the snooze, and now I sit enjoying the sounds of raindrops dancing on our fiberglass roof. The sound is hypnotic. I get a similar feeling when listening to the sounds of dry wood crackling in a fireplace. It makes me want to curl up with tea and a book, but running to work through the jungle in a storm sounds good too. If this deluge continues, I could make a raft and float to work. Talk about an ideal commute! For now, coffee and the Word have me feeling very content. There are worse situations in which I could find myself.

Yesterday we tried to watch a movie in bed, but you were determined to attack me from title to credits. Tugging my chest hair, biting my nose, you kicked and slapped like your life depended on it. I was not able to enjoy the movie. I don't even remember what movie it was, but I loved wrestling with you. At first I was annoyed, which I am sure any experienced parent would laugh at. I was under the delusion that you might lie beside me for a two-hour movie. I'm better off being irritated at the rain for being wet! Eventually, I remembered that you are my friend and will only be this age once. One day we will wrestle one last time before the season of father-son roughhousing will come to an end.

My irritation was derived from recent efforts your mom and I have made to develop a system which allows us to work smarter rather than harder. Little things like only owning three plates, establishing a laundry day, and keeping a shared calendar. We have recently recognized our witness will be taken more seriously if the thoughts and actions of our family unit are in sync. It is important for every family to identify the size of its plate and construct life in such a way that nothing spills off. This goes for both the individual family member and the family as a whole.

The tricky part with developing organizational habits is not obsessing. This is where people, including myself, can get all messed up if we are not careful. It can become more about the planning than the reason behind the planning. My friend has a 15-color, three-ring binder with the next five years planned to the second, but to do so she blocks out an hour each day, which could be spent playing with her son or taking a nap. You wanted to climb on me, but I got aggravated because that time was not allotted for roughhousing. For me, it was movie time. The truth is that life is far too unpredictable to be so rigid. Life is a balance, and outside of our most important needs (things like prayer, exercise, diet, fellowship, and rest), almost everything should be written in pencil.

On Sunday we go to the store with a meal plan for the week. This saves time, money, and stress, and ensures that we are putting good things in our bodies. Does that mean if we get a wild hair for Mexican food, we say, "No! Tonight is salad night." Absolutely not! If we can afford it, let's go. This is the balance. It is possible to be spontaneous and organized, driven and free-spirited, goal-oriented and content with how things are. Ask for wisdom; let it help you dictate that delicate equilibrium.

You whooped me yesterday,

V

■ ■ ■

19 March 2014
#159
Jeremiah 31:33
1537

Dear VI,

I recently won Sailor of the Quarter again. I did the dress uniform in front of a board interview and did my best to respond to their questions. I was nervous, but this time my confidence outweighed my nausea. I have stepped up my efforts: I am diving deeper into the Word, listening to sermons preached by men wiser than me, and poring over every word I write to you. Yesterday was encouraging because I felt like my vigilance was evident in the way I spoke.

I realize these simple letters may one day serve as a helpful tool for others; they may give me the opportunity to witness, and if that day comes, I want to have my act together which, as any wise man will tell you, is a double-edged sword. The more I learn, the more I realize how little I know. It is as if I am walking down a road where the further I walk, the further ahead I can see. The more horizon I see, the more I understand that the road is longer than I first anticipated.

One of the questions asked by the salty old sailors comprising the board had to do with homosexual marriage in the military. Specifically, how do I feel about it? I believe my answer pleased the Lord, but I was still left thinking, "I have a long way to go." Ironically, the additional diligence I mentioned earlier was both the reason I was ready with a quality response and what turned me onto how much better I could have been. I see much of my life has been spent limping by on the "Cliff's Notes Study Guide" version of the big questions. I have been scraping by with a slingshot, but I am in need of real firepower.

In college I was part of a weekly songwriters' workshop where I repeatedly heard the words, "Never use three words when two words will do. Quantity is the Enemy of the lyricist." I totally agree. With lyrics and talking in general, less is best. The accuracy of an answer is not based upon how many words are used. (These letters have been an excellent—and challenging—exercise in whittling down excess and using only words that pack a punch.) We all know people whose answer would have been painfully long complete with out-of-context verses and the alienation of everyone within earshot. A longwinded answer is good for one thing: making the listener think "I wish he would stop talking." The meaning is lost in the message.

That being established, education on all issues, but especially those regarding your faith, is paramount. What if I had responded, "Gays can't marry because the Bible tells me so." How does that answer represent Christ? Poorly! It makes Christians look like brainwashed fools. It would be wiser to say, "I don't know enough about that question to give you a respectable answer," instead of spewing what my mom refers to as "verbal diarrhea." A foolish response not only makes our King look bad, it also gives ammunition to the questioner: "So you're telling me you believe in God but can't tell me why same-sex marriage is a sin?" Without proper ammunition, anyone can quickly become painted into a tight corner. Don't let that happen. Succinct, precise, crisp responses are the ones that leave a mark. This is a delicate art that I am pursuing but know very little about.

Upon returning to my office, I gave a little prayer asking for help on the ever-lengthening journey ahead of me. I hope my words make Him proud on the way.

"It's our wits that make us men." I really hope you know who said that,

V

P.S. Tomorrow I take the advancement exam once again. I have studied all I can study. I am as prepared as I can be. Maybe this will be the one.

■ ■ ■

23 March 2014
#160
2 Corinthians 3:6, Ecclesiastes 3:11
0930

Dear VI,

Last night we had a small birthday party for your mom at our house. It was amazing. We grilled sausage and listened to music. Three years ago at my birthday party, my friend Grace made everyone say something they appreciated about me. It was an extremely humbling and surprising experience. I was shocked at the memories others carry about me. Things I have no recollection of doing are special memories held by others. From that time until this, I have made a habit of replicating this experience at every birthday party we attend as well as on our own birthdays.

What surprises me is how uncomfortable people get when receiving a compliment. You would think it would be reversed. The person forced to give encouragement on the spot ought to feel some discomfort. But the receiver always seems to have difficulty receiving affirmation, as if the gift is too great to accept. "I couldn't. Please, it's far too expensive; take it back." If I search my heart, I must admit that I have the same initial reaction when receiving encouragement. I can't just accept the fact that I actually mean something to someone. Instead, I find myself wanting to one-up their encouragement. I try to deflect the compliment to someone else—anyone else. Your mom started doing that last night. I told her how I admire her trust in me as well as my thankfulness for living the life of a military spouse, but before I could finish, she interrupted and began rambling on about how I am the one sacrificing: "Really, it's no problem, honey, honestly." Why is this?

Compliments are strange because people work so hard in the hopes of receiving one, but when the magic words come, the receiver practically begs them to stop. A big reason why humans both crave and fear encouragement is because most often those giving the compliments are either deceiving, have selfish motives, or both. It is likely that the compliment I gave your mom triggered a defense mechanism that was put in place after past accolades proved to cause hurt. Everyone has had his or her guard coaxed down by encouraging words only to be exploited by the encourager or told later that the opposite was true. That scenario is emotionally devastating.

The show, "American Idol," is a perfect example. With any luck it will be canceled by the time you are old enough to watch it so, in summary, the entire season is one long singing contest open to everyone. I used to watch the first few episodes because that is when they show the bad singer compilations. These shows are truly painful to watch. Traditionally, I would sit squirming in my chair, yelling at the television, "Do these people have no one who loves them enough to tell them they stink before they embarrass themselves on national TV?!" Shortly after everyone's ears bleed, the world famous singing talent would tell them "No"; they did not have what it takes. This launches the contestants into an all-too-predictable tantrum. "Screw you! People say I'm great! Y'all is deaf!"

No doubt these singers did have people tell them they were great. And the singer took the bait hook, line, and sinker—only to find out the hard way that they have no shred of musical talent or do not make the team or get asked to the dance or get the job. A double heartbreak is experienced. They realize that they are not as good as they believed, and their so-called "friends" tricked them. In an effort to avoid another crushing blow, walls are constructed and spirits are calloused. They will not take the bait so easily next time. They will deflect, they will deny, they will work for approval and then throw it away.

It is evil to tickle people's ears with false flattery. Proverbs 29:5 reads, "Flattery is a trap to the feet." But make no mistake; encouragement is encouraged (read 1 Thessalonians 5:11, Isaiah 41:10), just make sure that every one of your words is true. Otherwise, keep your mouth shut.

So far you have received more compliments than anyone I know. Maybe that is why your head is so big compared to your body!

V

P.S. I recently heard a friend suspiciously ask, "Are you just trying to butter my biscuit?" I thought that remark was funny.

■ ■ ■

24 March 2014
#161
James 4:1-3, 1 John 3:13, Galatians 6:2
1300

Dear VI,

It is fascinating to watch you develop a mind of your own. Your taste buds are deciding what to like, what to hate, and urging your brain to develop a system to keep "bad" food from entering. Spitting seems to work as does whining with your mouth closed. I sit on the other side of the spoon, half trying to hide how much I admire your creative determination and half weary of my attempts to help getting spit back in my face. You have also opened the door to self-mobility. Utilizing that skill has helped you in your never-ending quest to suck on stuff. Nothing is safe from your saliva.

It is remarkable how quickly a newborn transforms into a baby. The speed at which you are gaining strength, awareness, personality, and desire causes my pulse to quicken. I get a tightness in my chest, and think, "I am not doing a good enough job of soaking this in!"

It is equally remarkable to observe your selfishness. You want what you want because you have discovered the difference between want and need. Once upon a time, virtually anything served as a teether but now only a particular tag or toy will do. Your life was simple cause and effect. A teddy bear nose was gnawed on because that was its function, but now the why and how questions are entering the equation; things are getting thorny.

I understand selfishness. It is a natural talent of mine and a part of every human's DNA. It never goes away. It only becomes more specific. The toy eventually needs to be a certain brand, a certain color, a certain style. The food needs to be saltier, warmer, gluten-free, organic. It is a sickness that cannot be destroyed, only kept at bay. Give it its head and it will lead you to lie, cheat, steal and deceive—all in the name of getting what your selfish heart desires which, on second thought, never ends up being all it was cracked up to be.

It takes wisdom to look at a desire with perspective. There is great benefit in the ability to remove emotion from the equation and look at a situation objectively. Does what I want line up with my long-term goals? Is what I want in line with what my Lord wants for me? Will getting this put me in a hole financially?

Selfishness is so embedded in our sinful nature that selfless generosity arouses the same type of suspicion experienced while receiving encouragement. Instead of gratitude, the receiver becomes a detective trying to discover the angle of this generous giver. "You're giving me some of your food because I forgot lunch?" A person can't fathom the idea of no strings attached. They inspect the snack closely, as if I slipped a narcotic in their granola bar.

You are a baby. Giving is not on your radar yet. Your selfishness only further proves you are a healthy human. Because I am a father hopelessly in love, I want to give you everything your heart desires. My knee-jerk impulse is to spoil you. I am sure it will be harder to control that impulse as you discover my soft spots and hone in with your skills of persuasion. But in the same way, our Father in Heaven does not give me whatever sounds good at the time; I cannot run to your side at your every request. It would be foolish. It would be massaging your selfish muscle and creating a self-entitled monster. It would be horrible parenting.

Your daddy loves you,

V

■ ■ ■

25 March 2014
#162
1 John 2:15-17
0530

Dear VI,

Your mom and I are in a small group Monday evenings that is methodically working its way through a financial responsibility DVD. The amount of debt people are in because of selfishness is jaw-dropping. Babies and adults share the same motto: I want what I want, and I want it now. The difference is that adults have credit cards—apparently lots of them. They also have more command of the English language which enables them to justify and finagle. I keep hearing things like, "We pay $240 a month for DISH and are having trouble with rent, but it's not fair to expect us to live without the AMC channel."

Jesus has the ability to transform our desires by supernaturally changing the words "I" and "me" to "we" and "He." How else can you explain the desire for expensive clothes morphing into a desire to give the clothes off your back? He also takes the fun out of selfishness through conviction. I believe feeling convicted is excellent evidence in favor of the reality of the Holy Spirit for two reasons:

1) Animals do not feel convicted of their selfishness. They are not even aware that they are selfish. Yet their entire concentration is always focused on the most selfish of all interests—survival. If humans were not created in the image of God, their objective would be no different. We would not be flooded with a sick feeling every time we lied or deceived or swiped a credit card in the name of selfish gain. Nor would we ever have a need to justify. It would all just be another step toward trying to survive.

2) When a man becomes a Christian, he begins to feel convicted when committing selfish acts he has done habitually for years without a second thought. He begins to see things through the lens of the Spirit and realizes he has been drinking too much, he has not loved his wife as she deserves, he has spent more time playing video games than playing with his kid, he does not come home when he says he will. All the things he did simply because he wanted to are now seen as selfish, and the realization sparks conviction. It is an alarm that goes off in the heart of man to warn him when he is straying. This doesn't happen without the Holy Spirit.

The most beautiful part about God's desire for us to live unselfishly is realized when a selfless act actually gives more pleasure than the selfish one. God advises us to be selfless because He wants us to experience real joy. Does it feel better to get a present or give one to someone else? Do you feel better after volunteering at a soup kitchen or telling the waiter you want the soup of the day? What is more enjoyable? Snagging the last cookie or sharing it? I have never heard of a person regretting the sacrifice he made to go on a missions trip or say, "I just really wish I had kept that jacket instead of giving it to that homeless child."

Sin has turned us upside down, but God's teachings reveal to us that by doing the opposite of our natural instinct, we are placed back on our feet. We actually find more joy when we suppress the desires of our flesh and pursue the antithesis. Unbelievable! Humans are so naturally crooked, so altogether backward, that when we do the reverse, we actually experience more pleasure.

I realize this letter covers a lot, but it's your book, so feel free to hold onto it and reread,

V

■ ■ ■

27 March 2014
#163
Ecclesiastes 2:24
0554

Dear VI,

Yesterday was your seven-month birthday! This is a tough pill to swallow. You are now a little more than 18 pounds and 28.5 inches long. Translation: your weight is perfect, and you are slightly taller than most. Your mom deserves a lot of credit for this good health and growth. Her life has revolved around nursing and pumping. She puts in a lot of time making sure you sleep soundly. She double- and triple-checks your coziness level. She answers your call during all of those painful hours of the night. Because of this, you appear to be much stronger and healthier than many other babies your age.

Your seven-month mark brought with it a final round of immunizations and a tumble off our bed. Happy birthday! I hope you liked your gifts. Apparently, your mom looked away for a second and BAM! Your toughness shone once again. I was at work, but your mom reported that, on both occasions, you cried for just a minute, then looked angry for another minute before going back to exploring with new resolve. A little older and a little wiser. She said, "Today his strength proved more than ever that he is all boy." How proud do you think that made me!

The day's events wiped you out, which gave you the general attitude of fussiness seen in every other baby I have ever met. I act along these same lines after a long day that leaves me feeling poked and dropped.

Sometimes I wish that these letters were nothing more than a record of your daily life, how handsome you look in a particular outfit or how well you are sitting up. Enormous amounts of data have fallen off the paper. Routine touches most of the hours of a day. Life has the ability to fly by while humans only have the ability to watch it go. This is not my first time considering this. I scheme and devise ways to make these letters more of a historical journal than your dad's practical suggestions for life. I hate watching time soar by. But instead of hatching plans to capture the uncatchable, I am dedicated to sharing with you the reason we are alive. Besides, God did not tell me to document how cute your Hawaiian shirt is.

What I want is for you to enjoy this fast-flowing life. I promise I have done all I can to cling to the spirit God has given me. This is not because I am immature, despite what some would say. I have heard the desires of men older than me. They say things like, "I wish I had never stopped exercising," "I wish I had spent more time with family." Or simply, "I don't know how it came to this." While at the same time, everyone my age says, "I need to build my career," or "Life starts when you retire." The reason old people look back with regret is because they believed younger years were to be spent preparing for the future.

Young adults kill themselves in the name of moving up the ladder, developing habits and coping with depression along the way, only to look back and realize it was not worth it. Don't do that, son! Don't let the

Enemy trick you into squandering your very quick-moving life. Focus on enjoying this day. Grab it and shake it for all it is worth from this day until eternity.

I am off to work so you can continue to get big and strong,

V

■ ■ ■

29 March 2014
#164
Psalm 100:2-4
0956

Dear VI,

Yesterday we moved. That's right, our entire house. We didn't go far, just 45 minutes up the coast to Mayport Naval Station for the weekend. We are right by the ocean, living the dream. Yesterday was stressful because it was our first attempt at packing and moving our entire residence. Order and operation are critical, and I was sure of neither. Also, your mom and I did not really know how buttoned down the inside needed to be so we took down and put away more than was necessary. The truck made light work of pulling our 16,000-pound home. I could just as easily have pulled your red wagon.

As I cruised in the slow lane with you chattering away in the back of our big cozy truck, tunes pumping, our palace in tow, and your mom running her fingers along my forearm, I was the most blessed man in the universe. The feeling flourished even more when we got set up here in Mayport. The whole process took less than 10 minutes. The panels popped open, everything leveled out, nothing was broken, and I was smacked with the reality that the system works. Our dream to do exactly this has come true. I turned on a basketball game; we had reception! I looked in the fridge, and the food was cold. I flushed the toilet, textbook plumbing. I just could not believe it.

As I pranced around our mini-mansion, I spotted our new neighbor sipping a beer and slowly sucking on the end of a cigar while staring out to sea. I walked over to introduce myself, and he offered me a drink from the stocked ice chest duct-taped to his chair. I gladly accepted. The man is retired Air Force and a current RV professional—fat, tan, in the middle of three books, and content beyond belief. His whole system was a kind of customization that can only be made through decades of tweaking. The kind that can be set up and torn down in seconds. He and his wife spend the winter in Tampa and were currently in the process of heading home to Michigan. "We may get there around Easter," he said. "Depends on what we feel like." The contentment I have found among motorhome dwellers is straight from the Bible, whether or not they know it.

Today I am feeling extremely content. Your mom and I are lounging on a rainy Saturday. I could pout over my missed opportunity to surf. I could be annoyed that it was nice all week while I sat indoors. But no, I am going to go drink tea and watch a movie with your mom, but first I am going to pray and thank God for this new season we have officially entered into.

The system works,

V

■ ■ ■

30 March 2014
#165
Proverbs 3:5
1724

Dear VI,

Home again, home again! Back in Space 13 with much less trouble then the first time. Mayport was a blast! Greg, the old vet, and his wife invited us over when the weather broke. Lots of lounging and talking in the sun.

By the way, 30 seconds after I finished writing to you about all being right with the world, I found a fat leak in the skylight above the shower. It's my fault. I should have known something like that would happen. It was the Lord seeing if my content attitude would hold any water, or at least keep it from dripping into the house. Your mom and I sealed it with a team effort which included silicone and a hair dryer. It won't win a beauty contest, but it isn't leaking anymore!

Life can spring a leak at any moment, but it always seems to when you least expect it. That is why it is important to soak up a good situation. Maintenance may be necessary at any second, and the last thing you want is to be caught with your pants down wishing, "I should have appreciated that season when everything was working well."

You are my favorite son,

V

■ ■ ■

04 April 2014
#166
Proverbs 6:20-23
1236

Dear VI,

You, my friend, are off to spend a few hours at day care. Your mom is about to lose it, and your dad is not far behind. You are strong and active, always on the hunt for something to hit or eat. Your attention span is a maximum of 10 seconds. I could not be less surprised. My nickname growing up was "A.D.D. Boy" and your mom's was "Wild Indian." Our parents' dream of their children experiencing what they dealt with is beginning to come true. Our sanity sits on the edge of a razor, but admitting that to my parents would force me to listen to several minutes of laughter. I bet I would hear a champagne cork pop on the other end of the phone. We are passing you off to the professionals in a desperate effort to pray, regroup, and strategize. I am not going to let you in on the plan because, if you are as much like me as they say you are, you will devise some way to use the plan against us.

I am going old school and studying the Ten Commandments. I embarked on this adventure after studying Proverbs 6:20-23, which tells children to follow their father's commands, to keep them so close they are a lamp, and I realized that I am not only the child but am also the father. So what commands do I have? If my instructions are a light to your feet, then I had better chose carefully. Ultimately, our Father is King. Jesus is a big fan of the Law of Moses (see Luke), and I think it best to copy what He says. The main thing to keep in mind is that the Ten Commandments are made in love. You may get upset when, because I love you and I do not want you to get sick, I do not let you eat my filthy shoelace. Jesus says have no idols because He does not want you to be enslaved to a false waste of life. It is a simple concept, but things quickly get dicey when men start including rules of their own. I will elaborate on what I mean by this in future letters. Today I will end, as I occasionally do, with a challenge. Find for me something in life that is not bogged down with rules.

I adore you, my energetic son,

V

■ ■ ■

3 April 2014
#167
Acts 5:29
1310

Dear VI,

Again I find myself at the duty desk. It is all you might expect at a government job. I used to think having an office with a window would improve my situation, but I now know the opposite is true. It is perfect outside! It is one of those days where the sun would warm your back but not to the point of sweating. A day that leaves your skin a little tighter and convinces your freckles to come out. I can see boats in the water and kids playing on the dock. I feel exactly like I did from my first day of kindergarten through my last day of college while sitting in class—like a dog in a kennel.

I also tweaked my back, which doesn't help matters. I cannot touch my knees, and it hurts to breathe. This is not the first time this has happened, and I have recovered every time, but this one is so bad I cried, "Uncle!" and went to the doctor who, after a little bit of feeling around, said, "I can't believe you're walking."

I think I am scared. I cry at every touching commercial I see and do not even try and hide it. I'm scared to get old. Scared for the day I can no longer hurl my body around. Scared of sitting at a desk unable to encourage myself with thoughts like, "Two days until you get in the ocean," or "At least I have a basketball game tonight." It is unhealthy for a man to be cooped up like this.

As I continue to look into the Ten Commandments, I cannot help but believe that all of this boils down to one thing: rules! I have no clue as to why the vast majority exist or even what they are. No one does. Take a random poll asking five people how to properly alert the clinic of an armed intruder, and you will receive five different responses. All we know is, there is a procedure. It does exist.

In the military there are rules for everything (these are called SOPs or Standard Operating Procedures) from the length of your fingernails to the number of elective surgeries a person can have over the course of a military career and how many of those the government will pay for. Rules are tacked onto everything. Evolving, morphing, ever-changing, rules.

Why do we need them all? Because if rules are not established, some guy is going to walk around with a nine-inch-long, hot-orange pinky nail, or get his nose surgically enlarged on Uncle Sam's dime. Then when the man goes on a rampage and uses his nose or nail as weapons, the victims of the attack will turn around and sue the government. Stranger things have happened, I guarantee it.

These types of rules are not limited to the military. These rules are hopelessly tangled in any and all activities effectively choking the fun out of everything. The rules that run the world are created out of fear—fear of getting sued, fear of getting injured, fear of someone's feelings getting hurt, fear of the unknown.

They are a way of saying, "If everyone follows these steps, we will have an answer to all possible situations." This explains why the rulebooks continue to grow ever thicker. Time gives people the opportunity to do the unexpected, and every time the unthinkable occurs, the rule book gets meatier. A herd of corporate cubicles at Christmas is a simple example. Once upon a time there were no decorating restrictions. People were free to express themselves through the adorning of their six-foot square. But one year someone's Christmas lights started an electrical fire, and rules detailing appropriate, corporate approved lights, were rolled out. The next year someone was offended by a Nativity scene portraying the wise men as females, so that was out. Two years later, Santa fell out of a sleigh and a seatbelt law was incorporated. And let's not forget the secretary's under-cooked turkey which gave the entire accounting department 12 days of vomiting and diarrhea. An inappropriate elf email made its way around the spaces, and Tim's excessive eggnog drinking led him to harass his boss.

Every time something like this happens, the big boss asks, "What are we doing to fix the situation?" and his employees respond, "We are implementing new directives to fix the deficiency." After a couple of decades of this type of thing, Christmas is more depressing than a normal work day. No lights, no religious freedom, no eggnog, filtered emails, and Santa with a seatbelt.

The world's inability to create a set of laws capable of holding water for five minutes exposes how amazing Jesus is. He came into the world and laid down a set of rules that, if followed, would lead to the best possible life and, 2000 years later, it still works perfectly. But it gets even better because Jesus not only set up these rules, He then lived by them, and also gave every person the ability to live by them through the power of the Holy Spirit. It is impossible for a man to say, "The Bible is just a bunch of impossible rules." Christ proved we can do it, and doing it will be to our greatest benefit.

If you find a loophole in how we do things, I expect you to lovingly take advantage,

V

■ ■ ■

07 April 2014
#168
Psalm 34:17-18
0547

Dear VI,

Yesterday you were part of your first wedding party. Travis and Ashley got hitched with your mom behind Ashley and the Bradshaw men behind Travis. You did great! I held you the whole time, and you were content to suck on the toe of your shoe. It was a beautiful ceremony, which concluded with cake and BBQ at their house. It was a really meaningful day with a small group of family who sincerely love each other.

The day reminded me of those slow family days in Oregon I mentioned in Letter 114. I needed a day like that because I have been really sad for the last couple of weeks. A lot of it stems from work. My job is as uninteresting as it is stressful with patients who don't want to be there and coworkers who really don't want to be there either. So much so that they are literally gone much of the time. Either physically disappearing when the boss is not around or putting forth so little effort, it is as if they do not exist for any reason other than to make negative comments.

I am burned out on these letters, on work, on anything requiring a slice of my time. I don't care. I find that I hardly have a desire to speak, I have no appetite, sleep gives no rest. The majority of my effort goes into leaving my feelings at work, but I have not been great at this; I can see a rift beginning to make its way into our home. So why do I burden your young mind with your father's struggles? Because you need to understand that feeling as I am feeling is an important part of being human.

Keep in mind that *everything* God created is good. That includes emotions and feelings. The issues begin when a man hates experiencing a particular emotion. No one relishes the emotions felt when a loved one passes, but that does not make the feeling "bad." This would be like saying, "That flower is bad because I do not like the way it smells."

Complications also appear when feelings show up at inappropriate times. Anger, sexual desire, sorrow, love, despair, excitement, frustration... All of these are good and play an important role in a man's life. But when a man becomes angry because his team lost a game or sexually aroused when looking at his neighbor's wife, he must then acknowledge that his feelings are not bad but inappropriate under the circumstances. The flower is always good; it simply needs the right audience.

We get feelings at the wrong times because we are lost. Our flesh has no direction. This comes as a consequence of having a sinful nature. When a man becomes saved, the Holy Spirit enters the picture and starts pointing out when a feeling is justified and when it is destructive. Proof of this can be seen whenever a man starts walking with the Lord because he begins to dislike activities that once gave him pleasure. The pre-Christ man enjoyed the feelings that accompanied sharing his girlfriend's bed, but once he becomes a Christian, those same activities give him yucky feelings. This feeling is called *conviction*.

My situation is different because God, in His brilliance, is able to allow undesirable feelings to cling to a person for a time in order to make him stronger. (This goes way back to Letter 21's discussing refinement through fire.) My lifestyle has not changed; neither has my work ethic. If anything, life is easier and more prosperous than it was when I was gung-ho and constantly winning awards. Now that the new car smell has faded, I am left to prove that my motivation was not circumstantial. The accolades are over, and the time to attest that my claims of working for God has come. All my quiet times and pep talks aside, will I continue racing for my Lord? Yes, I will.

I love you, Lewis,

V

■ ■ ■

09 April 2014
#169
Proverbs 22:6
0744

Dear VI,

I have received more verbal counselings then I can count sitting in this very spot—the kitchen table in my mother's house. You are also here, upstairs with your mom, asleep. Yesterday we packed up our home and drove it over to the dealership where we bought it in order to get some work done. This was our first time properly securing our house for an extended period of time, and it was much more extensive than we thought it would be. Things like cleaning out the fridge, spraying for bugs, and disconnecting the battery were not on our radar until it was too late and a mad scramble had to be made. From the dealership we headed to the airport and boarded a plane that eleven hours later landed here in Southern California. I don't want to spend much time rehashing the particulars, but I will say pouring rain, a son who would not sleep, airsick parents, LA traffic, and two layovers were involved. At one point, your mom looked at me and said, "This lifestyle is not for the faint of heart."

You once again displayed great character. After 21 hours of packing and travel, you hardly fussed. You just kept giving me this look that said,

"I'm not sure what's going on, but as long as you stay close I'm going to allow it. I'm not a fan of the situation, but I won't freak out."

Sitting here at this table with you above me, I can't help but feel a mind-bending mixture of future meets past. From this very spot, I heard the words, "Someday you will have kids and understand what I'm talking about!" I also heard on more than one occasion, "You're not leaving this seat until you write a page about your day." I used to sit here at the table and, instead of writing as I was instructed to do, I would daydream about a day when I did have children and hope my future child was much better behaved than me. Now I sit here in the same chair, writing a letter to the son of my dreams who, so far, is proving to be above and beyond everything I ever hoped for.

Sometimes life is just weird,

V

■ ■ ■

15 April 2014
#170
Philippians 1:12-19
0600

Dear VI,

Let's recap: in the last week you have flown across America, met your cousin Duke (my sister's son who was born one day before you), got on a boat and traveled to Catalina Island where you attended your cousin Lyndsay's wedding, and were introduced to a lot of members ecstatic at meeting the sixth generation of Lewis Seeley Bradshaw. You did a photo shoot; I introduced you to my long-lost love, the Pacific Ocean; you took a nap on your grandpa; and now, today, we head back across this great country of ours.

You and your mom are passed out in the seat beside me. I would happily join you in dreamland if I came close to fitting in these tiny seats. My sister told me that kids change the word "vacation" to "trip" as in, "We are taking a *trip* to California where I will do the same things I normally do for my child without any of the comforts of my own home. On this *trip*, I will misplace critical personal items. On this *trip*, I will be horribly jet-lagged. On this *trip*, I will spend too much money."

Anyone who takes a trip back to his or her roots knows that travel produces change. I love this aspect of travel because it forces me to see specific ways that I have changed for the better and important reminders about who I am that I have since forgotten. I used to dread the idea of leaving home because I was afraid I might miss out on something. To my great relief, every time I come back, most of my childhood chums have very little to report. "Not much has changed around here. You missed a couple of good swells. Landon got hitched." Anyone who has come home after extended travel has had the same experience. People do the same thing and get the same thing.

The benefit of this is that their consistency reminds me of who I am. I was reminded by many dear friends that I am a skilled waterman whose love for the ocean surpasses anyone they know. Music I loved was played for me once again, some stories were told that forced me to acknowledge I am a leader, and many more stories reminded me of how goofy I will always be.

In my last letter, I admitted I was in bad emotional shape. I think this *trip* really helped me a great deal. I was lifted up by a lot of great friends and I got to do some things that charged my spirit. I feel motivated, refreshed, and ready to return to work.

You never know when the clouds are going to break,

V

■ ■ ■

16 April 2014
#171
Ephesians 4:27
1330

Dear VI,

When a man finds Jesus, he, too, is found. Together the man and the Holy Spirit make sure he stays that way. With Christ as the anchor, the man's lifelong goal becomes holding on to that anchor for dear life, while the Enemy's job is to coax him into letting go. As long as a man is diligent with his grip, he is safe, but relax for one second, and the darkness can grab hold and slowly peel his fingers away.

Think of it like this: a man makes his bed every morning until one day he doesn't. That night he crawls into his messy sheets but still sleeps soundly, so the next day he skips it again. Then laundry day comes, but he decides to leave the sheets because it takes hours and, besides, if not making the bed doesn't affect sleep quality, maybe smelly sheets won't either. His gamble pays off; he is still out like a light. But a few extra weeks of sleeping in the same sheets has given dust mites, dead skin cells, sweat, and germs the opportunity to make a home in the man's bed. Now the man awakes with irritating bites on his legs but decides at this point a few bites are less hassle than taking his sheets to the cleaners' for a proper delousing as they are now too dirty for the standard washer. To get them properly cleaned will involve money as well as a couple of nights with no sheets at all.

Do you see where this is heading? What started with one lazy decision ended with the man spending sleepless nights, scratching a moldy, bitten body. He lies there looking at the ceiling and wondering, "How did it come to this? I am so miserable." It is important to understand that it doesn't end here. Once Satan has a solid grip, things can always get worse. Maybe instead of fixing the problem, he starts popping pills to help him sleep. Maybe he spends all night staring blankly at the television.

It all starts with one day of skipping devotions, one night of going too far with a girl, skipping church for one Sunday, one night of one too many before getting behind the wheel, looking at that website one time. These actions create a small window of opportunity for the Enemy, which he will take advantage of every single time. Do not let the Enemy take hold. Stay diligent in the hills and the valleys. Cling to the things the Lord has commanded of you, and I promise you will look back and think, "I am so glad I made my bed."

When you discover the Enemy has slipped his hand in, be strong and regain position. Show the resolve to fight for what you know is the best way to live,

V

■ ■ ■

17 April 2014
#172
Psalm 128:1-3
0545

Dear VI,

Home at last! It is hard to believe that 48 hours ago I wrote from the West Coast. It feels great to be back in our cozy trailer. Without slipping into heated theological waters, I want you to consider why God created His law.

Imagine this scenario: two boys enter a store. The first boy knows where the candy aisle is, and the second is completely ignorant of its existence. Now because the first boy knows where the candy is, he also knows that he cannot have any without asking his mom. He knows he can choose one candy bar, and that he must then take it to the man behind the counter to pay. If these things are done, the chocolate is his.

The second boy knows nothing about asking or paying; his knowledge is limited to the fact that he likes candy. So the question becomes: is the second boy capable of shoplifting? Can he fill his pockets with treats and walk out of the store without consequence? No. Ignorance is not an excuse for committing a crime. "I didn't know" does not forgive the deed.

Prior to the law, we were all Boy Number Two: ignorant of the crimes we were committing but guilty nonetheless. Murder, theft, envy, adultery, gossip, slander, lying...all lead to a thin, sinful, unfulfilling existence. But until the law came along, it was impossible for us to know these sins were the reasons why life felt so horrible.

The history of God's law is lengthy when looked at as a whole. A lot has happened between the first law regarding the forbidden fruit, to the Ten Commandments, through the Pharisees, and into the everlasting rule of Jesus Christ. So let's focus on the present. Thanks to Christ, we live in an excellent situation. Christians have a very loving set of rules established by God to keep us from doing what will hurt us and lead mankind in the direction of doing that which will bring the highest quality existence.

We have the rules (serve others, for example), and we also have the Holy Spirit who helps us interpret when those rules apply ("Go and serve that lady by carrying her bags." "Go buy that man a sandwich." "Go shoot hoops with that kid"). By obeying these rules, we are greeted with a laundry list of rewards, most of which we never knew we wanted, but, once owned, become what we cherish most. Things like asking a stranger to church and becoming his best man.

Sorry to say but another letter regarding rules will be coming down the pipe soon,

V

∎ ∎ ∎

19 April 2014
#173
Luke 23
0530

Dear VI,

On Wednesday, as we pulled into Space 8, your mom and I were both very happy to be back in our neighborhood safe and sound. Then, as your mom and I were tightening things down and hooking up hoses, two things happened which proved we were neither safe nor sound. First, the RV shop that had been repairing our house while we were in California forgot to close the septic line, which means when I opened up the pipe to secure our hose a fermenting brew of the worst sort drenched my hands and bare feet. That sounds bad, and under normal circumstances it would have been, but then as I stood there doused in doo, checking to see if I had any open wounds, I heard a thud.

Somehow you managed to crawl out of your car seat and fell head first off of the bench in front of our house. We did not see it happen, but your mom and I both heard the distinct sound of baby skull on cement. Your mom saw you first, and her scream told me my ears were correct. Like a flash I was beside you. Your mom already held you close, and together all three of us bawled at what had happened. I came unglued and, for some reason, picked up the car seat and threw it as hard as I could into the woods while screaming, "Are you kidding me?!" I have no idea why I did that.

Five minutes later you were all laughs again, and I was walking through the woods with a bottle of hand sanitizer looking for your car seat. You cannot fathom how horrible your parents felt. The knowledge that your pain stemmed from our lack of parenting makes me sicker than my sopping septic sandals.

The doctor had a more relaxed approach. "He's a boy. You haven't seen anything yet." It is always refreshing to have the thoughts of the experienced. Because tomorrow is Easter, I decided to read Luke 23 which gives the account of Christ from conviction through crucifixion and into the tomb. This was the first year I read these verses as a father. I felt as though I was reading them for the first time. I responded to your skinned forehead by acting completely irrational. Imagine God watching His Son with whom He was well-pleased getting beat, spat on, and eventually crucified by people He had made in His image. He had the power to stop the proceedings at any moment by whatever means He desired—fire from Heaven, angels, turning the crowd into ants. But God, out of His love and devotion for us, let it happen because He knew that without His Son's going through what He did, you and I could not be saved. I write this letter with you on my lap. You are so strong and wiggly; it has taken me hours. I am continuing to better appreciate the power that lies in the love between a father and his boy.

I cherish you, my scab-headed child,

V

■ ■ ■

21 April 2014
#174
1 Thessalonians: 2 and 3
0600

Dear VI,

I have always imagined myself speaking to men about God, life, and how one does not function properly without the other. I have wanted that from a young age, and I do believe a time is coming when helping groups of men will take up a large chunk of my time. Only recently have I looked back on my life and realized that the experiences I have been through, good and bad, are critical to an effective ministry. In college I used to think I wasn't climbing the ladder fast enough, that God had forgotten my hopes and desires, and that I was ready to effectively impact the hearts of men. Those thoughts prove how foolish and unready I was. I look back on that season and thank the Lord for saving me from myself. I burn with shame when I consider how proud I was in possessing none of the right tools. It was as stupid as thinking, "My master needs a hammer; I've got a glue gun. Whatever, close enough." It would have been a complete embarrassment for a multitude of reasons. Obvious reasons like I was deathly afraid of speaking in public, and less obvious reasons, like the fact that I had no real-life experience.

How does a man relate to the brokenhearted without ever enduring heartbreak? How does a dad relate to fathers without being a parent? How can I effectively communicate to a world full of men stuck in stressful dead end jobs if I spent my life surfing and playing music? The exhaustion a man feels, the dread he battles each morning when the alarm goes off, the ever-creeping chest tightness…it is unimaginable until felt, but, once touched, it is permanent. The reality sparks sympathy which ignites a kind of passion that will motivate a man to do whatever it takes to truly impact.

Last night before bed, I read 1 Thessalonians 2 and 3. In 3:6-10 Paul talks about how he and his men worked for their food. He reminds the people that he is a full-time missionary and had the right to ask the Thessalonians to support his team, but, instead, they *earned* each meal. I dare you to call these men *lazy*. As I drifted into sleep with these chapters fresh in my mind, I was reminded that the Christian life is a game of endurance. I guarantee Paul did not hop out of bed every morning bright-eyed and bushy-tailed. He was constantly asking for strength, everlasting peace, and a deeper understanding of God. He did not, however, ask to feel *chipper* or *sprightly*.

In 3:13 he does mention the word "tired," but it is not used in the way you might think. "Never get tired of doing good." Take a second to make the distinction between that sentence and "Never let yourself get too sleepy." Living on mission for God is a strenuous grind. Endure till you can't then keep on enduring.

The purpose is worth the training,

V

■ ■ ■

23 April 2014
#175
Exodus 20:8-11
0612

Dear VI,

Like I told you a while back, I have been spending some daily time learning more about the Ten Commandments—10 practical guidelines that will help man have a fruitful existence. Today I wanted to touch on one in particular that I am discovering I am not obeying like I should. Commandment Four, "Observe the Sabbath." My last letter mentioned that the Christian life is hard. It is not always refreshing; we do not always wake up raring to go. Well, because Jesus loves us so much, He included a commandment that, when followed, is a major combatant against burnout. It is practical, it is healthy, it is genius. So naturally, people (the Pharisees in particular) created a long list of rules (1001 to be exact), which transformed a day of rest into a day of rules. Rules that answered questions like: If an old woman falls over on the Sabbath would it constitute work to help her up? Or can we leave her until the next day? How injured must she be before help is not a sin?

Until recently I have not taken Sabbath as seriously as I should. I confused the word "rest" with *lazy*, and they are not the same thing. The Sabbath was designed so we would be forced to recharge our batteries. We worship God through acknowledging He rested by doing likewise—just like we do during the week when we work hard, keep our house in order, and take care of our bodies. The Sabbath gives us a chance to put aside the toil of work and take a nap in the peace that whatever is in need of doing can wait because God loves us and says, "Put that stuff aside for now. It is more important to Me that you get your strength up."

It is worth recognizing that one man's Sabbath may look very different from another man's. I like to watch a movie or read a book. I play guitar some weeks, and other times a surf or a hike might be what my body needs in order to feel refreshed. Others may like to tinker around their garage, paint a picture, or talk on the phone. All of these are great so long as you are using them with the intention of refreshment, acknowledging that today my Savior rested so I will too. The human body simply does not have what it takes to work all day, every day. It can keep up with the demand for a while, but without the proper rest, it will positively be torn down. It is basic mechanics. Any machine without proper maintenance will break. It is that simple.

Our God loves us so much that He gave us the perfect ratio of work to rest so that we may stay sharp, healthy, and most effectively further His glorious kingdom.

Rest is as important as work,

V

■ ■ ■

25 April 2014
#176
Matthew 18:15, 2 Thessalonians 3:15
0603

Dear VI,

In a former life when I was bigger, stupider, and sported a gigantic mustache, I worked as a bouncer at a very swanky night club. I stood guard for famous basketball players, boxers, and musicians. You know the place with a long line of greased-up guys and women in tiny black dresses? I was the man in the front maintaining order. The money was decent, and my boss was fair. Overall, I enjoyed my time there, but looking back I see it did not at all help enrich my life in any way, shape, or form for all of the reasons you can probably guess. It was a den where wicked people got together and did wicked stuff. The experience taught me a lot of things I am not proud of (like how to properly exchange cash through a handshake). But it also taught me a lot about confrontation.

When people (especially rich people) get together with foolish intentions, there is always one who has to try and outdo the other. This goes back to the law of one-upmanship discussed in Letter 138. The man who will not stop touching a waitress, the girl doing drugs at the bar, the guy who drinks too much and starts getting physical. I was in charge of defusing the situation by walking up to a complete stranger to inform him, "Sir, you are making our guests uncomfortable. Let's take a walk outside. Please pay your $900 bar tab and come with me." Things didn't always go smoothly, but overall, I was good at resolving issues.

This morning I read Luke 17:3. Jesus tells His followers to rebuke a brother living in sin, and I looked back on all those people with whom I initiated confrontation. It was valuable training. I think if I can tell some obnoxious drunk to use his indoor voice, I must be able to sit down with a brother in Christ and bring up the awkward stuff. But despite my background, I still dread confrontation. I think everyone does.

My season in security also showed me how beneficial a little confrontation can be when done in the right way. Yes, I was swung at; yes, I was threatened; but you would be surprised at the number of times people would react positively. No doubt, a lack of accountability is a huge problem facing Christian men today. Men need to watch out for each other. But they oftentimes don't because it can be awkward, unpleasant, and rarely has any sort of foreseeable positive outcome. An evidence of man's lack of accountability to each other is seen in the names and threats that have come my way after confronting a brother. It is far worse than anything I ever experienced working at the club. There is a sick sort of desperation that shows up in the form of excuses, backpedaling, justifying, and shifting blame. It clearly shows that the person is not used to having these types of conversations.

Christian men are now so used to the dark corner of their lives safely hidden in the shadows that when the muck is suddenly thrust into the spotlight, they are caught catastrophically off guard. Most people make a mad dash to turn off the light instead of dealing with what it is shining upon. They might try to cover it up with a sheet or demand everyone averts their eyes. I have played the role of the light and the exposed. I know personally that the dread of bringing up the issue feels very much like the sick guilt and shame felt when your sins are on the other end of the flashlight.

We have not discussed one option. What happens if you do nothing? What happens if you think, "I'm going to keep quiet because I don't know if saying anything would do any good." Well then, when that person continues to slide deeper into sin and things keep going from bad to worse, you will think, "I wonder if it would have gotten this bad if I had said something back then." If you had simply said something about your friend's flirting with that coworker, he might not have committed adultery. If you had just mentioned his excessive drinking, he might have not ended up hooked on harder drugs. You may be the key to saving your friend from a world of hurt. So who cares if it's uncomfortable! It is the better option.

At the end of the day, the fact of the matter is that we are *obligated* as Christians, as Galatians 6:1 reads, to "restore with a spirit of gentleness." What will come of it is not for you to worry about. You can throw all of the options and scenarios out the window. Our job is to obey.

Finally, what happens when a Christian shows the courage to confront a brother who is willing to receive? What happens when the rebuked man realizes his friend is trying to help? Strength, restoration, testimony, and a million other good results that can only happen when two Christian warriors do life with their arms around each other. It is beautiful to experience and absolutely worth the cost. I'm sure this letter is not exactly motivating. I know almost everything about confrontation is unattractive. It is, however, a critically important part of being a man. I would be a coward for not discussing it.

I have been called out in love before, and it changed my life,

V

P.S. Scripture is kind enough to tell us how to go about confronting a brother. The words "gentle," "just between the two of you," and "forgive" are just a few of the words designed to give insight.

■ ■ ■

27 April 2014
#177
Hebrews 13:5
0901

Dear VI,

I hate to admit it, but you turned eight months old. Right now I am watching you naked as your first day on earth, crawling in a tight little circle on your blanket placed on the kitchen floor. We are in Mayport again, and this time, instead of horizontal rain and a leaky roof, we are enjoying a cool breeze and sunshine. It has been an amazing weekend.

You are turning into an abnormally content baby. You sit for 30 minutes at a time carefully examining the contents of your small toy box. You look at each one, chew it here and there, then set it to the side. I think your pleasant nature is due to situations like the one that unfolded right before my eyes. You decided to go potty on your blanket, which has made this trailer stink to high heaven. But your mom came to the rescue and mentioned neither mess nor smell. She only said, "Look at that precious paddy. It's like we're going all natural." She is exactly why you are such a content little baby. You feed off her calm vibes.

The older you get, the more you will realize that your mom's reaction to this situation and others is rare. Look at your friends' parents and guess how they would react to a soiled blanket in a brand-new home. I just witnessed a dad act as if the world was going to implode because his child got sand on his towel—*while at the beach*. His reaction should not be, but has become, the norm.

Jesus was very clear about what was unacceptable. He had standards and stuck to them. He was rigid on the things that actually mattered. But there is no record of Jesus being picky about dirt on His sleeping mat or reprimanding the cook for underdoing His fish. He was happy with calories in His body and sleep when He could get it. We know that Jesus got tired and slept deeply, but nothing is said about His needing a sleep mask to do so.

What an excellent way to live! This is the type of mentality we want you to be nurtured with, and it pleases me so much to see it happening. You pick on a kid or disrespect your mother, your life will get difficult quick. We have standards and things we will not tolerate. But if you break a cup or forget your backpack or most anything like that, life will go on, and we will overcome. If we, as parents, reacted the same to cheating on a test and not putting a smelly shirt in the dirty clothes, how would that response be Christ-like?

Pick your battles,

V

■ ■ ■

28 April 2014
#178
Proverbs 7
0556

Dear VI,

Yesterday, after returning to basecamp here at NAS, I rented a paddleboard from the marina and paddled out to explore the Saint John River.

This was not my first rodeo on a standup paddleboard, so naturally I took off the leash, set aside the life jacket, and left the help whistle behind. Mine was a great paddle. The still swamp air made the brackish water look like oil. I dove in a few times to cool off, but aside from that I stayed on the board and thanked God for the feeling a man gets when immersed in nature.

Upon returning, the manager implied I was a skilled paddler by giving me the backhanded compliment, "You're so big and hairy I was excited to watch you fall, but I'll be darned if you're not part fish." Thanks? After that insulting bit of flattery, he dove straight into a lecture explaining why I must always wear the life vest and have the safety whistle around my neck at all times. On and on he rambled until he finally climaxed with, "That way I can aid you in distress." Of course, my pride started to surface, and I wanted to argue. I wanted to point out the fact that he was aided by a walker, and looked as if a stiff breeze would blow him away. How was he supposed to "aid" me? I had grooves in my tongue, I was holding it so tight.

I wish I could say my self-control took over, but it's more likely that the amount of arguments I wanted to make caused my mind to overload, and all I managed to say was, "Lessons for next time."

Over the last couple of weeks, I have written several letters detailing various aspects of rules. Today I present the man who sticks to the letter of the law regardless of circumstance, a modern-day Pharisee. I can confidently say that the marina did not create the help whistle rule for men who seem to be part-fish. It's more likely that a six-year-old kid from the Midwest almost drowned, and to avoid any future lawsuits, the whistle rule was put into place. What annoys me is that my knight-in-shining armor was sitting inside with the television blaring and a ten-gallon bag of chips. Even if he had heard my whistle, he was going nowhere fast. But, you see, the rulebook doesn't state that someone must be outside with a watchful eye; it only details the whistle. There is no insight, no wisdom, and no logic. As you can probably guess I don't like this, but I do accept it. The next time I go out, there will be a whistle around my neck.

Looking forward to paddling with you,

V

. . .

30 April 2014
#179
Genesis 2:18, John 19:26, Mark 12:30-31
0552

Dear VI,

From Genesis to Revelation and everywhere in between, relationship shows up constantly. I would say a main Bible theme is God's desiring relationship with His people. The first thing God declared "not good" was man's being alone. Even as Jesus hung on the cross, He made sure His mom was looked after by asking "the disciple who He loved" (probably John) to look after her. God's greatest commandment is to love God and love others. The list of examples regarding the importance of relationships is as long as you want it to be. I challenge you to find other examples.

Last night I was shaving as I do every night, and your mom walked into the bathroom with her hair all messed up. She had on an extremely unattractive face and said, "My name is Cornelius Homely," in a voice you might expect to hear coming from a two-foot alien. (She does this sort of thing all the time.) Recently I heard her yell from our bedroom, "Honey, there are a lot of ugly-face options out there," and I assumed correctly that she had been making faces at herself again.

It dawned on me last night that no one on earth would think your mom is capable of being a "Cornelius Homely." I am so blessed to be in such an intimate friendship with my wife that she can try on her most repulsive look while still feeling totally confident in my feelings toward her. Not Facebook friends, not drinking buddies, not coworkers, not someone I am cool with at school, but real genuine friends.

I recently read that friendship develops in three stages. The first is *fact*. "My name is Lewis, my eyes are blue, and I graduated from high school in 2003." If my facts align with the stranger and vice versa, stage two, which is opinion, begins to enter the picture. "I think Kobe is too old to get a giant contract; West Coast surfing is way better." And finally, if the facts and opinion are found pleasing, the third stage (feelings) begins to be expressed. "I think God is telling us to move into a trailer. I am really upset about my dad never calling. Your profanity offends me." It is rare for a friendship to last in stage three.

A friendship free to express itself should always be cherished. A man and his wife are capable of higher echelons of friendship. Sex, first off, is the *most* intimate physical act two people can do. Start that before marriage, and you are guaranteed to alter and usually dismember whatever friendship there might have been. But I am talking specifically about the "Cornelius" stage. In the Cornelius stage, you can dance like an idiot or sing an improvised tune without the fear of rejection. You don't mind walking around in your underwear after a night of enchiladas. If you have food poisoning, you want your friend there for comfort—even when you are completely vulnerable and wrapped around the toilet. There is no secret too deep; there is no situation too embarrassing.

I pray with all of my heart that one day you will find a mate with whom you will share an all-encompassing comfort. You will never hear either of your parents say we have it all figured out or that we got the marriage thing on lockdown. But I am confident we are on the right track, and you, my little boy, will grow up seeing our Friend, Jesus, in the middle of your parents' relationship.

Half of your DNA is "homely"—the best half,

V

■ ■ ■

01 May 2014
#180
John 15:6-7
1024

Dear VI,

I have a day off! After your morning nap (which you are currently enjoy-ing), we are going to run some errands in the hopes of having a clear week-end schedule. I am sitting outside on our picnic bench acclimating to the humid Florida summer, which has officially arrived—much to the dismay of Floridians everywhere. An obnoxious amount of insects live here in the swampy south. My experience with this kind of weather is extremely limited. Ninety-five percent of all I know has been learned from movies, which never seem to have any bugs except for that one pesky mosquito that always gets squashed on the back of a sweaty neck.

This first trailer summer will be a totally new experience. The beauty of our home is the opportunity it affords us to spend time outdoors. But this climate is oppressive and wants to drive us indoors. If we submit, I foresee our small home becoming increasingly cramped. I refuse to be trapped in my own home, so I am forcing myself to acclimate to this new set of circumstances. People once lived here without air conditioning, so I can get used to it. Right?

As sweat drips from my nose to this page, I feel I must give Jesus more credit in the friendship shared by your mother and me. Our first two years of marriage were hell. We were one signature away from divorce. Our success is due to your mom and me working together and individually to place Christ in the very dead center of our friendship. You hear people throw around "Christianese" like, "Put more focus on the Lord" in a tone that might be used when suggesting I blink by closing my eyelids or walk by alternating my left and right foot. It's not that easy! Most times the issue runs deeper.

Focusing on Jesus sounds great, but it's hard to concentrate with all these habits and regrets interrupting concentration. Your mom and I walked a long, arduous road and lived to tell the tale. If you keep Christ as the center of your life from the beginning to the end, you will never need to travel this road. This is not to say you will never experience hard times. Of course you will! But you cannot break a habit if you have none in need of breaking. There is no need to soften the heart that is not hard.

John 15:6-7 reads, "Part from me and become a branch in the burn pile; stay joined to me and any request will be granted." Note the word *joined*. It doesn't say "visit me consistently" or "attend church semi-regularly." Be joined as an organism as critical to survival as a heart and lungs. I am a man who has experienced both Christian and worldly marriage with the same woman. I can say with authority that, while a worldly marriage is possible, it is puny and pathetic when put beside a marriage centered upon Jesus. Anything else is like eating candy with the wrapper on.

Don't settle,

V

■ ■ ■

02 May 2014
#181
Matthew 7:5
0615

Dear VI,

One of my collateral duties here on base is "Assistant Chief Fitness Leader." I get up early a couple of times a month and put sailors who are deemed "out of standards" through a workout designed by the command to drop some pounds in preparation for the Physical Readiness Test (PRT). This workout consists of measuring body mass index and watching every sailor complete the required push-ups, sit-ups, and the 1.5-mile run. I always look forward to the PRT because it means two weeks out of the office and the wearing of Navy-issued workout gear instead of my heavy work uniform. It also means observing 1,400 young men and women do the bare minimum physically. The Navy has set the bar low, and most put in just enough to ensure they stay even with that bar.

I always try and blow the bar away because I want to be an example and, selfishly, a high enough score is awarded two free vacation days that can be put in conjunction with a weekend. That's right! A four-day weekend for being healthy! Apparently, paid time of is not enough motivation for most people, but it is for me! Today is my day to take the test. I have spent a chunk of time training specifically for it; 101 sit-ups, 84 push-ups, and a 500-yard swim in under eight minutes.

From what I see, the pursuit of physical health is a seriously neglected part of the Christian faith. Mood swings, poor sleep, depression, and a lack of overall confidence are common mental side effects that come with a lack of exercise. A considerable number of physical ailments also accompany bad health habits, including back problems, bone and joint pain, hypertension, diabetes, and increased risk of stroke or heart attack. This line of reasoning is not biblical; it's medical fact. I would argue that a man is unable to be *as* effective in ministry if he is experiencing any of those avoidable symptoms. How can he be?

A Christian's poor physical health also gives nonbelievers a reason to employ the "pot calling the kettle black" strategy. "How dare you suggest I have a gambling problem? You eat everything you can get your hands on!" I have to admit, there is some validity to that claim. A lack of diligence regarding diet and exercise does result in visible signs suggesting laziness, gluttony, and a lack of self-control. This assertion is not biblical; this is a cultural fact.

Am I implying that all Christians should be physical specimens? Absolutely not! Obsessing over food and appearance is just as bad as paying it no mind. There is this idea amongst believers that as long as they are not partaking in any of what I call "the big three" (drinking, recreational drugs, and fornication), everything else is up for grabs. This is not so. Physical health needs to be looked at like devotions, or prayer, or time spent nurturing relationships; the goal is balance. I say eat the biggest piece of cake you can get your hands on—but not every day. I say enjoy an entire day of popcorn and movies—but not every day. The goal is putting forth consistent, genuine effort without getting consumed with the fine print or beating yourself up every time you slip. God calls our body a temple, *and* He created food for us to enjoy. That is a biblical fact.

As for me, I am going to eat some oatmeal and find out if all this training has paid off,

V

P.S. I think fathers have an extra charge to be healthy. It is important for them to be able to keep up and play with their kids.

■ ■ ■

04 May 2014
#182
Philippians 1:3-5
0900

Dear VI,

You are a minute away from crawling. Right now you're sitting on a San Francisco 49ers blanket that was a given to me by my grandma for my seventh birthday. We have so little, and somehow this raggedy old blanket made the cut. Just goes to show how much we value memories.

Yesterday you and I made a memory—one I will cherish forever. I decided to build you a small bed inside the top bunk we already have. But I needed a helper, and because it is your bed, I figured you were the perfect choice. We scribbled down some measurements then headed to Lowe's for supplies. We chatted most of the car ride until the excitement of a big home improvement store struck you speechless. The first thing we passed was home appliances, and I explained that the last time you were in this section you were in your mom's tummy, and I was wandering around completely perplexed how anyone can afford a new dryer. We had just moved to Florida and were learning the costs that come with homeownership. But now, in our new home, I am spending a fraction of the cost creating a cozy little bed for you. God is so good!

We picked up our supplies. I made sure to explain what each item was. You checked the quality by grabbing everything before it entered the cart. Then we went to Target for some final odds and ends. You were totally asleep, which I completely understand. Lowe's is a draining experience. Eventually, we returned to our little home where I shaped pipe, then cut and sewed cloth while you sat beside me, observing with a watchful eye. I doubled up your sleeping pad, put your favorite toys inside, and let you take her for a test drive. You really seem to love it!

Some day you will be too tall for your custom "cave." It will be time to sprawl out on the entire bed. Your size will push us into a new season, and our first project together will go into the dumpster. I am sure when that day comes I will feel a tinge of sadness. After all, that heap of PVC represents a day you and I spent being creative together. That's okay; life moves on and gives us constant opportunities to make memories. I cannot wait to make more with you.

Thank you for spending your Saturday with me, buddy,

V

■ ■ ■

05 May 2015
#183
Mark 6:3; Colossians 3:23; Proverbs 10:5; 12:11, 14, 24; 13:11; 14:23; 16:6;
28:19
0528

Dear VI,

It occurred to me as I sat here praying that Jesus built stuff all the time
with His earthly dad. His old man was a carpenter by trade, which means
Jesus' family had a business building stuff with wood. Back in His day,
however, there wasn't much lumber, so it is likely he also worked with a
lot of stone. Can you imagine our Savior, at 10 years old, hauling rock or
swinging a hammer in the hot Middle Eastern sun, doing His part to keep
food on the table? This is an awesome part of His testimony. Jesus was a
kid with calloused hands who stuck to clean Jewish eating, which means
He was probably pretty lean and fit. He honored His earthly father by
working diligently and obeying orders.

Consider this: With our God, no one can claim "Well, Jesus doesn't
understand what it feels like to work hard all day." The argument could
be made that making the Heavens and the earth, and everything on earth
constitutes hard work, but this is *God* we are talking about! The word
"hard" is not in His vocabulary. Neither is the word "easy." With God,
everything simply "is." God came to earth as a man on a mission to pay
our ransom and while on earth His physical body felt the strain of serious
manual labor. He saved the world while being a contributing member of a
humble family. That servility is incredible!

When you are older, you will be given obligations that will contribute to the maintaining of this household. Believe me, your parents are
excited to give you a fun childhood but, like Jesus, your help around
the house is a requirement. My personal opinion is that too many kids
sit in front of the television on a sunny day with a bowl of ice cream
while their parents do their laundry, carry in the groceries, clean their
room, and wonder why they are so exhausted. You will not run into

this problem—not because we have neither television nor ice cream, but because you are the type of person who desires an active role in our awesome family. I can feel it.

Your bedroom is a four-by-six square! How long could cleaning it take?

V

■ ■ ■

08 May 2014
#184
1 Peter 5:8-9
0612

Dear VI,

In 2011 I packed my Honda Element with your mom's and my most needed essentials and made the 19-hour drive up the coast to give marriage another try. My best friend Lucas flew from Oregon to Newport Beach to help pack and make the road trip. Three weeks earlier, your mom and I were on the fast track to divorce. If it were not for the constant prayer and pestering of Lucas and his wife, Grace, I don't think your mom and I would still be together. I probably wouldn't have anyone to write letters to. (This is a perfect example of Letter 176 discussing the importance of accountability among brothers.)

We did the drive in two days, stopping twice to surf in central California. Most of our time in the car was spent smoking pipes and listening to *The Screwtape Letters* on audiobook. We would listen to a track then pause and discuss what we had heard until we caught ourselves going down some tangent. At that point, we would start the CD again. After two days of surf, tobacco, and C.S. Lewis, we arrived at Lucas' home in rainy Salem, Oregon. Usually at the end of a road trip whoever is in the car hates the car and all its passengers, but not us. Both of us wanted to keep going to Washington and on to Canada!

But he had work in the morning, and I had a marriage to restore, so I gave him a hug, punched him in the arm, and said, "See you this weekend."

It's ironic that on one of my all-time favorite adventures, I learned a lot about the Devil. I am not talking about the learning one does to pass a test—memorize flashcards, circle in the scantron, and dump the data. I am talking about wisdom that comes from understanding. I gained applicable insight into the tricks and attacks of our Enemy. (Notice my wording here, "I gained applicable insight." I am *not* saying I solved the mystery and no longer get attacked.) For example, I learned that the Enemy's first wave of attack is often to make someone feel as if his mood directly correlates to something he is doing wrong or something someone else has done to him.

Keep this fact in mind while reading what comes next. For the last few weeks, your mom and I were riding a genuine spiritual high. I felt the lift of Jesus encouraging me, "You are looking for a new identity, and you are on the right track. Just wait and see how I can use you. You are going to be blown away."

Lately it has been a season where God has done huge obvious things daily. Visible examples scream, "I am here with you!" This all changed on Tuesday, I came home from work to a dirty house and a wife with a tear-streaked face. She told me she felt attacked and, like an idiot, I said she needed to "suck it up and stop making excuses," which I would normally *never* say!

We argued, did not pray over our food for the first time in years, and ate in silence. I did not pray over you. I went to bed alone and covered myself in a blanket of feeling sorry for myself. I totally fell for the Enemy's trick! "It's her fault I'm upset!" My feelings were justified because my wife can't keep my trailer clean. While I lay there blaming my spouse for my feeling poorly, the following verse came to my mind: "Be alert and of sober mind. Your enemy, the devil, prowls around like a roaring lion looking for someone to devour. Resist him, standing firm in the faith, because you know that the family of believers throughout the world is undergoing the same kind of sufferings." That verse sobered me up. I pulled back the covers to go make amends, but before I could, I was struck by a wave of fatigue. I did not move until my alarm went off eight hours later. That day

290 LEWIS SEELEY BRADSHAW V

was hands-down the busiest day I have ever had at work. The hectic day pushed yesterday's events out of focus until after work when, in the pool, all of this letter's contents clicked. It was as if I saw my life from my West Coast trip to that moment and understood that the entire chain of events fit together.

My household was under the first wave of attacks mentioned by Screwtape. How did I not see that? Your mom and I did a lot of praying that night and feel peace knowing that if we resist, he will flee. I am a prime example of what might happen if a man does not stay alert. I was on a spiritual mountain and let myself believe I was invincible. The Enemy attacked where it hurt most—my home. My wife, in her wisdom, said she felt the attack, and I stepped right on the land mine. Stay alert.

I take great joy in knowing that the battle is won,

V

■ ■ ■

09 May 2014
#185
Ephesians 6:12
0706

Dear VI,

Yesterday while at work, not one hour after finishing my letter detailing the spiritual attack our family is absorbing, one of my worst fears happened. You fell out of the bed I made you. Your mom didn't mention it until last night because I came home for lunch with a friend. How gracious she was to spare my feelings by not mentioning it in the presence of company! I still don't understand how it happened. I have examined every inch of that bed and see no possible way you could have slid out.

The thud of your innocent body hitting the floor woke up your mom. She said she was in there before she was conscious and found you wedged between the trash can and the wall, inches from the metal ladder we use to access the loft. But here is the kicker: that five-foot fall did not leave you with so much as a scratch. Your mom says you started to cry but seconds later you were all smiles and funny noises. My warrior! My little champion! Every night I hold you close and pray that our Lord will send powerful angels to protect you. It appears that prayer was answered. Your falling five feet is like my falling 18 feet. Yet you did it in such a way that you both landed safely and avoided many possible life-altering obstacles.

I do not believe your finding your way out of that bed less than an hour after my previous letter was coincidence. Neither is landing unscathed. I do not believe that every time misfortune or argument breaks out it is due to a demon. They are not flying around dismantling beds. The spiritual realm is as real as the words on this page, but the Devil is not the sole culprit of all misgiving. Your bed is fortified. If I took a wrecking ball to our trailer, your bed would still be in once piece.

Have a great day, tough guy,

V

■ ■ ■

13 May 2014
#186
Revelation 1:8
0541

Dear VI,

Right now you are staring at me from your perch on your mom's lap and making these little noises. It is a repeated loop of something like kisses followed by bubbles popping and baby laughter. It is a beautiful melody that hypnotizes your parents. Maintaining such a positive attitude while in your current condition is admirable. You are sick, very sick. You have developed a cough which, throughout the last few days, has gotten steadily worse. Now you are running a fever and coughing so hard that you are stimulating the gag reflex and vomiting. Your mom and I (especially your mom) have been up and down throughout the night to check your status. You hate everything that helps—like sucking snot from your nose and giving you baby Tylenol®. We cannot keep food in your gut, but we sure keep trying.

The most negative comment your mom has made was just now after banging her shin on the bed: "I have had better times." Your sickness coincides perfectly with your grandpa's visit, which is not ideal. He loves you so much. He is as easygoing as a leaf on a breeze, but it is not like we have a separate wing for him to stay. After three days in a 400-square-foot box with a sick kid and two sleep-deprived parents, anyone would be ready to move on.

So what does a man make of these situations? Honestly, I'm not sure. Each situation is unique, which is why wisdom is always a great asset to have close by. Life is not a piece of Ikea furniture, that's for sure. I can't tell you what to do, but I can recommend some things *not* to do. Do not let a tough situation define you. A worldly person is always searching for someone or something to define himself and, in turn, bring fulfillment. Most people seem to choose clothes. "I wear Prada; I am wealthy and classy but I still know how to have a good time." "I wear Volcom; I am an anti-establishment surfer." Social media usernames give people the opportunity to inflict their desired identity on others. I have a friend whose username is "benchking," and another goes by "skateboard_or_die" It doesn't get much more obvious than that.

Still others try defining themselves as "victims"—the divorced, the cancer patient, the unemployed. Some people cannot wait to let you know about their set of difficult circumstances. "Hello, I would shake your hand, but my arthritis is all flared up on account of my 60-hour work week on the computer. I got carpal tunnel right before I was laid off. Then my wife left me for an arthritis-free man." Talking in such a way does leave an identity impression, but never the intended one. If I talked to this man, I wouldn't remember anything except his woeful state. I would probably ask your mom, "What was the name of that guy with the hand thing?"

Situations in your life will no doubt explain things about you, but they should never define you. For example, I have a shaved head and face. Why? I am active duty military. My being in the Navy explains my look, but I am not just a sailor; that would sell my life short. Why is that woman living alone? Her husband passed away, but she is not just a widow! When all is told, at the very core, what we are is created by God in His image. We are His children. When a man applies this relationship to his situation, it will shed truth on the overall picture. I am about to go to work with watery eyes and a constant yawn because I am a sleepy dad. But I am going to labor as hard as I can and stay sharp because what I *truly* am is a child of the great I AM.

Get well soon, my boy! You have a doctor's appointment in a couple hours. Hopefully, we will get some answers. Stay strong and positive,

V

■ ■ ■

15 May 2014
#187
Jonah 2:8
0600

Dear VI,

You're such a generous lad. You passed along your sickness to your mother. The queen is down for the count. My medical scope of practice is limited, but I know if I were to look for help in the magazines at the grocery store, instead of a cure, I would find suggestions on how to transform into someone else altogether. "Get ripped abs in 30 days." "Look 10 years younger with this diet." These titles effectively say, "How you are is not okay. What I am offering is better than your current situation."

Without God, humans have no other choice but to forge ahead, searching for someone or something that might give insight into the mystery of who they are. "If I could only just..." is no doubt among the most common day-to-day thoughts rolling around in a person's head. "If I could only just... fall in love, get that job, drive that car, look like Batman," etc. But it's all pyrite—fool's gold. Nothing ever pans out, and when the novelty wears off, disappointment sets in. Falling in love is great, but marriage is among life's greatest challenges. A nice car is fun—until it breaks. And everyone knows there is only one Batman. Everything earthly—people and possessions—will fail, break, and then eventually pass away. Literally no worldly material or identity can fill a void long-term.

Our culture keeps falling for the same trick because if a man accepts the truth that worldly pursuits cannot form lasting identity, they must then conclude one of two things: 1) They either accept that life has no ultimate purpose, or 2) They accept there is a God and allow Him to become their Ruler. Either option has life-altering implications, some of which are undesirable; so instead of deciding, they try again.

I once heard a commentator say, "Everyone is holding a can of peaches, but Jesus is the only One with a can opener." Sadly, instead of going to God and asking for assistance, they smash the can with a rock, throw it, and find different implements to stab it with, which gets them nothing more than a dented can and an increased hunger.

I say the best way to avoid doing this is through a series of checks and balances while always remembering that the solution to the problem of identity lies in Christ. He is our identity, but the role He has for us to play is different every day. Some days we are comforters, other days we are leaders, and every day we are Christians. Our God is alive and moving, and if we are in Him, our lives will also be moving. The only way to avoid walking around with a dented can of peaches is by making the daily decision to identify the King who holds the can opener.

If I put my identity in my marriage, what happens to my identity when my wife is sick in bed? If it is held in my job, what happens when I get an annoying coworker? If it is in the ocean, what happens when the conditions are bad? If it is sports, what happens when my back is hurt? The very thing that was lifted up becomes despised. That which was idolized is demonized. The old is thrown into the pile, and another is lifted up until the man dies of starvation beside a can of delicious peaches. When a man puts his identity in Christ, he then becomes more *himself* than ever. It's as simple as that.

You are a stud,

V

■ ■ ■

17 May 2014
#188
Ephesians 1:1-14
0700

Dear VI,

I had duty turnover this fine Saturday morning. I had to be at work at 0530 to give a report of yesterday's happenings to two very hungover sailors. I do not envy the day they are about to endure. The report was more like a short phrase, "Yesterday nothing happened." I had to walk the two minutes to work in order to deliver that message during which time I praised God that my commute is literally a walk in the park. I was back home in bed at 0610, but instead of sleeping your mom and I got cozy; she showed me pictures from last week. The pictures were taken while my nose was to the grindstone. Here you are smiling with a saline bottle, your favorite toy we named "Salinea." Here you are outside in your walker, clapping your chubby hands. You're so beautiful. The thought of my missing these moments tears me up sometimes.

At the moment I am sitting outside surrounded by tall pine trees and listening to the pleasant tunes of the mockingbirds. It is cool, clear, perfect. I understand my role as provider will require that I am gone most days. But I have trouble accepting that I get to enjoy the sound of the birds maybe twice a week and experience your precious moments through pictures. As hard a pill as that is to swallow, I also recognize that my being gone during the week helps me better appreciate the time we do spend together. It's true, absence makes the heart grow fonder, but I wish that was not true.

It is very possible that the reason I love this picturesque moment is because I spent all week in a stuffy cubicle. Opposites accentuate. A mountaintop would not exist if not for the valley. We can always look at a difficult time with a tinge of thankfulness because, without it, a season of blessing would not feel as blessed.

Just because an action exposes its counterpart does not mean that a moment shouldn't be enjoyed for enjoyment's sake. I need to do a better job of enjoying each moment for no other reason than it is once in a life-time. Only when a man is walking with the Holy Spirit does he know deep down inside that every second in his life is a gift. He knows each breath has purpose and he can shape his attitude to enjoy every breath.

I know people like this—Grandpa Freeman, for example. I find myself battling spontaneous fits of annoyance coupled with jealousy when I am around him. I want to yell "How can you think eating that dry toast is so sublime!?" I feel this way because I am far from mastering the art of living in a given moment. My tendency is to stand in a valley, look up to the peak of the mountain, then put my head down and repeat, "I will get there. I will get there." But by doing this, my sole focus becomes the summit. I miss all the little stuff happening around me during the assent.

I have told you that following Jesus is an adventure that does not end until eternity, and today I would like to add that the adventure is just as full of little precious moments as it is grand memorable ones. Writing beneath the songs of birds, walking to work with damp grass underfoot, a casual conversation with a coworker, eating a good piece of fruit, all of these moments are precious. Make sure you never become so goal-oriented that you race past the subtle pleasurable treats. God placed them there just for you.

I'm excited to spend the day with you,

V

P.S. Little *choices* are also important! (Read Letter 84 for more.)

■ ■ ■

18 May 2014
#189
Ephesians 2:10
0710

Dear VI,

Again my letters capture how quickly things change. Let it serve as a lesson to the man who claims "Things could not be worse." Sometimes I think God takes that sort of talk as a personal challenge: "You think things are tough? Try this on for size!"

Case in point, I woke up with pink eye. My job as an optician has made me painfully aware of the signs and symptoms. I can't imagine what people would think if they turned on the television and saw our situation. Here is a family in a trailer; the wife and son look gaunt and sickly. Their slack faces suggest they have not slept for days. They lay in sweat-stained sheets and endure coughing their way through yet another humid day. Who is that man outside writing, and why is his eye discharging contagious goop? Why is he sitting on a wet park bench with a sizeable rip in the crack of his shorts?

But what an opportunity this situation gives me to practice the very thing I wrote about yesterday. If not for the conjunctivitis, my current situation would be extremely similar to yesterday's—same trees, same birds, same rip. With a little change of perspective, I could switch my focus from our less-than-ideal circumstances to an opportunity to soak in another blue sky. Instead of thinking "Things couldn't be worse," why not think "Things could always be worse."

Just a little optimism from your pink-eyed pops,

V

■ ■ ■

19 May 2014
#190
Ecclesiastes 5:18-20
1845

Dear VI,

You have given me great joy, you bring me daily laughter, you are always challenging me to grow, and today, according to my optometrist, you gave me pink eye. I know you're wondering what a family does when the bread winner gets eye drops and two days off work. Go to the beach, of course! The beach has proved to be an excellent yardstick for measuring development. Each time we go, you are able to enjoy it a little more. Now that you are a professional crawler, a beach trip looks a lot different. With your development comes a long list of places to go, flavors to taste, and people to meet, which really cuts into any sort of relaxation your parents hoped for. I crawled beside you for hours yesterday and marveled at your ability to live transfixed in the moment. You were a great example to me in an area of my life that needs work.

Of course, anyone would be content in the moment if their days mirrored yours. Your day is a sweet dream where you rotate from breast, to play, to nap. You are not concerned about current location or how you will receive your next meal. You are given a sponge bath, massaged with sweet-smelling oils, and your bottom is pampered almost hourly. Not too shabby!

But one day you will need to be certain places at specific times, you will need to think about meals ahead of time and leave room to practice personal hygiene. As you grow and take on more responsibility, you will have no choice but to look at me as an example. I am your dad; I am your friend charged with rearing you. In some ways, you will become more like me; in other ways, I hope to become more like you. Neither of us has it all figured out, so let's grow stronger as we walk together. Relationship is a handsome thing.

You have many years of eat, play, sleep, repeat ahead of you. I pray you enjoy every second,

V

■ ■ ■

20 May 2014
#191
Ephesians 3:20
1247

Dear VI,

And the plot thickens. I joined the sick club. To be honest, I figured I would catch the bug earlier as our close quarters makes avoiding a virus impossible. My joints ache, I am dripping with sweat then shivering with cold. My throat is on fire; my stomach is angry. Things could always get worse! Right?

The last couple of weeks has seen a real influx in medical paraphernalia around the trailer, items like syringes, inhalers, bottles of baby aspirin, throat lozenges, and snot bulbs. Putting you to bed has become a marathon, and the worst part is you despise the entire process. You scream and strain with all of your might. You work up a sweat, attempting to escape the incoming bulb. You must think it the worst type of torture. After I am finished, I wrap you in my arms and pray over your deafening shrieks before handing you off to your mom. This is where the magic happens.

I sit there with tufts of missing chest hair, surrounded by medical gear, and marvel at the beauty of breast feeding. No syringes or pulleys—just God's perfect design. Your mom's body feels your illness, so it whips up a special blend to soothe you, coat your throat, and build up your immune system. I can physically see your body melt into peaceful bliss. In 30 seconds, you go from fighting for your life to all being right with the world. It is one of the most amazing things I have ever seen.

When I read a verse like Ephesians 3:20 which explains God is able to accomplish infinitely more than we humans could ever dare to hope for, my mind goes to this type of situation. What kind of a creative scientific genius must God be to conjure up something as all-encompassing as breast feeding? It took a whole lab of geniuses a decade to develop cough syrup, which is a somewhat helpful tool, but a complete joke when put beside the Lord's design.

Every once in a while I see God's creation put into contrast with man's inventions in such a way that God's perfection is wonderfully accentuated. Spend a day under the hum of electricity then step outside during a sunset. Eat a microwaved hot dog then roast fresh fish over an open flame. There is no comparing man's inventions with God's creation. Breastfeeding, sunsets, fire look exactly as they did on day one. They are free, they are practical, they serve great purpose. Mankind has the gall to pat itself on the back for the computer or combustion engine, but never considers that its invention originated in the brain, which God created, and was constructed using elements God brought into existence.

Metal, momentum, wood, electricity, heat—He created it all from nothing! When you think of it that way, it is easy to admire the Creator instead of the created.

Never forget who is in charge,

V

■ ■ ■

21 May 2014
#192
Isaiah 40:31
0947

Dear VI,

Last night you shone in an entirely new light. You were crawling in a great circle around our trailer floor, stopping occasionally to lick the palm of your hands. Then you noticed my phone, which I had strategically placed on the edge of the couch to coax you into standing up. Once that phone was in your sights, you would not be denied. The first several attempts failed and resulted in your crashing to the floor. Tears were shed before another attempt was made, but at last your relentless efforts eventually paid off. With great grunting, you found your footing and reached out to claim your prize. I was beside myself! This was primitive man's natural instinct to explore the unknown and to push his limits. Bumps and bruises were thrown to the wind. All effort was pointed toward your goal, and once you accomplished that goal, you held onto it with two hands and made faces of excitement I had never before witnessed. I felt as if I had been given a glimpse of the future.

I would wager that most people would read this and conclude your mother and I are bad parents. Fear of injury or low self-esteem has driven parents to hand their children life on a silver platter. I recently heard a mom in a restaurant instruct her husband to "give him whatever he wants so he will shut up and sit still." When I saw that wiggly five year old prior to his mom's instructions, I profiled him as a young boy in a bright, loud, sweet-smelling restaurant. Of course he is wiggly! A clear-cut case of stimulation overload. Post-instruction he was "plugged in" as they say, headphones on, eyes glued to the tablet. Why not put a Valium in his food? I saw an engaged young animal get his adventure bug crushed. NPR recently ran a story detailing how government restrictions on playground equipment are so rigid, most kids are no longer challenged. There are no limits to push. There is no chance to conquer. The playgrounds around our nation are becoming little ghost towns. This is scary because once a man loses that spirit, it is hard to get it back.

I admit there are risks involved whenever a man pushes his limits; reward, injury, victory, and defeat are all possible outcomes. I see and understand that by limiting risk the chance of injury or that feeling of defeat is also diminished, but so is the stuff a boy needs to become a man.

The spirit I saw in you when you collected yourself and gave it another shot was special. You have it, son! I've seen it! I will work hard to nurture that spirit while working even harder to give you the wisdom needed to manage it properly. It is my job as your father to rear you to be a man who will one day kiss me goodbye and go off in vicious pursuit of whatever God tells you. And when that day comes, I want that spirit within you to be happy, healthy, and disciplined.

Your ever prouder dad,

V

■ ■ ■

22 May 2014
#193
Psalm 6:6; Psalm 84:11; John 6:54; Matthew 5:30
2245

Dear VI,

It's late, boy; my heart is heavy. I found out today that I once again failed my advancement exam. This is difficult for reasons I will go into later. The bulk of my sorrow stems from a spiritual debate I let myself slip into with a very fundamentalist Christian. I truly hate it when a conversation regarding Scripture turns heated. Nothing good ever comes from it.

A fundamentalist man does not abide by the golden rule of scripture reading which is *understand the context*. Instead he upholds a strict, literal interpretation of the Bible. This is a hard position to hold for many reasons, the main one being that the Bible uses all sorts of literary devices. It speaks figuratively and uses hyperbole. It uses colorful and emotional language.

There are giant books devoted to breaking down the different types of speech used in God's Word. Pick one up if you're interested. But to shed a little light on what I am talking about, here are a couple simple examples of hyperbole being used to drive a point home. In Psalm 84:11, God is called "a sun and shield." This does not mean our Lord is a giant gaseous ball or a piece of armor. It means He is our source of life and Almighty Protector. In Psalm 6:6, David describes his anguish by saying, "All the night I make my bed swim, I water my couch with tears." This verse does not mean his tear ducts are fire hoses. This poetic language is used to emphasize a point.

To take other verses literally would mean cannibalism or self-mutilation. John 6:54 states we can gain eternal life through "eating His flesh and drinking His blood," but He is referring to the communion elements. In Matthew 5:30, Jesus tells us to remove ourselves from the source of temptation when He tells us "If your eye causes you to sin, pluck it out."

The fundamental view of Scripture is unrealistic and impossible to apply to the entire Bible, so those Christians who hold this position are forced to pick and choose. They like the part about a woman's head being covered during prayer, but they tend to scoot over the part about the sinful hand being chopped off. This is a very dangerous game to play.

My heart aches for this man's lack of relationship with Christ. The way he views our loving Savior makes Jesus sound like a God I never want to meet. One day you will have a friendship so deep with someone that you know what they are feeling without hearing them say, "I am upset." Your understanding of their nature will help you determine what they like and don't like without their having to spell it out for you. Your intimacy will give you clues into how they would react to a given situation.

The man I spoke with today is desperately trying to find what he can and cannot do without allowing room for relationship with the Holy Spirit. His God is not a Person but a checklist. The frustration he displays when trying to decipher the Bible with this mindset proves the search isn't going well. With not allowing the Spirit to guide him, not accepting Christ's gift of grace, and not feeling the peace that comes from the Good News, he loses sleep worrying about what type of bread is acceptable for communion. He is completely missing out on the precious love our God promises us.

That is why I am sad. My new mission is to never again argue over minutia and lovingly try to show this man that his questions will be answered when a real relationship is kindled. I will keep you updated.

It is now 0130. I need to get some rest,

V

■ ■ ■

24 May 2014
#194
John 14:26
1208

Dear VI,

We pulled our home to Mayport for the Memorial Day weekend. Moving everything I own to another location still throws me for a loop. Here in Space 45, I keep thinking thoughts like "I hope I remembered to pack some sunscreen," before remembering that I never touched it, yet I did bring it, along with the entire bathroom where it is kept.

My mom gave me a devotional titled *My Utmost for His Highest*. I read it often, but I'm not sure how much gets through. The author, Oswald Chambers, spills wisdom from his pen like no one I have ever read. I feel like I need waders and a machete to make any sort of headway. My college music theory teacher is the same way. The man speaks in music lyrics. I hardly remember a word he said because I was too busy wondering how a human could string words together so perfectly. For me, writing is easier than speaking because with writing I get unlimited chances. My only hope of making your book readable lies in that truth. One of the lyrics my theory teacher once said was "To write is to rewrite." I wish I had thought of that.

Today I was feeling up for the challenge so I opened up Chambers' devotional to find the following:

> We are inclined to be so mathematical and calculated that we look upon uncertainty as a bad thing. *To be certain of God means to be uncertain in all other ways.* We do not know what a day will bring forth. This is generally said with a sigh of sadness rather than an expression of breathless anticipation.

Come on! Talk about a golden nugget! Now that I have traveled a little further into the world of words, I have an even deeper admiration for this type of writing. It is as muscular as it is inspiring while also serving as a solid reminder that I am just a baby.

I thought these words were timely considering my last letter describing my exchange with the fundamentalist sailor. The fact that these words arrived at so perfect a time is further proof they are true. You will find this sort of thing is common for a Christian. Look no further than your own letters. Because they span so great a time, I have unintentionally documented entire seasons of life where one day I write with a concern, and the next I write praising the Lord for the supernatural solution He provided.

Beyond the fact that He is the answer to the problem, there is no certainty with God. Even if that problem has several layers and no set of "how-to" instructions, He is the answer—even when we do not understand the question. Because He is alive, He cannot be limited to doctrine. We cannot understand His thinking through words on a page. He is bigger and, because of that fact, we have permission to stop obsessing about what we will never fully understand and focus our attention toward nurturing a relationship with the Answer.

Sometimes you just have to accept that some things are far too big to grasp,

V

■ ■ ■

25 May 2014
#195
Ephesians 2:5
0810

Dear VI,

As we enter into the latter part of your letters, I want you to appreciate the kind of firepower we are playing with as we live the Christian life. Christianity is a radical concept. Christians believe they become truly alive when they invite the Creator of the world to live within them while they, mere animals He created in His image, simultaneously live in Him and the universe He created. Try to appreciate how cutting edge this is, especially back in Bible times! Do you know what happened when the apostle Paul preached? Riots! He was nearly beaten to death several times and spent a good chunk of time in prison.

The principles of Christianity are looked at today as outdated or archaic, but no other ideals before or since have come close to the message of Christ. What is Christianity? It is a kingdom—the only kingdom in the history of the world founded on love. Jesus demands the human heart becomes His exclusive residence, and He gets it. The Christian God does not work within the confines of time or space, but He understands both and controls all. Humans are asked to make the conscious decision to hand their souls over to God unconditionally and, when done, they experience an actual supernatural fusion of love from Him and for Him. We are talking about an eternal life no man can earn. We are talking about a faith capable of moving mountains.

Because Christianity openly disagrees with secularism, and secularism is having its way in the world, Christianity is becoming increasingly disparaged. Make no mistake, we are disliked by a lot of people—entire nations. But that's okay, the Great Protector is on our side.

Be proud of who you are,

V

■ ■ ■

31 May 2014
#196
Romans 5:3-4
0531

Dear VI,

The period of time between this letter and the last marks the longest stretch I have gone without writing to you. I would love to have filled you in sooner, but my hands have been tied. It seems our trailer decided to fall apart in the thick of a heat wave while your grandma was visiting. It started on Memorial Day when, upon returning from Mayport, I activated the system that extends our slide containing the kitchen appliances. Everything was going smoothly until a gear stripped, plopping the entire 2,000-pound section smack dab in the middle of our kitchen. As you can imagine, this made our already cozy kitchen even smaller.

Our AC saw this as a good opportunity to make our lives that much more difficult and decided to blow hot air instead of cool. This act of treason slowly transformed our trailer into an oven as I educated myself as quickly as possible on both trailer slide outs and air conditioners. I eventually diagnosed both problems but was unable to do anything but curse the broken part for its inability to do its job. Tuesday through Thursday found me bouncing between work, home, and the phone, begging for the appropriate people to come save my family from their sweaty bondage.

Any man reading this can place himself in my shoes enough to imagine how his spouse and mother might react to isolation in a stuffy handicapped trailer with a baby. Gnashing of teeth might be involved, as would nagging and complaining. Unhelpful tips about the bowels of an air conditioner would not be out of the question either.

Well, in this scene, none of that happened. I waited, but it never came. Your family talked, then read, then talked some more. When I said, "Okay, try it now," your mom would. When I asked for a tool she would grab it, but besides her assistance, everyone simply lounged and fellowshipped. I consider this scenario evidence of Christ's ability to produce good fruit through Christians living in Him. I would argue that, without the Holy Spirit residing in each person active in the scenario, we would have had a very different outcome. A much more predictable one would be your grandma reminding me one too many times how warm she is, and I lose it, which causes you to cry and your mom to reprimand me sarcastically for scaring you. "Real nice, Lewis! I am so happy I have to deal with this now!"

The Enemy no doubt saw a golden opportunity to sink in his hooks and cause division, but the Holy Spirit protected us and transformed the situation into a strange, but pleasant, family memory. Your mom did not see herself as a victim of a precarious lifestyle, the wife of a man incompetent in the ways of RV repairs. She saw a husband trying to take pride in his home by attempting to fix something he knew nothing about in order to increase the quality of life for those he loved. This is a simple example of what Ephesians 4:23 talks about when discussing a renewal in the spirit of the mind.

Let me end with admitting that things don't always pan out this way. Many are the instances that argument was bred through minor setbacks. Does this mean that your family was not in Christ? No! It means that our ever-present flesh, which forever battles with the spirit (see Galatians 5:17), won that round. Not to worry, this will happen, and when it does repent and respond better next time.

Everything is fixed. The house is cool and, because the kitchen was in the living room for a week, our house seems huge,

V

■ ■ ■

01 June 2014
#197
Mathew 11:28
2211

Dear VI,

Another Monday is nearly upon me, but I cannot sleep until I write you. When I am writing, I feel as if I am as close to Jesus as my shadow is to my heals. I am doing precisely what God desires for you, for me, and for our family. I can only guess as to how, but I would place my life on it. I am writing to you now despite the hour because I need to feel this. I am not ready to go back to work. I would much rather be here in my home playing with you. I want to study and write. I want to learn about Jesus and understand more of the amazing things He did and continues to do. I do not want to put on the uniform. I want to be in bed with my bride. I do not want to examine patients; I want to crawl around with you.

Even after all the lessons I have gleaned from a long relationship with Jesus, I still feel this way. I understand being content, living in the moment, having joy during trials, and His refining by fire, but at the end of the day, I want things to be how I think they should be. Does that make me a knowledgeable fool?

No, the problem is that humans are able to feel good and bad separately but also at once. They can know what is right while craving what is wrong. They can be generous with an evil motive. They can be superhuman in charity and subhuman in cruelty. A perfect example lies in the fact that I know millions of men are staring up at their ceiling and dreading everything that comes after their alarm goes off, and this knowledge somehow pains me *and* gives me peace. How can I possibly feel sorry for men in my position while also taking solace in their pain? I feel sympathy, but misery loves company.

It is pride and the animal instinct to survive that drives non-believers to endure life's daily challenges. But when a man gives his life to Christ, he exchanges pride and the survival instinct for the strength of his Savior. This is why I can do all things through Christ who gives me strength, but apart from Him I can do nothing. This is why I cannot understand how people can experience such poignant emotions alone. Because I am saved, I cannot imagine toiling through each day with nothing but nonsense and temporary pleasure to look forward to. Alone, I am weaker than the agnostic; with God, I am the stronger man—the strongest type of man there is.

Someday you will feel as I do right now. You will know that you are right in the center of God's plan while dreading what comes next. I despise the feeling; but instead of getting worked up about it, I accept that as long as I am human, the feeling will sporadically become a part of my life. I have developed the habit of reading and praying through it rather than moping around, blaming life for my weakness. That has been a huge help.

Always remember that it is acceptable not to look forward to things, but it is unacceptable to blow them off.

I promise I will work my hardest every second of the day tomorrow, then come home so we can play,

V

■ ■ ■

02 June 2014
#198
Ephesians 2:11, 2 Timothy 1:9
0511

Dear VI,

This morning, after reluctantly peeling myself out of bed, I saw last night's letter sitting on the kitchen counter. Its contents may sound depressing, but my hope is that it might give you peace that dreading something does not mean you are flawed. It means that you are a human with the opportunity to build character.

Christ Himself did not cherish the crucifixion He knew was right around the corner. He asked that the event be somehow taken away from Him. The anticipation had Him bawling. He had anxiety. He had dread. But He obeyed His Father's will and because He did, the world was changed forever.

I feel it is important to add another small point as kind of a post script to yesterday's letter. We deserve nothing. A common reason why men begin to dread what comes next to begin with is because they have tricked themselves into believing that they deserve more. They wrongfully assume they have been given the short end of the stick. The promises, blessings, and plans the Lord has for us are a bonus prize for daily picking up our cross.

Whenever I can put beside my selfish desires and remind myself that every good thing I have is icing on the cake, I instantly feel better about walking through the woods to my office.

We have a lot to be thankful for,

V

■ ■ ■

03 June 2014
#199
Proverbs 13:22, Ephesians 1:13
0547

Dear VI,

Today I took a close look at Proverbs 13:22, which reads, "A wise man leaves an inheritance to his children's children." The logic here is straightforward but multi-tiered. If a wise man incorporates wisdom when both big and small life decisions present themselves, the result will benefit his life and the lives of future generations. Sound investments, healthy living, faithfulness, being present in the home, and hard work all have a part in leaving an inheritance. There is a direct correlation between his choices and the quality of life experienced by his offspring, their offspring, and on down the line.

The primary thing people think of when talking about inheritance is money, and yes, a wise man may leave his children and grandchildren with cash. But a wise man is not always wealthy because a wise man does not make a decision based on what will put the most change in his pocket. His soul focus is to do whatever it is the Lord desires for him to do. Look at Paul, though both formally educated and profoundly wise, he often went hungry. The Bible and our world today are full of good, wise men who fight daily just to make ends meet.

These people leave behind a second level of inheritance, including a work ethic, values, morals, and fear of the Lord; they leave the intangible tools necessary to be wise. The way I treat your mom will absolutely impact how you will view marriage, just as my view of marriage was partly shaped by what I experienced while growing up. Each generation inherits the wisdom of their predecessors and then adds their unique twist needed to better their particular set of circumstances.

While financial and immaterial wisdom are encouraged, Ephesians 1:13 speaks of a far greater inheritance, what I call a third tier:

> "And you also were included in Christ when you heard the message of truth, the gospel of your salvation. When you believed, you were marked in him with a seal, the promised Holy Spirit, who is a deposit guaranteeing our inheritance until the redemption of those who are God's possession— to the praise of his glory."

This supernatural heritage enables us to participate in the eternal fellowship offered by the Wise One. The treasure of eternal life is gained through simply believing. It is not gained through wisdom but chosen and, once chosen, added to our lives forevermore. An inheritance is traditionally passed on after the father dies. Imagine I passed away and left you with an arsenal of stuff that will improve every facet of your life, then I came back to life and hung out with you while you enjoyed the inheritance. This is what our Father and the Lord Jesus Christ actually did for His children— you and me.

While a man thinks "By making wise choices I could save up an inheritance that might be enjoyed by future generations," God says, "I died so you might have the ultimate inheritance, which will be your guide so that you might make wise choices that extend into eternity."

A Christian man's decisions are forever influenced by his Holy Guide. He respects his Lord and, therefore, he is very interested in heeding His advice. This choice is wise indeed.

I am going to work now. I pray you sleep in peace, knowing that you are very well taken care of,

V

■ ■ ■

07 June 2014
#200
Psalm 127:3
1150

Dear VI,

Hey, buddy, it's me, your dad, who is sitting in the sun on a Saturday awaiting the arrival of another repair guy, this time to fix our fridge. It stands to reason that the world is conspiring against me. Every weekend something major breaks while the Atlantic simultaneously turns into a lake. I am not saying I am the victim of a practical joke staged by karma, but it does seem awfully suspicious.

In addition to the weekend hassles, work has been exceptionally challenging. Coming home, I found it was literally difficult to speak. I actually struggled spitting out words without crying. But every day I would open up the door, and there you would be on the ground, sometimes naked, crawling around with a toy in your mouth. Our eyes would meet and you would give a squeal of glee and hyper-crawl to my feet. Then I would pick you up and kiss your tummy to hear you laugh.

When you see your daddy, it brings you joy; but trust me, the joy I get when holding you in my arms is far greater. You are therapy and encouragement far exceeding anything I thought possible. A man can learn more about life through holding his child then he can through memorizing every book in the library.

It's true; having a child happy to see you is everything it's cracked up to be,

V

■ ■ ■

08 June 2014
#201
1 Thessalonians 5:11
1949

Dear VI,

You will find in your Christian walk that you might sometimes feel what you are studying at the time. While pursuing the riddle of joy, you will no doubt spend time meditating on a text where the author is joyful and, in doing so, that emotion will spring out of the pages and into your mood. I have been sifting through the issue of discouragement since May 22, when I wrote regarding the fundamentalist Christian. I realized his inability to obey all letters of the law must leave him in a perpetual state of discouragement. I figured if I want to uplift effectively I should understand what I'm up against. I have tried to be a source of encouragement for him, and his mood suggests my words are lifting him up. However, in doing this, I have begun to feel my own pangs of discouragement.

   Today I read 1 Thessalonians 5:11, which commands men to "Encourage each other and build one another up." The words "one another" popped out as bold as if they were highlighted. Encouragement cannot be created out of thin air. It must be received in order to be given. My problem is I have been giving it away without going back for more. A man is not an encouragement factory; rather, he has a cup of encouragement which he pours out in order to assist in lifting up another. If he is not consistently filled himself, his cup will run dry.

This is why the design of Christian fellowship is so beautiful. Fellowship refills our cup. With Christianity, humans from all walks of life join together to pour into each other's cups so that they might go back out into the world and pass it on. Any thinking man will ask the question, "Where does the water come from?" It's true, there is a source for the waters of encouragement. For the non-believer, it could be any murky little puddle they want—Facebook "likes," sex, chocolate, exercise, vacations—you name it. Some things are healthy, others are wicked, all are a quick fix but unfulfilling in the long run.

The reason corporate worship and Christ-centered fellowship are special is because the source is a delicious well that goes forever deeper into eternity. Jesus is the bottomless well that fills without ceasing, regardless of circumstance, if only we come to Him with our cup. Imagine how different the world would be if, instead of splashing a muddy puddle into a cup, everyone had a cup filled to the brim with the encouragement of grace and hope in a Redeemer.

You're my buddy,

V

P.S. When you are searching for a wife, make sure this quality is high on your list. A supportive spouse is priceless!

■ ■ ■

9 June 2014
#202
Hebrews 10:24
1250

Dear VI,

Last night your mom sat across from me at the table and said, "I am so sorry work is so hard on you," then burst into tears. "I apologize for crying," she said, "I just love you so much it kills me to know how horrible you feel."

Like a dope, I did not take comfort in the amazing friend I have in your mom. I began to think what you are perhaps thinking: "You must be doing an awful lot of complaining."

Thankfully, a little more discussion revealed that while I am honest about my job, I make obvious attempts to keep a stiff upper lip and only divulge uplifting events in my day. Your mom knows me well. The strain on my face gave me away. Her tears came from her genuine love for me. You may wonder, with such a wonderful bride, how in the world can I ever get discouraged? It's a fair question, but you should know better than anyone that she is a girl. A man needs encouragement from other men.

The fact of the matter is that your mom cannot play the role of a guy friend. It is as impossible as her being my pet goldfish. Our biology is different and, because of that, we see and feel a situation differently. By acknowledging that we are opposites who complement each other, we are in the same breath admitting we are not the same. I have written many letters to you on the various reasons why relationship is critical. I have detailed why having a primary group of like-minded friends is a must and today I want to point out that if they are not the same gender, they are not like-minded. I believe one reason why I am feeling so discouraged is I have not found a brother with whom to live Hebrews 10:24 and "spur each other on in love and good deeds."

Any Christian man will tell you these men are hard to find. Godly men more than likely will not be sitting by the phone waiting to hang out. They have their own mission to complete. When I look to the men I know who are doing what they know they ought—nurturing their marriage, working hard, being involved in church, I cannot help but notice that there is little time for friends and hobbies. It is tough to be present in your child's life and a big-game hunter. It is not easy to volunteer at church and go watch a fight with a buddy. I respect this, but men must respect that intentional gatherings are critical in a man's life. In the name of being good husbands and fathers, godly men deny themselves guy time. However, their selflessness becomes a detriment because the lack of time spent with brothers results in a lower quality of leadership. But the encouragement received during a "man date" is felt through the entire family unit, effectively making everyone happier.

Gatherings like early morning breakfasts, quarterly camping trips, or arranging monthly ping pong tournaments lead to discussion about trials, the opportunity to lift each other up, and the occasion to re-member, "I'm not the only one dealing with lust, a whining kid, and an obnoxious boss." No matter what season of life you are in, make sure a good guy friend is within reach. This is something I have let slip through the cracks, which has given way to discouragement seeping into our family.

I am currently looking at you chewing on a sunscreen cap. It is putting me in an excellent mood. Thanks,

V

■ ■ ■

10 June 2014
#203
Romans 8:14
0548

Dear VI,

As you can imagine, this letter is particularly special to me. One year ago today, I sat down and penned Letter 1. I remember sitting at the table in our old house with a new coat of polish on my boots, ready for my first day in the Fleet. We had so many boxes to unpack, your mom could hardly squeeze her big tummy down the walkway. I remember finishing your first letter then staring out the window and daydreaming about future days at the beach together.

Sometimes while in prayer or Scripture, I feel the Holy Spirit whisper or guide me toward a particular thought or action. What I felt this time last year resembled a punch to the gut. I did not hear an audible voice; it was closer to a choir of emotions singing a tune written especially for me. I felt as if I was slapped with the hand of clarity.

I have no doubt God speaks to each man in a way that will best resonate with that man's spirit. He is our Designer; every man on earth is His custom masterpiece. When you look at it that way, is it so difficult to believe that He knows how best to communicate with His creation? A man who builds a house is intimately acquainted with its inner workings.

The Holy Spirit talks to me like a man who loves me deeply but has no intention of sugar coating. He tells it to me straight, which is historically the most effective way of communicating with me. If not for Letter 1, I would have no recollection of anything that happened that day. The ways in which life has changed since the original letter are so radical that, upon reflection, my circuits blow. I end up with glazed eyes and drool at the corners of my mouth thinking, "Whoa!" I do the same thing when I look at the stars and try to imagine the view from up there.

Through the grace of God, I have stuck with this documentation as instructed, and the entire transformation from that time to this is sitting in a two-inch stack beside me for you to read at your leisure. I don't think this will go on for another year. I am not quite sure when this season will end, but I feel as if I'm rounding third and headed toward home. How special it has been to be a part of this! How blessed I am to be your dad!

You are a great kid,

V

■ ■ ■

12 June 2014
#204
1 John 4:10
0520

Dear VI,

"Jesus loves me this I know, for the Bible tells me so." I am sure you have heard this song by now. It is a powerful hymn that got "stuck" in children's church. Pre-military I had either been a part of or led a worship team for over 15 years (that's over half of my life!), and I always loved starting off a time of worship with singing this chorus a cappella. Its simple, but profound, truth does wonders to prepare the spirit for worship. "Yes, Jesus loves me! The Bible tells me so."

It is obvious you have a strong musical inclination, which excites me to no end. Growing up a Bradshaw, you will have no choice but to listen to ears full of music. You will have a solid grasp on the evolution of music in America. You will have the ability to hear a timeless song and identify the group. I am not going to give you a textbook on the subject (unless you want one), but because music is such a staple in our home, you will have no choice but to absorb some of its magic. There are people in my command that have no idea who Beethoven is, who the Beatles are, or what a jazz combo sounds like. That, to me, is inexcusable sacrilege. I will always encourage you to study an instrument of your own choosing. However, I leave that decision to you.

It has always been a dream of mine to play *Amazing Grace* on the bagpipes,

V

■ ■ ■

14 June 2014
#205
Galatians 6:9
0900

Dear VI,

We moved to Camp Blanding for the weekend where it is currently pouring. One of my favorite things about the weekends is watching you go through the morning routine. You emerge from your room in my arms and view the landscape of our trailer like you have reunited with your favorite stomping grounds. You check all the spots. Yep, the window looks good. My tin cup is right where I left it. The vent still looks and tastes just as it always has. It is a treat to sit in on the morning regimen. I find it a satisfying blessing to know that this goes on while I am at work.

We live simply because we believe God wants us to. I strongly believe these beautiful mornings are a reason why. When it comes down to it, your daily exploration, the casual chatting between you and your mom, and all the other nuances of your day have come at the expense of making less money. In fact, it would be easier to stick you in daycare while your mom brings home a second paycheck, but I consider the daily nurturing of a mother-son relationship far more valuable than a big savings account or any of the opportunities more money would afford us. I would work nights scrubbing toilets if that's what was needed for your mom to stay home.

Now that these letters span a year, I am finding it fascinating to go back and see how life was exactly 365 days ago. On 14 June 2013, I wrote to you on the last day of my first full week at work and confessed to a gut full of nerves. I was stepping into a situation where failure was inevitable. It is almost comical to read now. Those things that gave me butterflies can now be accomplished with my eyes closed. Seriously; I tried it. I have even done things like make a spreadsheet with my fastest times and strategically positioned trash cans to make throwing garbage away more challenging. Sometimes I speak to my patients in an English accent, and other times I attempt to answer all questions with a question. What once made my palms sweat is now second nature.

Throughout the course of his life, every man is given a lifelong series of challenges. I always despised when I was young and struggling with homework or my awkward junior-high body and some adult would say "Just wait until you have kids" or "Wait until you have life insurance to pay for." Looking back at the challenges I faced a year ago, it is embarrassing to admit I ever had a problem—just like it is embarrassing to admit the amount of hardship I felt when it came time to shave, or sleep in my own room, or hold a girl's hand. At the time those challenges were the equivalents of challenges I have today. They were as difficult as nurturing a marriage or sticking to a budget.

When you see another man struggling, don't fall into the trap of comparing your life with his; you are not superior because you have been there before. Chances are if you already overcame the obstacle, you probably picked up some wisdom on the subject, so pass that on instead. I personally know a man who has a long, scraggily beard because his father kept teasing him about puberty. I shave every day while still half-asleep. You can see how easy it would be for me to think this man is weak for not shaving, that his issue is no big deal. But this is not true. He is not weak. He is unique; we all are. I bet a legitimate author would look at my letters to you and be tempted to think, "I wrote tens of thousands of letters to people all over the world.

How does it take you three hours to write a page?" Encourage others who are battling in their own trenches. Instead of comparing, lend a hand.

Sometimes the reason God puts us through things is so we might be the X-factor for others,

V

P.S. Letter 18 goes into greater depth regarding challenges.

■ ■ ■

15 June 2014
#206
Psalm 145:14
1457

Dear VI,

We are back at home base for Father's Day. This year feels different now that you live outside of the womb. You chose today to be exponentially fussier than at any other point in your life. It is the perfect Father's Day gift because it forces me to appreciate my dad a bit more. Both of my parents consistently remind me of how unfair it is that you are so sweet because apparently I wasn't. Today when they asked me how you were, I said, "Awesome!" instead of, "He is screaming nonstop for no reason. I'm developing a twitch in my eye." I didn't want to hear them laugh and say, "Yes! That's what you get!"

The reaction given to me by experienced parents is always the same. The first words are always "Just wait," then they break into a sort of sick grin as if they know I am one step away from slipping on a banana peel— the same peel they themselves slipped on many times before. It's a text-book example of yesterday's letter. Because they have slipped on several peels, they can look at mine and tell me, "It's nothing to worry about." A parent with a clue has only received that clue by going through years of challenges that I have not. But instead of giving me a heads up to the fact there is a peel behind me, they either allow me to slip or point out the peel while in the same breath reminding me that the peel I just avoided is nothing compared to future bananas. Your mom calls this process a "sick rite of passage," while I call it "twisted retrospective pleasure."

It seems every other step I take has me slip-sliding away. I might as well live on an ice rink. But that's okay. My goal is to slip, fall, then hop back up, massage any new bruises, and make the choice to not let that one get me again. The alternative is to fall, then lay there face down, feeling sorry for myself. The constant is the peel; the reaction is the variable.

As for me, to make sure I don't slip, I am going to sit in my chair, eat pancakes, and watch World Cup soccer.

V

■ ■ ■

18 June 2014
#207
Proverbs 29:17
0523

Dear VI,

A couple of times a week your mom and I watch old episodes of *The Simpsons*. I have a couple of the early seasons on DVD, and every so often we will plop in a disk. I remember when *The Simpsons* arrived on the scene; it was considered "edgy," and my parents would make me go to bed. They would laugh their heads off at the cartoon while I stared at the ceiling, contemplating the injustice of it all. Eventually, I got old enough or wore my parents down enough and was able to watch the show, only to discover I did not find it funny at all. Why was what Homer said so hilarious? I didn't get it! Well, 20 years later I am proud to say that I do get the jokes, and yes, they are, in fact, funny—brilliant, actually. (Back when I first started dating your mom, I was describing her family to my mom who asked if their personality could be described as "*Simpsons*-watching Christians," which is also pretty brilliant. I recently heard a pastor describe some Christians as "tight-shoed," which I think must be the antithesis.)

The reason we zoned out on cartoons last night is because your parents are worn out. Especially your mom who is thousands of miles away from the nearest grandparent. Last night she was crying as she fed you green beans. Not upset or depressed, just thoroughly exhausted. Bushed to the core. You are continuing to grow in strength, speed, size, and opinion. You can now climb the stairs to our bedroom, our last private sanctuary. Nothing is safe. Your mom spends her entire day removing you from things that may hurt you or out of areas you cannot be, only to listen to you complain about it. You know life has changed when a dad calls going to work "a break," and a mom calls taking a shower "a rare treat."

God has given us a child with lots of spirit, and I praise Him for that. It is an absolute answer to prayer to have a boy with such energy. While we are currently so drained at the end of the day that watching cartoons is the only thing we are capable of doing together, I wouldn't have it any other way. Our job is to mold you, to take that energy and channel it into good deeds, helping others, playing hard, and looking after those who do not share your exuberance. That is no easy task, son. But I look at the fatigue on your mom's face, I feel it in my bones and consider it all proof that maximum effort is being given.

If I could plug your spirit into the walls, we could power a city,

V

P.S. *The Simpsons* was recently voted to be "the most positive show on television."

■ ■ ■

27 June 2014
#208
1 Peter 4
0600

Dear VI,

The incessant talk I listen to at work about a new video game has led me to give you the skinny as to why we won't ever have video games in our home. Yes, they stunt physical development; yes, they hinder social skills; yes, they are full of images I would rather you not see. But to me, the greatest detriment of video games is giving the player adventure without the risk of suffering. They provide none of the trials a boy needs to grow up into a strong man, and all of the crutches a man needs to slip back into boyhood. Adventure is not adventure if, when you die, you simply start over. Sitting in a chair is not an adventure, either. Video games do everything for you, thus eliminating the need to push your imagination, muscles, relational abilities, and create your own memories in life. I am not some "tight-shoed square," either.

Here in the Navy, video games are king. They are a constant trend, and every time I say, "I do not have an X-Box," I receive a stupefied response that translates to, "I feel sorry for your lesser existence," to which I reply with some variation of "Give me a break."

Note that I never say video games are wrong. It is not a sin to play video games, but I find it foolish and extremely contradictory to the type of lifestyle we are attempting to pursue, so we will steer clear.

If you play video games at a friend's house, that is totally cool,

V

■ ■ ■

29 June 2010
#209
1 Corinthians 11:15
2050

Dear VI,

Your mom shaved her head. She was praying and felt the Holy Spirit tell her to, so she did. This was a couple of days ago. I came home for lunch to find her head shaved, hands shaking, and face stained with tears. I was, and continue to be, extremely proud of her obedience.

Your mom is my standard for women. When she is pale, I like fair women; when she is tan, well then, I find olive skin attractive. Now I have this thing for a girl with really short hair. This new hairstyle has compounded my attraction to her. My wife is more concerned with observing God than she is with the way she appears to others. My wife is brave enough to combat her own completely understandable fears and doubts in the name of obedience. Of course, she had thoughts like, "What if people think I have cancer? What if my husband hates it? What if my head is shaped weird?" Any man or woman reading this story understands how big a deal it is for a woman to shave off what the Bible calls "a woman's glory."

So why would the Holy Spirit lead your mom to cut off her hair? I don't know. No one knows except Him, which is all that really matters (Letters 5 and 21 allude to this). It is fruitless to ask the question and expect any answer beyond "Because Jesus said so."

But what if she was plumb exhausted from a long morning of parenting, and in her hazy state, she misread the Holy Spirit's nudging? What if her own wacky thought manifested as spiritual instruction? The answer can be found in 1 Thessalonians 2:4: "He is the one who examines the motives of the heart." Was your mom's motive good? Yes! She was praying with every swipe of the clippers. You had better believe her heart was pure! Whether it was or was not the Holy Spirit is not as important as the motive. Because hers was pure, the Lord gets great pleasure in her actions and will use them in the future.

You are the son of a very special mother,

V

■ ■ ■

8 July 2014
#210
Psalm 121:5
0556

Dear VI,

It is official; you love the water! I have witnessed it with my own eyes. On Saturday, July 5, we took a trip to the marina. The original plan was to go to the pool so that you and I could play in the water together, but the plan changed when thunder started. The Navy policy is to wait 30 minutes after any sign of a storm before reopening the pool. We ended up driving to the marina located about 500 yards from our house. It is a small manmade sand beach with a few lawn chairs. It was made as an entry point to the St. John's River for canoes, but on that day it was for you and me to play on.

It went like this: you and I would sit in about a foot of water while I held your waist, and you smacked the surface, screaming with joy. After this went on for a while, you would decide it was time to crawl up the sand to your mom's chair. Up the steep embankment you would march, stopping every few seconds to try and put a twig or rock in your mouth.

Where was I during all this? I was right behind you, trying to make myself unknown so that you felt as if your journey was your individual ambition while still keeping a sharp eye out for signs of fatigue, and a quick reaction whenever you tried to eat the treasures in your hand. It was hilarious to see your response after I snatched something from your palm. You would pick up a shell, bring it toward your mouth, and then, BAM! The item was suddenly gone. After looking at your now empty hand, you would make a face that said "I could have sworn I was just holding something," before resuming your journey up the hill.

The analogy here is obvious. Much of your life revolves around making your way up various hills that can be classified as trials, goals, or both. I hope your attitude of determination is always as it was at the marina. One foot in front of the other, slow and content, feasting on the world around you until the goal is reached. But as your mind develops and your reasoning matures, it would only be appropriate for you to ask the question, "What is the point of all this?" I can only say that the answer to those questions lies between you and your Creator, nowhere else. The closer your relationship, the easier those questions will be answered.

I will end with a promise God gives to His children. Psalm 121:5, "The Lord watches over you." Just as I stood over you making sure you did not choke on a twig, the Lord watches over those who love Him and ventures up their respective hills with them, making sure they don't hurt themselves. I am a child crawling up a hill.

Speaking of uphill battles, I am off to work,

V

■ ■ ■

12 July 2014
#211
Proverbs 31
0900

Dear VI,

The other night before bed, I called your mom "the woman of my dreams,"
to which she replied, "No, I'm not. You didn't even know a woman like
me would be the woman of your dreams." That response took the wind
out of my sails, but it is also one of the truest statements I have ever heard.

She is currently singing "It's a small home after all" while making you
a fort. The song, the fort building, the fact that she made banana pancakes
for breakfast is all proof that man does not know what he wants. Growing
up I was dead set on a wife who surfed, played sports, and was really
outgoing—in that order. Notice how "little" aspects like respectful, warrior mother, selfless, trustworthy, godly, or willing to sell it all and move
into a trailer never made the list. To my credit, while I never considered
these things valuable, neither did she. It all evolved. We wanted marriage
the way God designed it to be and then pursued it. The pursuit is what
brought the desire for these virtues.

From time to time I send a photo of your mom to the family. The
one I sent today was commented on by her brother who said, "That is
a Proverbs 31 woman." I verified his claim by reading the chapter and
concluded his analysis checked out. Your mom is, in fact, a Proverbs 31
woman. Now why has this parallel never occurred to me? Why didn't I
grow up longing for a woman the Bible describes as "most ideal?" The
easy answer is one I have already given you: men do not know what it is
they want in general, much less in a life partner. Secondly, it is because
after enough failure and frustration, I threw up my hands in the air and
said, "God, I want only what You want because obviously I don't know
what's best for me."

Forward progress is made only after the thought process is changed.
Now I can look at my wife, head to toe, inside and out, and think, "Yes,

she is exactly what I want." I use this day in my marriage as an example you might look to in the future. But also to remind you that your parents are perfect for each other because Christ transformed our way of thinking, *not* because we knew exactly what we wanted and managed to find a mate who put a check in every box.

I love you, my boy. I hope this letter helps.

You're my big buddy,

V

■ ■ ■

17 July 2014
#212
Genesis 3:17-19
0555

Dear VI,

I spend a lot of time thinking about or doing something that pertains to money—not because I want to and certainly not because I like to. All of my money thoughts are tied up in when payday is, when a bill is due, how much gas I can get, how many diapers we can buy, or my least favorite but most nagging thought, will we get proper nutrition?

Your mom and I couldn't care less about flashy clothes or luxurious cars. Given a choice between a posh house and a trailer, we would choose the trailer every time. We spend more time imagining ourselves off the grid than we do in a big house. That being said, between Monday and Friday, I work between 50 and 60 hours. This is not done for my health; in fact, I am sure it puts a strain on my health—both mentally and physically. Rather, it is spent earning the money that keeps our trailer wheels rolling.

The Bible is very specific about the way in which a man should handle his finances. Your family attempts diligently to follow its example. We tithe, we save, we have no bad debt, we are not frivolous. So when I put in so many hours and do as I'm told with my earnings, I become thoroughly discouraged when I am still unable to put healthy food in the bodies of those I love most.

I am not alone in my discouragement. This is a very common tune around the world. Men who work far longer hours at much more difficult jobs barely scrape together enough cash to keep the lights on. The vast majority of the working class manages to only keep the basics covered—food, water, shelter, and a means of traveling back and forth to their place of employment.

This is the curse of man and has been since Adam was punished for eating the forbidden fruit: "To Adam he said, "Because you listened to your wife and ate fruit from the tree about which I commanded you, 'You must not eat from it,' cursed is the ground because of you; through painful toil you will eat food from it all the days of your life." Notice how the words "painful toil" are used in conjunction with "all the days of your life." God's punishment was not for Adam only, but for all mankind. It is a sentence to be carried out until death.

A common rebuttal to this line of thinking is, "Well, what about rich people? What about pro athletes and those who inherited great wealth?" The problem with that question is that all answers are subjective. No human can point to another and say, "They don't toil." Just because the man is seen sunbathing on a yacht does not mean he has never experienced the harsh grind of work. Who can tell me that the movie star or football icon doesn't sacrifice constantly to get where he is? Who can tell me their day to day is without drudgery?

When I get discouraged watching our money fall between my fingers like water, I remember two facts:

1) Self-worth is greater than net worth. In the grand scheme of things, how valuable we are to others far outweighs the figure in our savings account.

2) The Bible tells us to be "happy with our toil." It is a gift from God because many of His good gifts and lessons occur while toiling.

We are doing just fine,

V

■ ■ ■

20 July 2014
#213
Genesis 1:25
0908

Dear VI,

Most weekend days you and I go on long nature hikes. We wander down to the water's edge and hunt for creatures, which is easy. There is no shortage of wildlife here in the dead of summer. The humidity is palpable, the world is green and trying to sit as still as possible, yet is "teeming with biology," as your grandpa puts it. Living in a little trailer motivates all those living inside to spend more time outside, and while eight months out of the year Florida is a great place for this, right now the idea needs serious massaging. The heat is oppressive. It is as if the sun has strapped me into a weighted vest. I now know why the South has a reputation for having a slower pace.

Yesterday we were both shirtless as we marched along. My favorite way to carry you is with one of your legs on each side of my shoulder so that your chest is against my ear. This way I can hear your heart beat as we explore. You wrap one arm around my head and use the other to beat my sweaty bald head like a bongo. We saw turtles, ospreys, various swamp herons, giant grasshoppers, toads, fish, giant banana spiders, a centipede, three kinds of lizards, a butterfly, and two alligators. All these were just a few hundred yards from our house! Each one had its own individual heartbeat.

Today I felt it was important to document one of the many adventures we have gone on together, so I did. I had a blast exploring with you!

Looking forward to many years of adventure to come!

V

. . .

23 July 2014
#214
Ecclesiastes 9:7
0606

Dear VI,

I was having a beer with a friend Monday night and he said, "I didn't think you would drink; I heard you were one of those uber-Christians." I told him I love the Lord and, therefore, take His advice, but I am far from "uber" at anything—especially Christianity. I told him drunkenness is sinful and foolish for both the Christian and the atheist, but I am free to enjoy alcohol. Drinking in and of itself is not a sin; it is pleasurable and has positive benefits. Just as eating has its advantages, gluttony is sinful and causes harm. To all of this, he replied, "You're not converting me today, so let's change the subject."

This response has become so commonplace that I find it hardly worth mentioning. It's like mentioning "I put pants on this morning." It is a very direct, real statement: "I do not want what you have to offer." And while I do find it disheartening, I have learned to respect the fact that so many of the non-believers I encounter are forthright about their feelings, which is more than can be said for many churchgoers I know. People whose marriages are in shambles, whose children are in the hospital, who are in toxic friendships or financial peril seem to exclaim through gritted teeth, "God is good all the time."

I've told you before that the Enemy's first wave of attack is to persuade Christians into believing that life is tough because of something they did. If Christians believe their negative circumstances are due to personal wickedness, then it makes sense why they would lie. Who wants to invite harassment and chastising into their lives? The problem is that their lie is a direct result of believing the one spoon-fed to them by the Enemy. The Enemy lies to the Christian; the Christian then unknowingly furthers the Enemy's progress by lying to another Christian. All the while it is likely that the muck in their life is not a direct result of sin, yet there they stand isolated and full of self-loathing.

Your mom and I have run into a lot of these situations lately. So much so that I feel led to bring it to your attention. Honesty is critical among Christians because they have the power of prayer on their side. How can I ask the Lord to help my friend's debt problem if all he says is "I'm in the Lord's hands"? How am I supposed to pray for him and lift him up? How can I direct him toward believers who specialize in finances?

If believers were honest with each other the way that my non-believing friend was, if the church was up-front like Proverbs repeatedly commands, we would then be in a position to help. And if that happened, everything would be different.

Let's always be honest with each other,

V

■ ■ ■

01 August 2014
#215
Jeremiah 1:5
0549

Dear VI,

What a difference a year makes! We have officially hit your birth month. Twenty-six days from now, you will have your first birthday. As you can see from the length of time between letters, this season of documentation is tapering off. If I had taken a week off six months ago, I would feel extremely convicted. I consider my inner peace proof that I am almost done. The time is coming when my efforts will go into refining the letters that already exist instead of creating new material. For your first birthday, I will give you the gift of no more letters.

A part of me is relieved. Staying consistent with these letters has been a giant undertaking—much larger than I first anticipated. I don't think I will miss writing so often, but I am extremely thankful for the opportunity. I have grown leaps and bounds through this assignment. All praise and glory to the Lord.

Thanks for giving me such great content,

V

■ ■ ■

12 August 2014
#216
Job 6:24
0545

Dear VI,

I am recovering from a horrible sickness. I thought it was due to a long paddle I took. I thought there might have been some bacteria in the water, but that is not the reason. The doctor's final diagnosis said my body was too torn down. I have not been resting enough or eating enough for recovery. I was not giving my gut enough calories to fuel and heal, so eventually my systems could not keep up with the demand. I am doing much better now, just weak still. I have been looking back on all the mornings I skipped breakfast because I just needed a few more minutes on your letter. Or all the times I had a granola bar for lunch because of my self-inflicted commitments at work. Or all those creative dinners we ate because, frankly, it was all our budget would allow. I find myself thinking, "I have been faithful to You, God. How could You let this happen?" The answer I receive? "No one told you to starve yourself."

This is one of those free-will moments that people too often blame God for. I know one guy who hates God because his sister died of cancer, but she smoked a pack a day for decades. God did not strike her down; she was taking a risk by smoking.

It is important to keep in mind that everything cannot be broken down into God's trying us or God's disciplining us; there is also a "user-error" option. If I had to classify this situation, I would file it under "self-inflicted trial."

It is amazing to me that the prior letter outlines Christians who falsely accuse themselves for their situation, and therefore keep the problem under wraps. Then I become sick due to my own foolishness and cast the blame on God! I guess the moral of this story is that sometimes our own idiocy does land us in a tough spot.

I am going to go make some breakfast,

V

■ ■ ■

09 September 2014
#217
Luke 8:19-25
0551

Dear VI,

I wrote that date nice and slowly. It is time to end, and it seems appropriate to finish where I started—450 days ago, 217 letters ago, Luke 8:19-25. Twice in these six verses Christ talks about obedience. Once in verse 21: "My mother and my brother are those who hear my message and obey." And again in verse 22: "Who is that man that the wind and the waves obey him?" When I read these scriptures, I always think about how important it is to obey the Lord and how most days I do not. These 217 letters to you are one instance I can confidently say I obeyed. I hope you enjoy them.

Saturday we had a birthday party for you here at the trailer. What a time it was to see the wonderful people God has placed in our lives! People from work, church, and our neighborhood along with their kids came. I rented the spot beside ours, cooked burgers, and stocked a big cooler full of drinks while your mom decorated the inside of our home to look like a jungle. Our friends brought lawn chairs, and that was that. We were like one big family, sweating together in the Florida sun. It was obvious that no one enjoyed the fellowship as much as you. Your love for people was the topic of conversation throughout the day, which had your parents beaming. You also had no problem crawling with bare knees and feet along our gravel street while all people not Bradshaw walked gingerly with shoes on. You are so tough! When we sang "Happy Birthday," all 30-some-odd people wedged into the living room. You had your own little chocolate cake and, because we did not have a birthday candle, your mom carried a scented one. Yours was the only chocolate cake in history to smell like a pine tree.

Before I continue, I want you to see how our lives have changed in the last 450 days. Read Letter 01 and notice the confident tone I write with when I talk about where we will live for the next five years. How I painted your room and how you were nothing more than a bump in your mom's gut. You must understand the Holy Spirit did not just instruct me to write some letters. He instructed me to obey His commands and write what He said to write so that this life transformation could be put to ink. Never in our wildest dreams did your parents think your first birthday would look as it did, but we agree that we prefer how it happened to how we imagined.

I believe this will be my last letter; at its conclusion, I am to transcribe every word from my miniscule, barely decipherable scribbling, edit what I have written to the best of my ability, send the collection to my mom to proofread and to a mentor and pastor for theology verification. I suspect because I am a slow typist and don't know how to edit, this will take years. But know, just as I stuck with constructing these sentences, I will stick to revising them. I am excited and a little nervous to see what the Lord has in store for this next season. I am about to jump into writing waters that I have never come close to touching, and fulfilling that task makes me uncomfortable.

I have previously mentioned the Bradshaw family tradition of going around the room and praising the birthday person. You couldn't possibly sit through 30 people individually speaking to you, so I gave a toast. The waterworks were on full display; tears poured down my face. We have a video of it. With my hand on your head and your mother, my very best friend, scratching my back, I said:

"I just love you so much. You are such a good boy with a genuine spirit. You have an amazing attitude and true sense of adventure. I pray you never lose that, son. All these people are here because they love you. They have played key roles in your life from the time you were born. Thanks for your amazing attitude when your parents are stressed and tired. Thanks for being patient during our constant new-parent mistakes. I pray beyond everything that you feel the presence of our King in this house. Get to know Him intimately. Lewis, thanks for being my special friend. And that's it… Let's eat cake!"

To a lifetime of memories to come,

V

# ACKNOWLEDGMENTS

Savannah, my better half. Your unwavering support does more for me than you will ever know. The genuine enthusiasm you greeted me with every time I tried out a letter on you or told you about some little writing accomplishment was a huge shot in the arm. Thank you for trusting me. Thank you for doing life with me. You're the hero of my heart. You're our son's champion. You are beautiful from flesh to core.

Jennifer O'Connor, my mom. If not for your pesky red pen, this thing would still be a long ways off. I give a grateful smirk when I think about your sitting at the very seat you taught me from—that one at the kitchen table looking out the window, a coffee to your right and water to your left, considering the grammar of your little boy. Thanks for the lessons in comma usage and for enlightening me as to what in the world a semicolon is. Thank you for infecting me with a love for the right words. Thank you for taking me seriously when I said it was our Lord's will that you come beside me in this. I feel our relationship has grown leaps and bounds. What a blessing it is that my mom is my writing partner!

Lewis Bradshaw IV, my dad. You had no clue any of this was going on, but you should know that your consistent presence in my life was not taken for granted. Thank you for always being ready to play with me. Thank you for letting me watch you fillet the fish you speared. Thank you for showing me how to do a handstand on a skateboard and diving in the freezing pool with me. Thank you for passing on your love for the ocean. Thank you for never missing a game. Thank you for working so hard all those years so mom could stay home with Jordi and me. You are a great friend.

Jordi, my sister. You gave me the reason to protect. The duty I feel deep inside to protect those in a tough spot is evident in this book. I have you to thank for that proclivity. It developed because I always wanted to make sure you were safe, but I have always been inspired by your excellent example of looking out for the lonely. Thank you. I know I never really needed to look out for you. You are one of the strongest, most capable people I have ever known. But I am your big brother. I will forever be teasing you and making sure no one messes with my little sister.

Sean Solomon. There is an adage that suggests we never judge a book by its cover, but no one abides by it. Without an enticing cover the book is never opened. This truth had me at a serious disadvantage until you gave me your creative talents. Thank you for wrapping these words in beautiful art. Thank you for believing in this project. Thank you for taking care of my sister. Thank you for being such a faithful friend.

Stan Myers. When I let you in on the fact that I was writing a book, you looked me in the eye and took it seriously, which further compounded my respect for you. Often, when I feel tired or burdened, I think of your relentless commitment to family and Kingdom, which gives me the strength to keep on grinding. Thank you for reading every letter and making sure the Biblical principles I am giving to my son are accurate. The relationship you share with your wife shows me how awesome marriage can be. Thank you for your example.

Lucas Myers. It is obvious you and I are made of the same stuff. You are my likeminded friend—wise as a serpent, loyal as a dog. I am sure one day the Lord will bring our families together on the same plot of land. One day our sons will be best friends. But until then, we have a lot of growing to do so let's keep grinding away side by side like brothers in Christ were always meant to.

Keisha Napier. I have never met a harder working woman or mother. I owe much of my success in the military and this book to your generously picking up my slack. You took my patients so I could study. You scanned those documents so I could edit these letters. We have spent close to four years in the same eight-by-ten box, and I still look forward to seeing you every morning. Thank you for making me laugh and tuning my ears to the accents of the South. You are an inspiration and the most special part of the Bradshaws' time in Jacksonville.

Johnathon Evans. Like Keisha, you knew what I was up to and picked me up. I could not have balanced home life, military life, and this book without your selfless work ethic. Thank you for being such a hard worker. Thank you for being my friend.

Bear Grylls. You are a great example of a godly man. I am very thankful for you and the example you set. If you ever want to meet up and grab a drink, I will more than likely be available.

Made in the USA
San Bernardino, CA
30 November 2016